Praise for
***TODAY'S THE DAY!* AND WENDY TUCKER**

In the masterful oral history tradition of Studs Terkel, where the interviewer is deceptively quiescent and unobtrusive, journalist Wendy Tucker brings to the page the fully realized life story of Mel Fisher. *Today's the Day!* is Mel Fisher's memoir, in his own straightforward and unfailingly fair and optimistic words. It is many things on many levels: a humbling and touching read, a testimonial to the resilient fabric of the human spirit, a paean to family and friendship and loyalty, and a sweet, joyous, and ultimately rocky ride into the heart of the hunt for treasure, both tangible and divine. It is a headlong plunge into a world where the magical and unforeseen are a given. And the quest is not just for any treasure, but for one so immense in its historical value alone, and so seemingly out of reach, that only someone who had truly felt and heard its faint but still clear heartbeat across the centuries could heed and honor as his life's work. That man was Mel Fisher, and it would not be a stretch of the imagination to say that he was born to find the Spanish galleon *Nuestra Señora de Atocha* and her sister ship *Santa Margarita*, lost to a hurricane off the Florida Keys in 1622.

Mel Fisher was a modern-day alchemist who understood on a very primal level the mysteries of the alchemy of old and the spiritual concept behind the transmutation of base metals into gold. In his own words he proclaimed that gold never tarnishes, gold never stops, gold just keeps going and going from man to woman and woman to man, and on and on and on. Gold was not a god to Mel, but rather a touchstone that shone a light onto his life's path. When Mel states that it was never about the money in his quest for the *Atocha*, we believe him, because there is no greed evident in these pages, no avarice, no meanness of spirit. There is instead a rare and certain purity of heart that shows itself throughout the book, but most poignantly when Mel talks about how he felt as he held relics from the galleons that sank in 1622—a shard of olive jar, a piece of jewelry, a cross with tiny gold nails piercing the body of Christ. He wonders what those who drowned in the hurricane that took the *Atocha* were feeling, to what demon they had borne witness as the sky opened up, how much they must have suffered. And there is great empathy that comes across in his words, which are reverent, spoken almost to himself, as if he had known each man or woman or child who had been lost. And who's to say he didn't?

Joseph Campbell might call Mel's a hero's journey. This reader disagrees. I believe Mel would call it simply a journey—certainly one filled with adventure and fun and romance, as he often states in the book. But one suspects that is at times a catchphrase to mask what Mel would like to keep to himself: that he was bound by destiny to this journey before he was born, and that he knew it. He said that there is nothing that can compare to seeing the ocean floor covered in gold. His alchemist compatriots of the Middle Ages would have agreed with him, and they well may have knelt in prayer at that very sight. If you are able—just for a moment or two—to suspend all belief in the simply rational and instead believe in magic, transmutation, destiny—whatever one chooses to call it—then one can entertain the notion that a certain precise alignment of stars in Indiana at the exact moment of Mel's birth foretold what was to come. There are "coincidences" aplenty in Mel's journey in *Today's the Day!* And who is to say this is just one Mel forgot to mention?

—Lorian Hemingway is the author of three critically acclaimed books: Walking into the River, Walk on Water, *and* A World Turned Over *(Simon and Schuster). She was nominated for the Mississippi Arts and Letters Award for Fiction for her novel* Walking into the River. *Her work has also appeared in* GQ, The New York Times Magazine, Esquire, Rolling Stone, Westchester Magazine, *and numerous other*

publications. She is the only woman to have received The Conch Republic Prize for Literature—other recipients include Russell Banks, John Updike, James Dickey, and Harry Crews—for her dedication to encouraging the work of new writers of fiction.

As an experienced journalist and a reporter for many years with the *Key West Citizen*, Wendy Tucker has weaved together a fascinating insider's account of the inner workings of Treasure Salvors Inc. as Mel Fisher and his "Golden Crew" found the *Atocha's* mother lode and the treasure of the *Margarita* after searching sixteen years for the shipwrecks off the Marquesas Keys. Wendy's gifts as a storyteller make it impossible to put the book down as she gives the reader an unforgettable narrative of the day-to-day salvage operations from the Key West office and out on the sites forty miles at sea—much of which is described in Mel's own words. It's a great read for divers, history buffs, and all those who want to know something about the cultural legacy of the 1622 Tierra Firme fleet rescued through the recovery of priceless artifacts from the seabed.

—*Dr. R. Duncan Mathewson III is a marine archaeologist and author of* Treasure of the Atocha: A Four Hundred Million Dollar Archaeological Adventure, *now in its sixth printing, in English and Spanish.*

In the many years that I have known Wendy Tucker, I have always looked upon her as a consummate professional, both as a photographer and as a journalist. Working with her has been my pleasure and good fortune. Her biography of Mel Fisher, which details his most notable achievements as well as his struggles with disappointment, offers additional evidence of her talents.

—*George Sullivan is a best-selling author who has published more than two hundred adult and young adult nonfiction books in a career that has spanned several decades. He came to know the Mel Fisher family, Wendy Tucker, and the Key West community on a number of treasured annual summer visits there.*

Today's the Day!

The Mel Fisher Story

Today's the Day!
The Mel Fisher Story

WENDY TUCKER
with
MEL FISHER

Brick Tower Press
New York

Brick Tower Press
Manhanset House
Dering Harbor, New York 11965-0342
bricktower@aol.com
www.BrickTowerPress.com

All rights reserved under the International and Pan-American Copyright Conventions. No part of this publication may be reproduced, stored in a retrieval system, or transmitted in any form or by any means, electronic or otherwise, without the prior written permission of the copyright holder.
The Brick Tower Press colophon is a registered trademark of J. T. Colby & Company, Inc.

Library of Congress Cataloging-in-Publication Data
Today's the Day!—The Mel Fisher Story
Tucker, Wendy, with Fisher, Mel

BIOGRAPHY & AUTOBIOGRAPHY /
Adventurers & Explorers
HISTORY / Maritime History & Piracy
HISTORY / Caribbean & West Indies / General

Copyright © 2022: Wendy Tucker & Mel Fisher's Treasures LLC
Trade Paper 978-1-899694-02-0, Hardcover 978-1-899694-04-4

Editor and Interior Design/Typesetting: Mike Slizewski
Content Consultant: Taffi Fisher Abt
Front cover photo: Fisher Family Collection
© Mel Fisher's Treasures LLC
Ship line drawing: Bill Muir, © Mel Fisher's Treasures LLC

Information:
Mel Fisher's Treasures LLC
605 Simonton Street Suite B
Key West, FL 33040

First Printing 2022

To the Fisher Family
and
Members of their Golden Crew
Past and Present

ACKNOWLEDGMENTS

Many people deserve thanks and appreciation in connection with this book, and any attempt to name them will in no way diminish the contributions of those I meant to name or should have named, but in the press of time and the failure of my aging memory somehow overlooked.

Other books have been written about various aspects of the quest for the *Nuestra Señora de Atocha* and *Santa Margarita* and the 1622 Spanish Fleet, and the ships of the 1715 Spanish Fleet. They include Dr. Eugene Lyon's *The Search for the Atocha*, R. Duncan Mathewson III and his *Treasure of the Atocha: A Four Hundred Million Dollar Archaeological Adventure*, John S. Potter, Jr. and his *The Treasure Diver's Guide*, and Mendel Peterson's *The Funnel of Gold*.

This however is a memoir of the long and amazing life of Mel Fisher—*in his own words*. Because Mel has "crossed the bar," and is no doubt with his beloved wife and partner Deo, it has been my honor and privilege to write this book with Mel using interviews I taped in the latter 1980s. I also taped several interviews with Deo Fisher. Now I am sharing the adventure further with their daughter Taffi Fisher Abt most directly, and with her brother Kim, brother Kane, her husband Michael Abt, and her children, Joshua, Nichole, and Melvin. Although they are gone, I want to remember Grace Fisher, Mel's mother, and thank her posthumously, and Mel's son Dirk, who died, with his wife Angel and diver Rick Gage, in the long, arduous, and often unrewarding search for their ultimate prize, the *Nuestra Señora de Atocha*, and her sister Royal Guard galleon, the *Santa Margarita*.

Over the long years of the searching for the *Atocha* and *Margarita*, as we began in Vero Beach, I have been close friends with the Fisher family, and also with the "extended family," including the Treasure Coast 1715 Fleet family, and over a longer time, the 1622 Fleet Florida Keys family of all those who have joined the Fishers in their quests. This includes people with the Mel Fisher Maritime Heritage Society.

Also, I have joined with "family" members from California as well, including Fay Feild and Eddie Tsukimura. Then there is Demostines "Mo" Molinar, originally from Panama, where he first encountered Mel, and over the years joined Mel's adventures, first into California and finally to Florida.

During all the years of the searching, and finding, the shore-based as well as those at sea were intimately involved, and "hard times parties" welcomed all to the "family." The discovery celebrations included everyone as well.

In Key West, especially in the 1970s and 1980s, and still a little in the 1990s and early 2000s, there was traditionally more of a small-town feeling, where everybody knew everyone. So everyone was genuinely glad when Mel "found it," and shared in the glory, welcoming the attention of the world.

Wherever anyone once connected with Mel Fisher and his adventures, they are connected forever with their wondrous memories.

—*Wendy Tucker*

FOREWORD

by Taffi Fisher Abt

People often ask me what it was like to grow up with famous treasure hunters for parents, Mel and Deo Fisher. As the youngest child and only daughter of the world's greatest treasure hunter, I can only say, I really didn't realize we were different from any other family. We ate dinner together, watched TV, went to movies, ate out sometimes, joined the Boy/Girl Scouts, and visited distant family on vacations, just like all the other families did. I suppose I did notice that no other kids brought silver "Pieces of Eight" to school for "Show and Tell," and my folks did appear in magazines (like the January 1965 issue of *National Geographic*), which I didn't notice any of the other kids' parents doing. A little later, I would sometimes get my feelings hurt overhearing someone say my dad was a kook, a lunatic looking for something that was a myth, or that he was a con artist just trying to swindle people out of their hard-earned money. It didn't really bother me too much, because I knew the truth. I was only two years old when my parents started treasure hunting full time, and they were *very* successful. I grew up watching my parents find authentic shipwreck treasures.

As a child, I just didn't realize how hard it was, and how different we were. In reflection, I realize that my life has been a tapestry of vivid, rich and colorful events. I am truly only just beginning to fully appreciate the depth of the unique and historic events that I have been an active player in. My parents were not only loving and supportive, they shared with their children a level of optimism, positivity, and adventure that most children (and some adults) will never get to experience. I am full of gratitude to have been born into this family as well as being a part of the extended family of believers, supporters, and adventurers who have shared our journey and dreams.

Because of my parents' notoriety, I have met many reporters over my lifetime, and when I first met Wendy Tucker, she was a reporter working for the *Key West Citizen* back in the 1970s. Wendy was a journalist so talented that Reuters (International), the Associated Press (AP), and United Press International (UPI) often picked up her articles and ran them nationwide and internationally. And Wendy always seemed cheerful and interested—you could just tell that she genuinely believed in my parents and their quest. She was there through the hardest of times, the tragic loss of my brother and sister-in-law and a crewmate, and through the leanest years, when we were living on boats and sharing "hard times stew." She was there through all the years of court battles with the government (we won every single one, all the way to the US Supreme Court). Wendy covered the good and bad news, including a ridiculous investigation by the SEC (Securities and Exchange Commission), which was thrown out. She covered the sinking of the *Golden Doubloon*, our full-size reproduction galleon that doubled as a museum and office headquarters, and in that same month, she wrote about our discovery of more than $20 million in treasure on the *Atocha*'s sistership, the *Santa Margarita*. Finally, after my parents had been searching for sixteen years, Wendy was there on "The DAY" in 1985 when we found the mother lode of the *Nuestra Señora de Atocha*, laden with more than forty tons of silver, gold, and artifacts valued at that time in excess of $400 million.

Wendy and my parents became very close friends over those many years, and she graciously agreed at my mom's request to take on the task of recording interviews with my dad for his biography. In the meantime, she got hired as assistant city planner and had a full-time job. Wendy got together with my dad as much as possible during the next decade, but he was hard to catch, a very busy man and—not surprisingly—very popular to interview. Many things have been printed about my dad, but Wendy captures his true personality, his eagerness to learn new things, and his definite tendency to be a nonconformist, taking and trying "the road less traveled." She covers his childhood life and years before "treasure hunting" like no one else has.

I am so pleased that she has written this book and honored that she asked me to be the first reader. I believe she has done a *fantabulous* job in passing along, throughout this book, what I would consider Mel's most important messages to future generations. I know Dad (and Mom) would be proud, as am I. Thank you, Wendy, for sticking with it and making this book a reality.

Today's the day!

—Taffi Fisher Abt is Mel and Deo Fisher's youngest child.

Taffi Fisher Abt with Atocha *gold spoon.*
WENDY TUCKER PHOTO

TABLE OF CONTENTS

Introduction ... *1*
Preface – Meet Mel Fisher: The Summer of 1964 ... *4*
Chapter One – In the Eye of a Hurricane: Winds of Time and Sea Combine ... *14*
Chapter Two – In the Wilderness: Water Child in Midwest Culture ... *22*
Chapter Three – Into Adventure: Homemade Dive Helmet and River Voyage of "Huckleberry Fisher" ... *40*
Chapter Four – Vision and Leadership Come from Unexpected Places ... *51*
Chapter Five – Man of War: Across the Ocean ... *67*
Chapter Six – Into the Sunshine: Postwar Freedom and Florida Adventures ... *89*
Chapter Seven – Diving in: "Fearless Fisher" Spearfishing Sea Monsters ... *96*
Chapter Eight – Fun, Romance, and Adventure: The World's First Dive Shop ... *105*
Chapter Nine – The Other End of the Line: Making Underwater Movies ... *127*
Chapter Ten – High Road to Danger: Attack of the Leopard Ray ... *164*
Chapter Eleven – Hunting for Gold on Silver Shoals ... *181*
Chapter Twelve – Pioneering Treasure Hunting for Spanish Galleons: Florida's Treasure Coast ... *203*
Chapter Thirteen – Quest for the *Atocha*: Dare to Dream Big ... *223*
Chapter Fourteen – Today's the Day! Mother Lode and "Heeeeere's Mel" ... *253*
Chapter Fifteen – Treasure Is Where You Find It ... *270*
Epilogue – Follow Your Dreams! ... *313*
About the Author ... *317*
Index ... *319*

INTRODUCTION

As with Mel Fisher and his first home in Indiana, I started in the Midwest but hungered for the waters where he began to wander, then venture forth, and down, into the waters of the two oceans that border our country. And before he died, Mel was also part of other explorations in the Caribbean, South and Central America, and even Africa.

First, however, Mel, with a carpenter father, a creative mother, and an engineering brain, had to venture into ponds and pools, with homemade diving helmets, and always learning, into the rivers and lakes of this nation. His story is the story of a man of twentieth-century America, which was a nation a-building, and Mel Fisher went with the tides that carried him into an incredible life, taking many of similar independent persuasion with him, first through the Midwest, then west to California, and finally east to Florida and the Florida Keys.

For Mel Fisher, "Today" was always, always "the day." For me, as a journalist, today was also always "the day." So it was a natural fit that I would track his adventures finally in Florida, and in the Florida Keys, where Mel found his ultimate achievements in the glory of finding the final trails of *Nuestra Señora de Atocha*, the richest sunken Spanish treasure cargo ever found, and her sister ship, the *Santa Margarita*, the two Royal Guard galleons of the Spanish Fleet of 1622. He had already found ships of the 1715 Spanish Plate Fleet, in ocean waters off the coast of Florida, and there are to this day museums of their final yields of history and treasure in Sebastian and Key West.

Mel's words are his own, with a few exceptions for modern propriety, and they are taken by me from lengthy tapes recorded primarily in the 1980s, after the finding of the "mother lode" of the *Atocha*. My writing draws from the classic Greek Chorus style, introducing and ending each chapter in italics, tying together the amazing stories of his life. Mel's words are written directly *as is* into the narrative. And that also includes people like his wife, Deo, his daughter, Taffi Fisher Abt, and Capt. Ed "Eddie" Tsukimura. Taken together, they all reflect the amazing story of a most remarkable human being.

Deo and Mel Fisher circa 1954–55. FISHER FAMILY COLLECTION

PREFACE

Meet Mel Fisher: The Summer of 1964

The summer of '64, it was. At Vero Beach, Florida, dunes covered with sea oats meandered along the shoreline of that part of Florida, near where the subtropic weather zone begins. You could hear the surf with its powerful *shhhh* roll and slap the shore along that magnificent stretch of beach.

Condominium developments hadn't been created yet. Real adventure was still possible in post–World War II America, and the ocean was a frontier.

Among the older motels on the beach was the La Posada, a one-story, U-shaped building that reached toward the Atlantic Ocean, built of stone and cement, with Spanish hacienda influences from red tile roofing down. The aging air conditioning system, such as it was, was centralized, with ductwork extending room to room. If someone opened their windows, the other rooms' AC was affected. Guests learned that quickly and stayed or didn't. In the center of the motel's "U" was a large rectangular swimming pool. Adding to the Spanish hacienda ambiance was a huge brownish log. First thought: alligator! Not. But there was a huge old iron cannon, encrusted with sea growth, smack in the middle of the pool. Along the southern side of the hotel there was a small sign on one of the units, and a little museum of pieces that belonged to some most unusual guests.

Just down A1A (the beach highway that parallels South Florida's shoreline all the way to Key West) from La

Posada was a rustic old hotel of some fame that sported a great restaurant and bar, known as the Driftwood. The sea was in charge of its own real estate in those days. Buildings and uses were in harmony with their seaside location. People were tuned to the same harmony, calling distantly to sea chanteys of old.

Driven by my own sense of adventure, I had decided to accept a summer journalist "internship"—at student pay—with the *Miami Herald*, even though I was graduated from the University of Nebraska School of Journalism. I had applied to the Columbia University Graduate School of Journalism but did not know whether I'd be accepted. *Herald* Managing Editor Larry Jinks said that was his offer, and I took it, gambling on a positive future, whatever decision came from New York. My compass headings were set south back to Florida and eventually Key West—as were those of the amazing Fisher family.

As I was a summer intern journalist, The *Miami Herald* used me primarily in the Fort Lauderdale Bureau. But as vacation times occurred in that summer of 1964, I was sent on a "bureau swing" to fill in as the "chief" of the one-person *Miami Herald* Bureau in Vero Beach, covering Indian River County. Relationships built there that summer would last a lifetime.

In Vero Beach, I was immediately captured by the idea of new adventure in a new newsbeat location, and intuition took me to the La Posada. At the motel front desk, I learned that some people who discovered Spanish treasure were often there, and of course, that sounded like a news feature story. No question, that was where I'd stay.

For me, the sound of the surf at the La Posada was all new and enchanting. For most of my first night there, I listened to the roar and slap, the powerful shoreside landing movements of the sea. I left the windows open and didn't at all mind any lack of air conditioning. Several times during that night, girl journalist from landlocked Nebraska that I was, I slipped quietly back along the building to the dunes and the incredible, living ocean. The sea—and Florida—had called me to what would be a new life.

A very unusual family was well-known in California but yet unknown in Florida. They and their extended "family" of treasure hunters had decided to make Vero Beach, and the La Posada oceanfront motel, their home base. They were Mel and Dolores "Deo" Fisher, and their four children, Dirk, the oldest at about ten, Kim, Kane, and Taffi.

The wonderful little family-style restaurant at La Posada was particularly awesome for its breakfast time. Mornings—and I will always remember the first view—you could see flaming red hair come flashing into the sunlight as the Fisher family arrived for their first meal of the day. A shapely "Mom" and two children, a boy, and the littlest, a girl, all sported brilliantly red hair that no one could miss. The oldest of the four had red hair too, but the sun had bleached it so much I thought it was blond. The children swirled and darted around their parents, "Dad" being tall, well-built, and sun-bronzed. This was Mel Fisher, with a beaming smile that lit up the area around him. Deo had a figure to match her hair, a beauty queen with her own beautiful smile. The second oldest boy was equally a "sun child," hair bleached to a brownish-gold, already taking after his keenly observant father.

I learned that one of the big events at that friendly, low-key motel was the daily arrival of the locally famous Fisher family for breakfast and coordinating their treasure hunting efforts. When someone was available, they'd open a small treasure "museum" in one of the motel units. I wanted to observe first and did not approach them right away. I hoped to meet them informally, find out about what they were doing and how, and get a story! The stories I soon started writing also began my coverage over time of a Spanish-treasure and history-hunting news "beat."

West of the Great Divide of America, though,

great things had already happened for the Florida-bound crew from California. Mel and Deo had separately and together made big marks on California, and no one really believed the word "retire" when they heard that conversation from the Fishers.

Mel was always looking for old-fashioned "fun, romance, and adventure"—and treasure. He dug gold in the mountains and chased critters and treasure in the sea. He became one of the first to acquire an "Aqua-Lung," an underwater rebreathing system developed by Jacques Cousteau (whose dive belt Mel found during an underwater adventure in Panama). "Fearless Fisher" had already engaged his family and others as pioneers in the dive world. They had already roamed from California to the Caribbean on their adventures. They had operated a pioneering dive shop, leading dive trips, teaching, and making their own wet suits and underwater movies.

By 1963, an expedition to Florida had been planned and prepared by the Fishers. A nucleus crew of like-minded adventurers included a diplomatic negotiator, a construction veteran, an engineer and expert welder, an electronics expert, and a marine diesel mechanic.

With the Fishers, others who had come east from California were also staying at La Posada. One was Fay Feild, an electronics wizard, whom I remember as lofty of stature and mind, serious-looking and serious-minded. He represented a real reporting challenge, and our friendship lasted too. Each person among the Fisher associates was a unique individual, each worthy of getting to know, and worthy of respect.

The band of adventurers included Feild, electronics expert; Rupert "Rupe" Gates, the diplomat; construction veteran Walter "Walt" Holzworth; and engineer and welder Richard "Dick" Williams. There was also Panamanian-born, dark-skinned diesel mechanic Demostines "Mo" Molinar, found and recruited by Mel on his earlier Panama adventure. In spite of the times being pre-desegregation, Mo was treated like family by the team. Working through the years with the Fisher family in good times and bad, "Mo" was always an inspiration with his abilities, intuition, experience, persistence, and outlook. The group called themselves "Treasure Salvors," and they were heading to meet up with a Florida man, Kip Wagner, who was seeking Mel's well-known expertise to salvage shipwrecks.

The original Treasure Salvors group teamed with Kip Wagner's Real Eight Company in Florida. They committed to each give a year's effort to find treasures from shipwrecks of the 1715 Spanish Plate Fleet. History revealed that the ships were lost that year off Florida's East Coast, along a stretch of about thirty miles off the Vero Beach-Fort Pierce area. In the spring and summer of 1963, the Fisher family and friends pulled up stakes in California and headed east for Florida in a car, trailer, and boat caravan. The children, who over a decade later added so much to the *Atocha* saga, ranged in age in that first Florida year from Dirk, nine, to Taffi, nearly two.

The handshake deal between Mel and Kip was a "fifty-fifty" one, with the Californians having to survive and salvage at their own expense for one year. Anything they found would be divided evenly, also subject to the state of Florida's division sharing.

Almost the full promised year of efforts passed before the rewards came. The team had been using Fay Feild's unique, towed magnetometer equipment on the surface, looking for "hits" of ferrous metal, iron that was used for such things as barrel hoops. Tall and remote, the eclectic Fay Feild had his mind most of the time on innovations or repairs of the all-important electronic equipment, even when sipping his beer.

For the closer-to-shore, shallower, and rough-water 1715 wrecks, Mel and his team developed what they called the "mailbox," an elbow-shaped metal tube that, lowered aft of the boat's propeller, deflects the prop wash downward and blows away layers of sand from the sea bottom.

Treasure hunters look for "anomalies," unusual patterns, while searching the sea bottom with towed magnetometer equipment. For the hunters, a special "anomaly" happened on May 8, 1964, but no iron was involved. That was the date "Mo" Molinar found two gold Spanish disks. An irony of history was that the "Douglass Beach Wreck" site was located offshore of a once-segregated beach area, and the man who found the first gold was a man with dark skin. Mo, sometimes "Momo," would forever be teased for having the "gold touch," an uncanny sense of where gold treasure could be found.

The golden gamble paid off. Starting in May, the treasure hunters made what was described as the biggest treasure find since Sir William Phips salvaged $1 million off Hispaniola in 1687. Mel and his dive partners found the ocean bottom "covered with gold." That day, they recovered an amazing 1,033 gold coins! In a week's time, they brought to the surface an even more amazing 2,700 gold coins as shiny and beautiful as when they were lost those hundreds of years earlier in 1715.

"Once you see the ocean bottom covered with gold, you never forget it," Mel told me and many other interviewers in the summers of 1964 and 1965. He meant it, because he never forgot it!

A year later, the team made another amazing find of 1,128 golden Spanish coins in one day, salvaging at another Spanish Plate Fleet wreck area.

Leaving aside the serious storms of government negotiations and business realities, the informal association of Treasure Salvors became incorporated, and salvage on the 1715 Fleet wrecks continued in cooperation with Wagner's Real Eight Company. And the finds continued. There was more: nine-foot cannons, silver chunks, and silver "cob" coins by the thousands. From a "mailbox"-equipped barge they called the *Gold Digger*, on their first day of work on a site known as the "Riomar" wreck, the salvors found two golden crucifixes, one a marvelous gold cross with 120 spikes that had once been encrusted with pearls. Looking back one later day, Mel's face brightened like a sunrise. He remembered how he was just going overboard to check on his young son Kim when the ten-year-old surfaced clutching a handful of gold coins.

There was an exciting *National Geographic* magazine article about the 1715 recoveries in January 1965. That was the first time for such world-touching events. For the Fishers and their friends, history would eventually repeat itself.

What was required was a wondrous sense of adventure, the willingness to work very hard and take many risks, incredible optimism and self-confidence, great salesmanship, and the ability to recognize opportunity. These were assets Mel Fisher possessed. Liabilities were the high costs of treasure hunting and the slower return of financing, and these meant perpetual money needs.

In 1964, the world had not really heard for hundreds of years of the lost Spanish treasure galleons *Nuestra Señora de Atocha* or *Santa Margarita* that disappeared in New World stormy seas in 1622. It would be some years before Mel learned about those lost 1622 ships during a side trip to the Florida Keys.

Then the diving weather got "terrible" and the water offshore "really muddy" earlier than usual at those 1715 wreck sites, and Mel decided on a late 1960s visit to the Keys. He was overjoyed at the "flat, calm water" he saw. In the Middle Keys, he threw a get-acquainted party for fellow treasure hunters in the area. Mel said that was when he first read and learned about the fabulous riches of the Spanish galleon *Nuestra Señora de Atocha*, lost during a hurricane in 1622. Someone produced a copy of *The Treasure Diver's Guide* by John S. Potter Jr., rated as a Bible for treasure hunters. The *Atocha*, he learned, had the highest rating among lost shipwrecks listed. That was intriguing, and his chess mind started to work. The date was certain but not the location, and everyone at the party began to speculate about that very important problem.

The Fishers kept their ties to Sebastian, Fort Pierce, and Vero Beach, but the new horizon was southward, and so began their search for the *Nuestra Señora de Atocha*.

There was no immediate glory in the 1715 shipwrecks, as there never was for the 1622 galleons. The glory was in the search effort, the rugged daily challenges of the sea to puny if athletic humans with great goals always ahead and unseen. The seas gave hints, tantalizing little rewards now and then, but not more. Every minute, the ocean could surprise. This lifestyle demanded physical strength and endurance, and a constant readiness for the unexpected that could mean injury, life, or death. Being ready for anything was required.

Dreams of Spanish gold treasure under the sea started for a young Mel during high school library time, reading *Treasure Island*. And he was adventurous and mechanically gifted enough to make his own first dive helmet and air supply using a bicycle pump on a raft. He never learned anything in his whole life, Mel said later, that he didn't use somehow for his treasure hunting life.

Years of effort, triumphs, and tragedies would occur before Mel's dive mask finally pointed at the unforgettable sight of the "reef" of silver bars that marked the "mother lode" of the *Nuestra Señora de Atocha*, the richest Spanish Royal Guard and treasure galleon ever found. But that's another part of the Fisher family saga.

Mel came originally from Indiana, and Deo from Montana. They were from landlocked Midwest and western soil, but both found their most dynamic personas in the ocean. Together they founded what has become a saga of hardworking adventurers, farmers of the sea. Children, grandchildren, great-grandchildren of the Fishers, and members of their treasure-hunting and archaeology-inspired private enterprise family still carry on through generations and across time.

Now, in 2022, there are two museums, at Sebastian and Key West, that share with the public the events, research, and physical proofs of nearly four hundred years of history that, because of Spain's global empire, have enriched and educated the world.

"There's always a beginning," said another friend of a lifetime whom I met in the summer of 1964, "Captain Tony" Tarracino. He was supportive of the treasure hunting family from the hot July day when the Fishers and their dog arrived in front of his saloon on Greene Street in Key West. The children all had cold Cokes, the dog a bucket of water, and maybe—though Tony didn't say—Mel had a rum and Coke.

Key West had cast its spell on me too. Visiting the island for the first time at the end of that summer of 1964 with other *Herald* interns, I heard my own voice saying aloud, "So this is Key West; so this is where I'm going to live." The words amazed me then, but they came true, and I still reside there today.

Years after, I was relaxing one evening at the Fisher home on Key Haven. Deo and I sat at the counter that divided their kitchen from the dining room. Mel was standing at the end of the counter. "Gosh," I said in a rum-fogged reverie, "I wish I had been there in Vero Beach when it all first happened!" Mel shined his big smile at me.

"You were," he said.

—*Wendy Tucker*

Deo and Mel Fisher hosting a March 1986 screening of the National Geographic Society documentary Atocha: Quest for Treasure.
WENDY TUCKER PHOTO

CHAPTER ONE

In the Eye of the Hurricane:
Winds of Time and Sea Combine

*A*lone *on a hand-built search tower that he and his crew rigged at sea west of Key West, Mel Fisher's past, present, and future came together when the first feeder band winds of a growing hurricane sprang to life around him.*

The winds of time that whirled around him gave only hints of what was to come. But he was too busy to notice. There was no fear, as usual. He was skilled with his mind and hands; he could face any challenge of the moment. Then too, he had chosen to start his quest of a lifetime where he and his beloved wife Deo had first visited as newlyweds.

That day when we started our search, I was on this tower, way out of sight of land there, all by myself. And I could see squalls in all directions. As it happened, this was the first time I'd ever been in the eye of a hurricane as it was forming. The thing started right there on the *Valbanera* spot where that ship had its disaster back in 1919.

It was ominous in the first place when we started. It just kept getting worse and worse. We didn't know that a hurricane was coming. I think this hurricane was spawned right where we were—right on the side of the *Valbanera*. That would be kind of unusual, I know. Most usually, hurricanes start way over by Africa and come across the ocean. But I have seen a couple of others start out here since then during the last twenty years. Several other hurricanes have started right here and then went over and hit in Louisiana or Texas.

That first search day after we'd built the tower, I told the crew, "Today's the day, men. I know there's big squalls all around. And it's really rough. But with Gene Lyon's pinpointing the area where he thinks the *Atocha* went down, we very well could find it today.

"It's a big ocean out there. It takes men and ships. But we're gonna reverse things, find this ship, recover its treasures, and let everybody in the world look at it!"

We had all packed up and headed down to Key West in 1969. We knew we were going to be doing some searching, probably west of the Marquesas Keys. Before that I had figured that I could find the *Atocha* in the hundred days that I took in our Middle Keys search. But I couldn't, so I began to think that maybe it was going to take six months to do it.

First, we thought maybe we could do it in the winter season, but we didn't.

I decided to just stay there until we found it, and forget about mainland East Coast Florida and Vero Beach, where the state had given us a hard time with the 1715 wrecks. They had so many new rules and regulations about them owning the treasure, you just couldn't run the business.

We sold out our interest to the Real Eight Company, and in 1969 started hunting for the *Atocha* full time.

It was the spring of 1969 when I decided to launch our search for the *Atocha* about thirty miles west of Key West, near the Marquesas, at the site of the same shipwreck where Deo and I were on our honeymoon.

To start our search for the *Atocha*, we went first to the site of the *Valbanera*. We never dreamed we would be going back there to put up a tower to hunt treasure. That's where Deo and I had made the movie *The Other End of the Line* for Voit Rubber Company. We were honeymooning and on a working vacation—right on top of where we later started our search for the *Atocha*.

In 1985, after we finally found the "Main Pile" of the *Atocha*, Deo—I don't know how she found out—but she noticed one of the charts, with some bottom readings, and the start of our search at the *Valbanera* was *the same date as her birthday! Boy!*

We built a theodolite base tower on top of the sunken hull of the *Valbanera* wreck. I found out that ship had a load of women and was refused entry to Havana, then went on toward Key West with a hurricane coming on, and the ship was wrecked, with everyone aboard killed.

The day we started to build the tower, we didn't need to use metal detectors. We could see it a block away, a big dark spot on the west end of the "Quicksands" area. There was a ripple of water over it from the high tide that was going by.

We had brought along a couple of "burning bars," which are pieces of pipe with magnesium inside. We went down and burned four holes through the steel hull. When you light up a burning bar, you light it with a cutting torch. That starts the magnesium burning and then you have pure oxygen going through the pipe. It makes a big ball of fire about six inches in diameter. A burning bar keeps burning when you go underwater, and it makes a lot of bubbles. It's pretty spectacular! When you get to a hull, you just press the end of it against the steel, and it's so hot that it burns a hole right through.

After we cut the holes, we went underneath the ship—which was upside down—and entered the decks.

We went down some stairs that were going up, and down a hall, through a doorway. We went down a stair to the next deck—going upwards. There were all kinds of shadows moving in there, probably grouper and jewfish. We were using underwater lights and got into the engine room.

Finally, we saw some shafts of light coming down into the total darkness. I hammered on the bottom.

I think it was a fellow named Gino on the outside

who came back with a bang. I had the bolts with me, and I put washers on them, then pushed the bolts up through the holes—one at a time. He would put the nut on from the outside with the washer.

Now we had somewhere to start to build our "Eiffel Tower." We built that tower out of angle irons until it stuck up above the water, about ten feet high. Then we tried it out with a theodolite, which is a survey instrument for measuring angles, and a communication radio to navigate by.

But we found the tower at first was a little shaky, so it wasn't very accurate. We had to run four cables in different directions to it to hold it steady.

Then we set up a search pattern, and the *Virgalona* (our converted treasure hunting boat) headed out from the *Valbanera* site for "Tail End Buoy," which we were going to use for the other end of our baseline, a distance of about seven miles.

The boat headed out, and after about three miles, it began disappearing and reappearing from sight on the theodolite tower, because it was going over the horizon.

So I told the guys to take a break. I took one of the black plastic bags and attached it to a long cane fishing pole, so as the boat went over the horizon, I could still see that big black ball floating in the sky. And that way, I could keep them on course heading out toward "Tail End Buoy."

Sometimes they'd get ten or twenty feet off to the west, or ten or twenty feet off to the east, so I'd just talk them back. I'd say, "Ten west, 9, 8, 7 west, 5 west, 3, 2, on course!" And they'd keep heading for "Tail End Buoy," dragging Fay Feild's underwater proton magnetometer to detect iron below.

Once the fathometer on the *Virgalona* showed they had passed the edge of the reef and dropped off into the Gulf Stream deep water, they made a U-turn and came back at me, and I'd move the theodolite instrument over a couple of seconds on the compass and guide them back toward the *Valbanera*, where I had my tower. That way they were searching the whole area like spokes of a giant wheel out from the tower. Back and forth.

We did get quite a few readings on the New Ground-Quicksands area, near our first tower location, but we didn't check those out because our information from the Spanish archives said the *Atocha* should be in fifty or sixty feet of water. Maybe one of these days, I'll go back out and check those anomalies that we originally located, since they could mean one or more of the sister ships that went down the same night [in 1622].

At the time, I guided my crew back and forth on the *Virgalona* for about three or four hours. The squalls kept getting more ominous, and the winds kept getting higher. Sometimes a big squall would go between me and the *Virgalona*, and I couldn't see them. So they had to stop and wait for the squall to move by.

Once the *Virgalona* was in the middle of one of them. They told me on the radio it was like a miniature tornado, blowing things off the boat. But after it passed, we kept on going with the search.

Then I looked around, and while the boat was turning around, I could see about sixty or seventy squalls in all directions. I'd never seen that many squalls all at once before. It was kind of frightening.

A waterspout headed for me, and I was wondering if the tower would hold up if it hit us, hit me. Fortunately it went on by, off to the side. But a big squall did hit me, with winds about fifty miles an hour. So I had to shut down the radio and hang on for dear life to keep from getting blown overboard. I got thoroughly soaked and was unprepared to keep my logbooks dry.

That day when we started our search, and I was on this tower, way out of sight of land all by myself, I could see squalls in all direction, and as it happened, I believe this was the first time I'd ever been in the eye of a hurricane as it was forming.

While the *Virgalona* was making runs back and forth, I was talking to them on the radio and was telling them "ten feet left" and "eight left," seven left," "five left," until they got on zero, and I'd tell them "straight ahead." But they disappeared into one of those squalls of rain that was coming down very hard, so we took a break for a while.

But the wind kept getting stronger and stronger and stronger. Soon it was blowing beyond gale force, up to about fifty miles an hour in a hurry. The squalls were getting thicker. There were lots more of them all around me. Quickly it became one big storm.

The crew was out of sight. I couldn't see the *Virgalona*, and they couldn't see me, and I was hanging on for dear life with all that wind and rain out there. I was hanging on to the angle iron railing we had around it [the theodolite tower].

Finally, they found me. I jumped off and we headed for the Marquesas—where the palm tree was. They picked me up, but we had a rough trip going back to the Marquesas. I could imagine if you were on deck on the *Atocha* trying to hang on. It would have seemed almost impossible. I guess that's why most of them were down below. Of those that were up, two or three that were up topside, they were tied down. I remember I was thinking about that, thinking how it must have been, back then.

That storm went on down to Texas and hit there with hurricane force, giving them flooding and a lot of damage.

I was just out there hanging on. The waves didn't get high enough at that point to be coming up over the platform, because we had about a ten-foot height over the water. But it was close. If the waves had gotten much bigger, I would have probably been swept overboard, or the tower would have been knocked over. Fortunately, the boat got to me. They saw me between the rainstorms and picked me up.

Today's the Day!

I learned on the radio a couple of days later that this was the beginning of a hurricane which hit the coast of Texas with more than hundred-mile-an-hour winds and a bad flood. It really didn't matter about the logbook though, because they hadn't yet found any anomalies in the proper depth of water to check out to see if it was the "Big A." That logbook got wet and ruined, so I threw it away. That was just the first day of our hunt.

So I told the guys, "Well, I figured we could find it and recover it in about six weeks, but considering the storms and the big, powerful ocean, it might take us a little longer. Maybe tomorrow will be the day!"

We continued searching down the spokes of that big wheel, gradually working toward the east for a couple of months—until we could no longer see the boat. Then we decided we would have to move our tower to Cosgrove Shoal lighthouse. That lighthouse is about twenty miles east of the *Valbanera* and about seven miles south of the Marquesas Keys. It stands on the edge of the Gulf Stream, where the bottom comes up fast and there is a ten-foot shallow reef that could have been the reef where the *Atocha* struck.

We found several anomalies along that outer reef near the drop-off. One was a Civil War ship that I may go back and dig on some day. Another was an extinct lighthouse that had been blown over and destroyed by the ocean, by the powerful ocean! Also, we found several more modern shipwrecks.

While the winds of a coming hurricane blew up around him, Mel persisted, as did those who believed in him. He told his crew "Today's the day. . . . I know there's big squalls . . . and it's really rough. . . . But . . . we could find it today." He knows, as always, that it may be rough in the moment, but research plus hope spells eventual success.

Mel as a young boy. FISHER FAMILY COLLECTION

CHAPTER TWO

In the Wilderness:
Water Child in Midwest Culture

*P**lains, open sky, lakes and rivers, nature, and farms make up the Midwest that was the first home to Mel Fisher. The Midwest also bred a spirit of "can do" creative, independent thinking and action. He was good with his mind and his hands, a natural leader who always said he used everything he learned from life in his quest for treasure and history under the sea.*

I was born in Hobart, Indiana [August 21, 1922]. Hobart's a little town halfway between Valparaiso and Gary. It was a rather small town on a lake called "Lake George."

I don't remember Hobart as a kid, but I went back there as a teenager an awful lot because I enjoyed the fishing and paddling around on the lake, camping out and exploring there, even going there in the wintertime and ice skating and using an ice float there, playing hockey and ice sailing—something like surf sailing.

There's a dam there at Hobart across the river, and that created this lake. The river backed up for several miles, and the lake is real long. Gosh, I don't know—maybe seven or eight miles long. Crooked. I followed the path of the river, and it gets wide, and skinny, and wide, and skinny, but there is always this channel snaking its way through the lake. I was curious to go to the headwaters of the lake. I explored up through several different little lakes, up into little creeks and tributaries by water. In the wintertime, I would explore them ice skating.

Then I decided to go the other direction and go down from the dam. That went for maybe thirty or forty miles and finally got to where the river ended up not being a river and became what they called "Burns Ditch"—which was just like a canal—that went from the river on out to Lake Michigan. So all that water ended up going out in Lake Michigan.

My grandmother they called "Mama Sprencel," "Ma Sprencel." I'm not really sure what her real name was, but everyone called her "Ma." A real heavyset gal. Her husband, my "Grandpa Louis," was very tall and skinny. He was traveling most of the time. He drove trains and he built bridges for trains. Maybe that's where I got my engineering incentive. I'm not really sure. That's probably why I became an engineer. I was doing the same thing he was doing. My middle name was given for Grandpa Louis.

Grandpa Louis and Mama had a great big old house in Valparaiso—they called it "Valpo." Down in the basement there were tunnels all around cut in the earth, and all kinds of things stored down there. I remember finding hundreds and hundreds and hundreds of lead musket balls. I guess they used them in a war, I don't know. I'm not sure whether it was the Civil War or what.

In fact, I had one of my grandpa's muskets on my houseboat in Key West for a while. I don't know what happened to it. I think somebody swiped it; I am not sure. It was a real antique.

I remember asking Grandpa Louis if I could use some of his musket balls to melt down to make my lead soldiers, and he said "sure."

Then I melted the soldiers down and made a diving helmet. So the diving helmet was from the Civil War days, probably.

That reminds me of the gold that we are finding now [in the 1980s] and the lead we're finding now. The gold just keeps on a-goin' through the centuries. It doesn't rust, it doesn't turn green. It just keeps on going from hand to hand, and man to woman, and on through the centuries and centuries and centuries and lots of lifetimes. The gold just keeps on a-goin'.

I don't remember my grandparents on my father's side. I don't think I ever met them. I think they both passed away before I can remember anything about them.

My mother, Grace [née Sprencel], said she met my father, Earl [Fisher], when he first came to town from his family farm to Valparaiso, Indiana. She said that she met Earl when he came to town to go to school, that he needed to rent a place to stay, and rented a room at their big house.

My Dad was a carpenter for many, many years, and he felt great pride in being able to cut stairsteps and roofs; cutting—designing and cutting gables, and different angles on the roofs on houses—is quite a skill. And he could figure all the angles of a lot of mitered cuts. He really wasn't a highly educated guy, my father. I don't think he completed high school or college. But he was pretty sharp, and he could do a lot of stuff naturally. So they usually made him foreman of the different carpenter gangs, because he could lay a job all out for them, and tell everybody how to cut all the hip joints, gables, angles, and stairs. I've been told he ran away from home so he could finish school, because every time it was harvest, his father would take him out of school to help on the farm.

My mother, Grace Sprencel, had five sisters. They used to have a little vaudeville show in Valpo. At a big old house, they built a kind of dance studio on the side of it, and a theater. They would charge people ten cents to come to the vaudeville show, and see a black-and-white show, about a fifteen-minute movie, like Charlie Chaplin. Usually comedy movies.

Then the six girls would put on their ballerina dresses, [and] toe shoes or tap shoes. My mother played a cello, one played a piano, and one played a violin. My Aunt Mary was a ballerina, and Aunt Lillian was the pianist. My Aunt Agnes was also an exotic dancer. All of these six girls would put on shows for all the college guys. They would come and pay ten cents to see the show. I think I have some photographs. My Aunt Agnes and probably most of the other sisters were out on a beach at Lake Michigan, doing beautiful ballet routines. All in white dresses and toe shoes. Pretty neat pictures!

I remember also seeing pictures of my mother and dad. I think they met at Wauhob Lake, where I tried out one of my first diving helmets. And my dad and mother both had black-and-white-striped bathing suits on—like jailbirds. That was when they met. They met in bathing suits. Very sexy! They were kind of long-legged bathing suits, you know. I think they came down to their ankles, and they were very well covered up with black and white stripes all around. My dad said later that he went home and told his sister Ruby that he had met the girl he was going to marry. That was Grace. How about that?

After we started out in Hobart, and moved to Glen Park, which is really the south end of Gary; we stayed there for a long time. I don't remember moving from Hobart to Glen Park. South from the Calumet River there was called Glen Park—which was more or less a suburb of Gary.

Well, gee, I was trying to think back about the earliest thing I could remember in my life, and I seem to remember being in a Model T Ford, riding across, like, desert, a lot of cactus and stuff, prairies, going out I guess to Colorado or somewhere, with my mother and dad. There weren't any paved roads, or highways, just dirt roads. It seemed like we were going forever and ever, trying to go across the country like pioneers. I vaguely remember that. I think I remember Kansas, somewhere along the way. Just dirt roads, and mud puddles, and ruts in the road, getting stuck. It seemed like a lot of nothing out there. Nothing but cactus and desert.

One way to get in touch with my early years was to go back through old pictures my mother always saved. She must have known people someday might get a kick out of seeing a successful treasure hunter start out on a bear rug. It was always very important for her to keep records, scrapbooks of clippings and pictures.

I remember two pictures—one was marked "Melvin Fisher, aged three. Before 'let's play barber'." This guy and I were going to play "barber" one day. He was going to cut my hair, and I was going to cut his. I sat in the "barber chair," and he put this towel around me and started cutting. It didn't really hurt very much, but I remember there was blood coming down my face. He was cutting my head, I guess, while he was cutting my hair. He cut it all off—I mean he cut *all* of it off, almost. Then the kids announced it was my turn to be the "barber." But he started crying and he ran away. He decided I looked such a bloody mess, he didn't want me to cut his hair! I don't remember his name, but it might have been "Sonny." The second picture, of me "balding early," was marked "After playing barber. Age three, Melvin Fisher." Someone also wrote on the picture: "New hair style. Lost besides hair, a few drops of blood and some skin." The back of one photo says I was "38 inches tall at age two and a half, and weight was 41 pounds." In another picture, at two and a half, I had a cap pistol in a picture that was probably taken at our home at 4195 Fillmore Street before we built the enclosed porch on it. I used a window as a door to the enclosed porch. My own first little private room was out on that porch.

One picture says Mel "two and a half," and that looks like I had a cap pistol. I was wearing a cowboy hat in another picture, and if you look close, you'll see I had a cigarette in my mouth too. That was a habit I picked up early. At two, there's a picture with my cousin Edward Noel and my teddy bear. Other pictures included some with Mary Comeford and Julia Sprencel, two of my aunts, when I was "two and a half." Another one showed "Grace Fisher and Melvin, past three. Mary Sprencel on the right, at the beach." Louise Theroux was another aunt, and there was Aunt Agnes Sprencel and Aunt Lillian Barman. My mother had five sisters. That picture of them must have been at Miller Beach, where we went most of the time when I was small.

By the time I had a tricycle, we had had concrete streets put in at our Fillmore Street home. One of our pictures shows "concrete mixer in front of our house. We have concrete streets now."

One other thing I vaguely remember from my early childhood was when I was down in Tampa, Florida, with my mother and dad visiting relatives—I think it was my Aunt Louise, and a hurricane came. They had all us kids get under the bed, and the roof blew off the house. When we came out from under the bed, there was no roof. But nobody got hurt! I'm not sure whose house it was, because there's a picture of me at age three with Gail, who was Aunt Agnes' daughter, and they had a house in Tampa. We were just down there on vacation, or visiting.

Some photos show my dog Prince. He was a real neat little dog! Prince would ride in my bicycle basket, and I would drive him from Glen Park out to Hobart every weekend so my buddies and I could go boating. He'd run part of the way, until he got too tired. Then I'd put him in the basket. At Hobart, we kept a boat underwater, so nobody would swipe it. We'd splash the water out of it with paddles.

As I grew, starting at about fifteen, I began to tower over both my parents in our family pictures. Deo says she thinks the same thing happened to our son Kane, at fourteen—happened to me at about the same age. From being "a little bit round" I shot up to tall. Apparently I took after my Grandpa Louis Sprencel, who was tall! He was six-foot-three! Some pictures of me were taken in Valpo, where my grandmother and grandfather had their great big two-story house with pillars.

My Dad, Earl, was a carpenter, but during the Depression, he did landscaping for the city park system.

Dad built our house on Fillmore.

There wasn't a lot of money around to do things when I was a youngster, but I never really thought I needed it. I was always trying to do things with whatever I could find that didn't cost money but worked. The first radio we had, I think we used earphones, but it was hooked up to bedsprings. My Dad told Deo about that too. We had a wire hooked up to the bedsprings of my mother and dad's bed. I guess that was the antenna. Also, we had a little rock, a white rock that was jagged, and we'd stick the wire around in different holes in this rock. It was a crystal, like a crystal radio, and that brought us the different radio stations. When you'd get the wire in a certain hole, you'd get music. You'd stick it in another hole, and you'd get somebody talking. That was a different station. That's how we moved our radio reception from station to station.

My mother always did earn money doing different things. She started her dancing school in Glen Park, Indiana. She charged thirty-five cents for dancing lessons—tap dancing, ballet or toe dancing, ballroom dancing, tangos, and all that.

I remember at first there they didn't have an extra bedroom for me, so we built a place on half of our front porch with screens and canvas awnings that rolled down on three sides, and I slept on the front porch. I'd be trying to sleep in, especially on Saturday, and my mother would be teaching all these kids tap dancing. All I could hear was clickety-click, clickety-click, "Off to Buffalo," stomp, stomp, and "The Train" step, and the "Suwannee River" step. Tap dances were pounded into my brain in my sleep. I had all of the clickety-clicks memorized, so I could do them all myself too. I was a pretty good tap dancer, and ballet dancer, and toe dancer. Then my mom even got me to come in on the ballroom lessons and the tango lessons, help her teach and dance with the girls who wanted someone to dance with them. She became an Arthur Murray–licensed instructor and took lessons in Chicago with the Arthur Murray Studio. My dad did too, and they were great dancers. They had a lot of fun dancing together. They'd go to dances everywhere, all kinds of dances. They would usually take me with them. Sometimes I would sleep in the car or fall asleep on a bench at the dance. They would keep dancing and having fun, and I was there too.

Once when I was twelve years old, I was in a dance recital. I put on a blond, curly wig, a ballerina skirt, and toe shoes, and did my ballet. Everybody applauded. When I came back to take my bow, or curtsy, whatever you call it, I took my wig off. Then they all laughed and clapped. I quit ballet then, after that.

There was one picture when I was a little older that read "Mel Doing the Charleston." At the time I was copying one of my mother's great dance steps, the "Charleston." She was a dance instructor by then.

Then we added another big room on the back, my dad and I. That was my room until we put the roof and the porch back up again. Then my mother's costume business was doing well, making so much money we lifted the whole roof up, and added a second story on the house for the costume business.

The inside of the house got a little more fancy when my mother got very angry once. She bought herself a rug. And furniture. All of a sudden she was going to be a sports girl. She always looked great—even into her late eighties. It was fun to have a sexy mom, even when I was in high school. All of the high school guys used to whistle at her. I'd really surprise them when I'd say, "What are you doing, whistling at my mother?"

Underneath this house, we also had a big basement. That's where I had a workshop with all kinds of tools. There I built things and grew things.

We had a big furnace down there, and a wine factory that my mother and dad had during Prohibition. I had a root beer factory. I made root beer—but I think the root beer had a dash of alcohol in it too. The wine had 4.5

percent, but the root beer only had about .4 percent alcohol. I remember when I was six years old, my mother and dad and another couple used to play pinochle twice a week. They'd gather at our house or at the other people's house. This was in Prohibition, when there was no alcohol—nobody could buy booze. But we used to go up into Michigan each year, and we'd go out in the vineyards and pick grapes. We got a real good buy on them if we picked our own grapes. We'd bring back a whole mess of grapes from Michigan to Indiana. We'd take them down into the basement, and we had a press down there, a scoop press, where you'd squish all these grapes, then you'd ferment them, and pour the juice into kegs and barrels. So down in our basement, we had this real neat distillery where we'd make wine. And their friends had one too. One night, the two couples were there playing pinochle and their boy and I went down in the basement. While they were playing, we took turns lying on our back, underneath the keg, and opening up the spigot of the wine barrel, letting the wine drip in our mouth. After we drank it, we got real dizzy. We couldn't even stand up anymore. So we crawled up the steps from the basement. We crawled up on our hands and knees, and we came out there where they were playing pinochle, and I remember I said, "I'm drunk, and I know it!" I really didn't know whether my folks were going to, you know, spank me, or what. But they just laughed, and they really didn't punish us all that much, but they didn't let us go down in the basement anymore while they were playing pinochle.

All my childhood I remember as being in Glen Park, Indiana. I remember going to kindergarten at Lew Wallace Grade School there.

One big surprise in early school was in art class. I enjoyed the art classes. The art teacher had some project for everybody to do, something she drew on the blackboard, and everybody was supposed to copy it. While they were all drawing this thing, butterflies or something, I was working on a sheet of graph paper instead, and I was coloring in the squares, making a big thing, like a snowflake. It was symmetrical, all over the graph paper, and I covered it up with the butterfly page when the teacher would walk around. So I was drawing butterflies, and after she'd go by, I'd go back to making the snowflake. Then the teacher came up behind me and surprised me, and took it away from me. I thought I was going to really get bawled out. Instead, she took it up in front of the class and said "Look at this beautiful snowflake! Now this is really creative!" She went on and on about how neat it was, and symmetrical, an original idea, and all this baloney. That surprised me. So that was kind of gratifying as a young kid. With all the other kids looking and listening, it was just the opposite of what I expected.

It was good to get praised by an important person in your life for something that you did that was different. Yeah, I learned that it is good to praise people, now and then, for their good work, instead of just criticizing all the time.

And then, let's see . . . I think in first grade, I was about six or seven. I remember the little girl who sat in front of me had a pigtail one day, and I couldn't resist. I stuck the end of her pigtail in the inkwell, and she turned around and slapped me. I didn't know what was going on. What did she do that for? Really surprised me.

In Glen Park, which is the south end of Gary, we lived at 4195 Fillmore Street. Broadway was the main street, and all the other streets were named after Presidents. I think I was about twelve blocks away from Broadway, so Fillmore must have been the twelfth or thirteenth president of the United States! I had to walk about a mile to school each day and had to go up a big hill.

Then I got a bicycle. It was quite a challenge to see if you could ride the bicycle up the hill. Usually, I got about three-quarters of the way and had to get off and walk and push the bike. Going home every night, we'd get to going real fast down the hill.

We used to take shortcuts when we were walking. One of the big shortcuts went through the cemetery. There were a lot of trees in the cemetery, and in the back part it was like wilderness—a lot of bushes and shrubs. We used to go swimming in the pond in the cemetery. We built a pretty big raft and paddled around on the raft on the pond. We used to stop by there almost every night on the way home from school and go for a ride on our raft. It was fun. On that pond in the cemetery, we would ride the raft and tip it over on purpose sometimes to make sure everybody got dumped in the water. We built a kayak from pear crates and paddled around there on that too.

Also, on the way home, we made some rabbit traps. We would bend down a willow stick and have a string going to a peg under a fork. On the end of the peg was something the rabbits liked to eat. You try a carrot, you try this, and you try that. We were trying to lasso a rabbit by the leg or something. Really, it's how you do it. It is really tough. I don't know if we ever caught one or not. I don't think we ever did. We could see the little rabbit turds around, the footprints, and the bait would be gone, but we never caught a rabbit. It was just something we were trying to do for the hell of it. We'd inspect them every night on the way home to see if we caught any, but we never did catch one. We made all kinds of rabbit traps but never caught a rabbit.

We found tadpoles out there too. Sometimes we found thousands of tadpoles. It kind of amazed me the way they were pollywogs, then later they grew legs, and before you knew it, they were frogs. It was pretty amazing to watch them grow. I remember seeing tadpoles in the little puddles around down there and watching them grow each week and become a frog.

My mother and dad used to always have a garden in the backyard. I remember transplanting a lot of tomato plants. I guess we sold tomato plants. We planted the seeds, and then when they'd sprout, we'd transplant them into bigger boxes, and then we'd sell the plants to people, and they would grow tomatoes. Then also tulips. We sold tulip bulbs and cut tulips and tulip plants. Also pansies. We had all different colors and types of pansies. I remember even selling the tulips out in front of that same cemetery gate on whatever day it is when you decorate graves—Decoration Day, Memorial Day.

I used to go out on the farm—my aunt and uncle's farm about three miles west of Crown Point, Indiana. In the summertime, I'd go out to Aunt Lillian and Uncle Tony Barman's house for a couple of months for vacation. His brother's name was Leo.

They'd give me little jobs to do—pitching hay and shoveling cow manure, feeding the cows and feeding the chickens, feeding the hogs and milking the cows. I wasn't very good at milking cows. My uncle did it well and fast, and the cows were real nice. But when I did it, they'd kick the bucket over or kick me over or swat me with their tails. I guess I didn't pull on them just right and they were saying, "Ouch! Get out of here!" I carried a lot of buckets of milk from the milking barn up to the windmill, where we had cold water. I guess the cold water came from deep down in the ground, I don't know. But they always had this cold running water going around the milk cans to cool the milk down, because when it came out of the cows it was hot. We had to put it in these big milk cans, and they would kind of float in the water with the running cool water going around them. I guess the windmill did the pumping so it didn't use any electricity. That was about thirty or forty miles inland from the lake.

One time I remember this other little kid and I were in a ditch full of water catching carp. We were catching them with our bare hands. We would hide up underneath the overhang of the ditch. We couldn't see—it was real muddy—but you could feel them when you would catch one, and then they would flop all around and try to stick you with the spines on them. You'd thrown them out on the bank. Then I looked at this other kid and he had about ten or fifteen great big leeches on him, blood leeches, so I tried to pull them off, but they were too slippery. Then he looked at me, and I had about a hundred of them, and then I figured out how to dig into them real hard and pull them off. Then he started pulling mine off. I looked back at him, and he had about a hundred more on him. And he looked back at me and I had about a hundred more on me. What it was, they were little teeny things when they were on you at first, and you don't even notice them, but they get big, they get all full of your blood. So they were really sucking a lot of blood out of us, so we kept pulling them off and pulling them off, and then more of them just kept growing. I'll never forget that one! We pulled them all off. But you couldn't hardly even get them off when they were little. I don't remember them being on the carp. Just us. We went back, and did it again, but instead of getting in the ditch to get them, we would get them with a pitchfork, a hay fork. I think we ate them. I took them home to my aunt to cook.

We also caught some huge frogs. Gigantic frogs! I didn't know they grew so big. They must have weighed ten pounds, fifteen pounds, and they would jump big jumps! Fifteen to twenty feet they could jump in *one jump* when you were trying to catch them! They would be jumping all over the place. They were just in a little swamp there, and we took some and put them in—well, that same windmill that I've been talking about. It had another concrete tank outside the milk cooling building that was always full of the ice-cold water for the horses to come up and help themselves whenever they wanted a cold drink of water. They would just come over there and get a drink. So we put some of the big frogs in that tank and we thought they were safe there. But the next day, we came back, and they were gone! I don't know if my uncle let them go, or if they just jumped out and got away.

We didn't ride the horses very much. They were great big horses for pulling the wagons and plows and stuff like that. Although I remember my uncle did have some buggies in the barn there. He had one barn that was just full of buggies and stuff like that. I bet those would be good antiques now. Then he had a Model T car and a Model T truck. He let me drive the truck a couple of times. That was exciting, great! I liked that. He finally got a tractor to use instead of the horses.

I remember as a kid we used to get on the bus in Glen Park, at 41st and Fillmore, and pay 'em a nickel. We'd get a couple of transfers, and transfer paper slips, so we could ride from Glen Park to downtown Gary, Indiana. We had a bus depot at 5th and Broadway in Gary. There we'd catch a bus, and we went out to Miller, Indiana. We would transfer there and get one that went out to Miller Beach. I spent a lot of time swimming and hiking around the sand dunes and swimming in Lake Michigan. The water was crystal clear, and you could even drink it. You could see everything clearly, even without a mask.

I remember we had a kind of a game, or a challenge for us, which was to be able to swim underwater and catch a duck by the feet. That was really hard to do! I think they were wild ducks, mallards, or something like that. Then when you'd catch one, when you'd come up for air, it would flop its wings on you and peck you and really give you a hard time!

The water was kind of chilly, though, in the lake, and we'd get goose bumps.

After a while we'd go over the dunes to the lagoon, a great big freshwater lagoon that went for miles and miles. In wintertime we'd go ice skating there, and in the summertime the water was real warm. We'd go swimming there. We liked that spot!

Miller Park was right on Lake Michigan. They had public beaches and a big park there and the big lagoon. Sometimes we'd get a transfer from there and go farther out into the sand dunes. I think it was my friend Romano Gibbs and I who used to go out to the sand dunes. We'd get off and just hike around in the wilderness there.

We went out there both in the summertime and the wintertime. One interesting area out there was a huge factory of some kind that was shut down. I don't know if it was an old steel mill or what. But it was a huge factory that was completely inoperable, and we had a lot of fun playing around up in the attics and steel ramp locks.

In wintertime, I remember, they had a toboggan slide on the end of the lake in Miller Park. We'd go down in the toboggan and out over the ice on the lake. Then you'd whirl around on the slippery ice. One time when I was a teenager, we took a Model A Ford out there, or a Model T, I guess it was, driving around on the ice. We did a lot of ice skating, played a lot of hockey, and sometimes we'd go ice sailing.

We did something like what is now called sail surfing. Only we did it with ice skates. We made our own big sail, something like a great big kite made out of canvas or something. We'd hold that and go lickety-split! I just built it myself. I saw a picture of it in *Popular Mechanics*, or a magazine like it, and built one.

Then we used to ski out there in the wintertime. We'd carry our skis on the bus. They weren't skis with shoes on them. They just had a toe strap. We'd ski down one side of the sand dune, walk up the other and ski down another side. Go for two or three miles. Sometimes we just walked for miles down the beach in the summertime on Lake Michigan. Then in the wintertime, we'd walk down the beach, and, once, there was ice on Lake Michigan, but then some of the ice was just mush. I remember going out on part of it right next to the edge where the water was, and it would build up real high and thick there at the edge of the water.

We had some .22s, and we were trying to hunt for these ducks with the ring, the green neck. I guess they were mallards. We couldn't hit one, and we kept trying and trying. But we couldn't hit a duck with a .22.

We thought we would be able to find a place where we could walk back to the beach, but we couldn't. We were on a kind of peninsula made of ice, so we had to walk about a mile back down this ice floe to get back to the beach.

I guess I did more of that than other kids.

I enjoyed camping out on a lake. My folks would take us out there and leave us for maybe three weeks—me and a group of kids—and we were supposed to exist on the land. We would go fishing and try to catch a rabbit. I remember one time we found a cow out in a field, and we decided we would get some milk. Man, that cow was really hard to milk. Kept switching his tail at us and kicking us. Maybe we weren't pulling on the nipples right or something. I remember that Romano was lying on his back underneath the cow, and I was afraid the cow might step on him. I was trying to squirt the milk out, and I was squirting it all over his face and head and everywhere. Once in a while I hit his mouth. That milk really didn't taste all that good, since it was hot. But anyway, we finally got some milk out of that cow, and nobody got stepped on.

We were getting hungry because we ran out of food. We found a crab apple tree. I don't know if you ever had any crab apples. But you eat one and they are very bitter. They're really crummy-tasting. They don't taste like real apples. But that was the only apple tree around. So we picked crab apples. It made us a little bit ill eating the green [apples]. They had worms in them too. Lots of worms. We tried to cut the worms out. Then we decided that night we would make some applesauce. We built this big fire and had this big old pot full of crab apples. We figured it would take a couple of hours boiling, so we kept cooking and cooking. But they wouldn't cook. We kept making the fire hotter. Finally, about 3 o'clock in the morning, they turned into applesauce. So that solved the food problem for that day.

We were just doing it on our own, learning how to exist in the wilderness. We were figuring out which things were poison and which ones were OK, you know. Once you got poison ivy, you knew what poison ivy was. I remember one time we found these neat javelins or spears growing. We cut them off and stripped all the limbs and leaves off of them. We were having a javelin-throwing contest to see who could throw the spear farther than the other guy. They were really good spears. They would really go a long way. The next day we found out they were poison oak. We all broke out with poison oak all over us. It was awful. So we walked—we heard there was a drugstore in some little city, village—and we walked three or four miles to get there. We bought a bottle of calamine lotion for our poison oak, and that really helped. It worked very well. Also, we got a bar of Ivory soap, and that Ivory soap seemed to cut all the poisons off our skin, helped us get over our poison oak. There's a good plug for Ivory soap! We also got a bar of Fels-Naptha soap, and between the Fels-Naptha and Ivory soap, we got all those poison oak juices off us.

I liked the water a lot. Did a lot of swimming and looking at girls on the beach. I enjoyed all kinds of water activities. The water in Lake Michigan was always real cold, but it was real clear back then. You could even drink the water you were swimming in, it was so clean. Sadly, I hear it's more polluted now.

I just did what I thought was fun and enjoyed life.

Mel Fisher had a capacity from his earliest times to minimize the challenges, not give them a life of their own. Instead, he would maximize the pleasure from exerting real physical effort to solve the immediate problem and keep moving while he kept looking—at the girls as well. With his imagination, and his reading in "library" periods, he decided adventure lay ahead in and on the water, just like in the books of old.

Mel and his parents, Grace and Earl. FISHER FAMILY COLLECTION

CHAPTER THREE

Into Adventure: Homemade Dive Helmet and River Voyage of "Huckleberry Fisher"

Mel gets his start early as a waterborne pioneer, building his own dive helmets and related equipment while for the first time reading in high school library periods about treasure and pirates. And Mel also built boats in his basement, not all of which he was able to remove except in pieces, like a submarine. But he discovered the art of improvisation very early, along with mathematics, and the two would set him on a lifetime pioneering course. First, Mel and his childhood buddy had their own "Huckleberry Finn" adventures in the nation's Midwest—Lake Michigan, Chicago and the Chicago River, and the rivers that flow south from the nation's center.

I actually attended Lew Wallace Grade School and Lew Wallace High School—graduated there. Twelve years in one school! We had a work-study-play program at Lew Wallace High. We had two study periods—one in the morning and one in the afternoon, an hour apiece. I would study in the morning and do all my homework. Then in the afternoon, I would just read in the library, things like pirate books, *Treasure Island* and *Blackbeard the Pirate* and history, Spanish-American history books. *I was always fascinated by the treasure and the pirates.*

A lot of kids took books home every night and did homework, for two or three hours a night. But I never did, so I didn't really study all that hard. I did best in—I think the first "A" I got was in trigonometry. I did pretty good in math—algebra, calculus. Then when I got in college—

the first time I got in doubt as to whether I was really going to have to study—I was taking college chemistry, and I couldn't hack it. I didn't have—I didn't take high school chemistry, while everybody else in the course had already had it. So the professor was going from "there" on, and I didn't know what I was doing. So I had to really buckle down and hire a tutor to try and help me catch up. Almost flunked that. But we're still using that "trig" out here treasure hunting, you know.

A kayak was one of the first boats I built. Bought two pear baskets. I guess they were about three feet or three and a half feet high, and a foot on one end, and a foot and a half on the other—they taper. Then I put some slats or laths between them. I covered the whole thing with muslin and painted it with—I don't know if it was Elmer's Glue or flour and water, but something like that. It made the cloth get tight and waterproof, and then I painted it with paint. It worked real well. I had a good kayak. I built a couple of them. I had a double paddle, with a paddle on both ends, and you have to paddle like mad. If you sneeze, then you tip over, and you are upside down in the water!

Let's see, I remember I built an iceboat in the basement of our house in Glen Park. I must have been a real genius engineer at that time, because when I got it all done, I couldn't get it out of the basement. I had to cut one of the main pieces of it to get it out of the basement.

I built a submarine down there too. I never got it done because it got expensive when you started getting to the part where you had to somehow have air or oxygen, or a way to absorb the CO_2 [carbon dioxide] and things like that. I never did take that thing out in the water. I think I finally ended up trashing the submarine.

I did make diving helmets. I made several of them. I tested my first diving helmet in Lake Michigan, and I also tested it in the lagoon there at Miller Park. Also, I did tests on one of my helmets in the high school swimming pool at Lew Wallace High School.

First one was out of a five-gallon paint can which was turned upside down. I sacrificed my bicycle and my lead soldiers. I cut one of the tires and wrapped it around just below the lip of the paint can. I put some baling wire into the tire and twisted it tight. Then I made a circular belt that fit all around the can, and it was just the right amount to make the helmet go down and hold me down too.

We tried it that way, without any hose or anything, and without a window. Just a can, and it worked pretty good. You could stay down two or three minutes. Then you'd come up, get another bucket of air, and go down again. Every time you'd take a breath, the water'd come up in the helmet, then go down, up, and down. After you'd used up all the oxygen, you could still breathe, but you'd black out. I just wanted to see if I could go down with it, and I could. At the time, I don't think I knew anything about air embolism, but I never got it. So I guess I always exhaled when I was coming up.

Then I took a valve core from a tire on a bicycle, and I drilled a hole in the bottom of the paint can—which was the top of the helmet. I don't know if I soldered it in, or I bolted it in, or what—but I made a place for the air to come in. Then I had a garden hose clamped onto it. I had about twenty feet of hose with a bicycle tire pump on the other end from my helmet. This other kid, my buddy Romano Gibbs, would sit in the inner tube and be pumping air. I would be down on the bottom with the helmet, counting sunfish and croppies—little fish. Every once in a while, I'd goof around and pinch his rear end, or tickle his feet. So he would get even with me and put the tire pump under water. Then he'd start spraying water down on me through the hose, like a shower. Sometimes if he kept doing it, I'd come up and flip him over.

With that helmet you could see down a bit, but you never were—you couldn't see very well. This was in a gravel pit. Evidently, they'd taken big chunks out of the bottom with a giant clamshell. So every now and then it would suddenly get six foot deeper. Then it would get shallow, and then deep, and then in some places it'd drop way off!

I finally decided to put a window in the helmet. You could see a little bit by looking at the bottom, because the bottom was open, and you could sometimes see a little bit. Then I put in the window. It was from my dad's automobile. He had a car, I think it was a convertible, and what it had was not a glass window. I think they called it "isinglass," which is maybe a forerunner to clear plastic. You couldn't see out of it like you can out of glass. But you could see out. Also, we could bend the shape of the helmet. I just taped the "isinglass" window on with tape, white adhesive tape. They didn't have waterproof tape back then, just regular coarse, cloth-like tape. So it blew off, didn't work too well. Finally, I made a frame to go around it, and bolted it down. Also, I had crosswork, a crosshatch of little bars on the inside of the helmet so the water pressure wouldn't push the isinglass in.

When we got it working real well in the gravel pit, we took it out on the weekend to Wauhob Lake near Valparaiso. The water was deeper there, about thirty-five feet or so, and we went out to a raft they had tied up offshore for swimmers to swim to. Romano Gibbs, who was one of my best buddies back then, was pumping air to me with a tire pump from the swimming raft. He was worried because it was deeper water than we were used to, so he was pumping away like mad, as fast as he could pump.

I went down off the raft, and sank waist-deep in this really soft, oozy silt. I was almost stuck in that real black, deep mud. I was weighted too heavy with the helmet.

The bars I had put into the helmet were on the inside to keep the pressure from blowing it in. But my buddy was pumping so hard with the tire pump that it blew the window off the helmet. So I took the helmet off my head, pushed it down in the mud, stood on the helmet, gave a shove, and swam up.

I came up on the other side of the big raft from where Romano was still pumping away like mad. He didn't know there was anything wrong. I got up behind him and tapped him on the shoulder. He turned around and was so surprised to see me standing there that he just kept pumping.

Then we gave up on the helmet that weekend. We remodeled it again, put wires inside and outside. It worked pretty well after that.

Later on I made a helmet out of a hot water heater tank, a twenty-gallon water tank. I cut the end of it off and cut it to fit my shoulders. Then I hung a bunch of window sash weights on it.

The first test of that helmet was at Lew Wallace High School. The coach let me take it into the swimming pool to test it out. I had the window sash weights with hooks on the end of them hooked onto the helmet. While I was down there, I tilted sideways or something, and one of the weights came off and hooked me on the forearm. It took a big slash of meat out of me. I remember that. That one finally worked well too.

We would go to Lake George quite often for swimming, fishing, boating, and camping. To go swimming and practicing with our diving helmets we used to go to lakes like Flint Lake, Wauhob Lake, Cedar Lake. We went to Lake Michigan; first we'd go to Miller Beach—for the beautiful beaches. From there, we'd walk over the sand dunes to a lagoon, where the water was nice and warm and clear. The water in Lake Michigan was always real cold, but it was real clear back then, and you could even drink the water you were swimming in.

One time we were watching the boat races, the speedboat races, at Flint Lake [Indiana]. I think it was on a Fourth of July. One of the speedboats went out of control. The boat headed straight for the pier I was standing on and ran into the pier right in front of me. The boat filled with water and sank. I asked the guy who was standing in the boat as it was sinking if he wanted to sell it. He said "Yeah," he'd sell it to me. I think it was $10. So I bought it from him. That was about like me, getting his boat for $10.

Last month [1987], I sold the boat *Virgalona* to [Demostines] "Mo" Molinar for a dollar when I made him a partner on a wreck we've been salvaging together all through the years. He called one morning recently at 8 o'clock. He said he had the boat all ready to go and he was boogyin'! He was heading out to sea. I wonder what he found!

Probably my first real great adventure was when I got talking with Romano Gibbs, my best friend back then. I'm not sure exactly what age it was—probably thirteen or fourteen or fifteen. We decided we would like to take this boat that I had bought, remodel it, and make it into a combination sailboat, rowboat, and home. We wanted to sail from Miller Park near Gary, Indiana, across Lake Michigan to Chicago, and enter the Chicago River that went out from Lake Michigan, then go through Chicago and on down to where the Chicago River met the Des Plaines River and became the Des Plaines River. Then our plan was to go on down to the Illinois River, which dumped into the Mississippi River, and along the Mississippi River, and then go on down to the Gulf of Mexico and sail down to Tampa, Florida, where I had some relatives.

My folks said they thought it was a good idea, and they approved it. Romano's mother wouldn't let him go. Anyway, we started working on the boat and getting it ready. We kept talking to his mother every day or every week. Pretty soon we had a cabin on the boat. We made it the same way we made the kayak, with some muslin—cotton muslin. I think it was eleven cents a yard. I put the glue on it—powder mixed with water—and made it waterproof.

We got some oarlocks and put them in the side of this hydroplane speedboat I had bought for $10. We patched a hole in the bottom, which was very, very expensive. I think it cost us about $17 to patch that hole in the bottom. We were only on paper route money, so that was quite a bunch of money. Then we put a mast on the boat, a sail, and a rudder. We saved up some money for food, cameras, and film. You know we had to have pictures of this epic voyage.

Finally, Romano's mother said, "OK," when she saw we had the boat ready and all the money we needed. When summer vacation came, she finally said, "OK, go for it."

We took off, and it was a weird feeling to leave land and head out into Lake Michigan and see all the land disappear and just water everywhere, you know. It was my first experience of having no land visible and knowing it was kinda lonely out there!

Fortunately, we had a compass. It was a Boy Scout compass, and it worked pretty well. We kept sailing west and we got to—we spotted the skyline of Chicago and actually found the mouth of the Chicago River or the Chicago Canal. And went into it. It was more like a canal. We went down it, and soon it turned into a nice river. We didn't stop in Chicago. We just went right on through. There wasn't much current, so we had to row quite a bit. Once in a while we'd get the wind going in our direction, and we'd take advantage of it.

Then we actually got down to the Des Plaines River, and that was like wilderness. There were no people, no houses, no cities, just open country. The current was going pretty good and just taking us along. We hardly had to do any work. We stayed on an island one night in the middle of the river there.

It reminded me about this book I had read about Huckleberry Finn and Tom Sawyer. It was like reliving that experience.

We headed on downstream, and when we got to the Illinois River it was kind of disappointing to us, because it got real wide and real big. Gosh, the river's half a mile wide or something, and the current got real slow. We were just barely moving along, and the wind stopped. So we started rowing. We'd take turns rowing, and we'd get tired and hot, so we'd jump in the river to swim and cool off. We went on down the river.

Then along came a speedboat with a siren and horns. They had a loudspeaker saying, "There's a tornado coming!" There was a tornado watch, and everybody got clear out of the river. No boats were allowed. We rowed over to one side of the river, and there were just sheer cliffs there. We found some ladders going up the cliff. We went up the ladder, and there was a cabin up there.

We knocked on the door, and nobody answered. We tried the doorknob. It was open. By then the winds were blowing real hot and heavy, and it was raining like mad. We went inside for shelter and stayed there for the night. Next morning, when we left, we left them $2 for rent. That seemed like an awful lot of money to us then.

So then we went on down the river. Soon there was no wind and no current. We got so tired of rowing we couldn't row any more. We were so hot and sweaty we decided to dock the boat and go somewhere where there was civilization.

We hiked through a swamp and found a little city somewhere in Illinois. We went to the public swimming pool and went swimming. Then we went back to the boat and went further down the river and got to some big locks.

They were like a big fence across the river. We found out that the water wasn't moving very fast because they had a dam there. Then all the boats had to go through these big doors into a lock, and we had to fill out all these papers. Very complicated papers, they were, I guess by the Coast Guard, US Army Corps of Engineers, and everybody. We got some guys to help us figure out how to fill out the papers. We had this little, teeny boat—I guess it was about a fourteen-footer, but pretty wide.

Then they lowered the water down. When they lowered the water, it was like a big whirlpool. Our boat was spinning around real, real fast, and we were really dizzy. We were going round and round like a top.

When the water got about halfway down on the lock, they opened up the doors or the gates on the other end, and we went roaring out of there about sixty miles an hour down a mountain of water and were carried on down the river.

There was a slight current then—maybe about a mile an hour. We got tired and fell asleep that night.

About 3 o'clock in the morning, all of a sudden we heard this huge "BOOOOOO!" We woke up, and there was a huge oil tanker coming right at us. We paddled like mad and just barely got to one side of the bow of it. It almost tipped us over, and we swished down the side. That really scared the daylights out of us!

We went on down another day or two and got to Starved Rock State Park. That was a park that had natural canyons, rivers, tunnels, and caves carved out of the stones. It was such a neat place that we docked at a pier there. We took hikes up some of these canyons, looking in some of the caves and exploring. It was like a tourist resort. We really enjoyed that. When we got back to our boat, though, somebody had gotten into the boat and took our cameras and all the film and pictures that we had shot on the whole trip. So you can't see any of them in this book. And they took all our money. All the money we had in the world, and our cameras, and everything we had. Everything on the boat! They just cleaned us out. Since we didn't have anything left, we wondered what to do.

I finally told one of the park guys what happened and asked him if I could use their telephone to call my dad. He said, "All right." He let me call my dad, and I told him what happened. So my mother and dad jumped in the car and hooked on a trailer—I had a boat trailer too. They came down to Starved Rock and picked us up, put the boat on, and we went home.

So we never did make it to Tampa, and we didn't get to the Mississippi River, but we sure had a good vacation. We had figured on, I think, three months. But it took us about a month before we got cut short, ran out of money and everything. Romano's mom was glad to see him back home and safe. We had called them a couple of times along the way.

Not all rivers flow to the sea, but Mel Fisher was a mighty "river" of a man whose life flowed seamlessly overall—despite many setbacks and bumps—through his universe, and after a practice boyhood run toward the Mississippi (which he didn't make), found his way home after a "good vacation."

Mel with his band. On saxophone, he sits front row, second from left.
FISHER FAMILY COLLECTION

CHAPTER FOUR

Vision and Leadership
Come from Unexpected Places

Musical Mel? Yes, it's true. Mel Fisher was a lot more than a treasure hunter, as you might have guessed. But a musician? Probably he came by it naturally from his mother, Grace. In high school he decided to join the band, which again started him on a lifetime of separate activity. Leave it to Mel to choose an instrument as tall as he was at the time, a baritone saxophone, but more important was a lesson in people vs. perfection, a lesson he carried through his life. He became a real bandleader, as his band, Mel Fisher's Orchestra, went to a twenty-one-piece band playing Glenn Miller and Tommy Dorsey orchestrations. But practical as always, as he got to college, Mel figured out a "people" way to make money and ease his way from musician to engineer.

A true son of hardy middle America in times of "you try stuff and you find out," the young Melvin Fisher had started learning early from each of his parents how to use his hands, brain, and showmanship in carpentry and music, and the benefits of education and idea-making from math to reading on his own in high school library periods. He had already experienced the accomplishments that came from adventures in nature and in her waters as well. But as an eager young man, he was soon to awaken to more adult experiences of life, including World War II.

Then I decided to join the band in high school. I signed up to be in the band, got in there, and the teacher said, "What instrument do you want to play?" I said, "I don't know," and he said, "Don't you like any certain instrument?" I said, "No." I said, "What kind of instruments do you need to make your band complete?" He said, "Well, I don't have anybody in the saxophone section." So I said, "OK, I'll take saxophone lessons."

At Lew Wallace High School in Gary, Indiana, I became a sax player in the military band and also the concert band. I'd play in the parades for the football games. I'd play all kinds of parades in lots of other cities, and in different kinds of celebrations.

Also, for another band, my mother became a baton twirler and the leader of the band who struts down the street out front—drum major? She was the head cheese and would lead all the other drum majorettes. My dad was a bugle player in the American Legion Drum and Bugle Corps. He would play in the drum and bugle corps, and my mother would be leading the Auxiliary Legion Corps Band, and I was playing in the high school band. We would all be in the same parades together!

When I first started my musical career, I was playing a baritone saxophone. I wasn't very tall then, and I think the saxophone was just about as tall as I was. When I was wearing it, it was only about an inch above the street. That was kind of tough when I was in these parades, because once in a while the saxophone hit the street and jarred my teeth. I was thinking about putting wheels on it. It was awful heavy too. But then I grew taller and didn't have that problem. I got a little stronger too, so I could handle it.

A proud moment came when I was chosen "first chair" in the band. That means you're the best player—something to be really proud of achieving. I remember this one kid was taking private lessons from the band director, and he challenged me. They "challenge" you when you're "first chair." Each "chair" can challenge—third chair can challenge second chair, second chair can challenge first. This kid came up from second chair, and so he challenged me, and we went in there to play clarinets in competition.

By then, I played clarinet half the time and

saxophone half the time. Every time the band director would pick some song or something for us to play, this kid had it just perfect. He'd been practicing and practicing. He played everything just perfect. I was goofing all up, and making mistakes, because I'd never seen the music before. Fortunately for me, the band director was reasonable, and he said, "Well, even though he outshone you in the challenge, you're still the first chair player." That surprised me, that even though this other kid had . . . I knew he'd beat me. The band director had good judgment. I've remembered that, since.

I've applied that system several times through life. It's not necessarily who can do something perfect. There's a lot more to it, a lot of understanding about people.

We played a lot of football games, but we also got into some unusual musical situations. A trumpet player—Joe Hlodnicki, a guy who played an accordion, and I, found out we could play music for money at a Lithuanian wedding. They said they'd pay us $3 a night to play at this wedding. We decided, "Let's do it." That was my first dance band job. I was horrified to see that the music of these Lithuanian polkas was all in five sharps and six sharps, which I never played before. Most music that we played in the military band and the concert band were in the key of C, or G, or F, or D, or some kind of normal music. But these Lithuanian polkas were in five and six sharps, so that meant that every note you played was cockeyed. We really sounded sick for the first two or three hours. Finally, we got into the gist of it, and it just kind of got natural for us to play everything cockeyed. We learned the melody, got it all memorized. I don't know if you know about a Lithuanian wedding, but they go on for three days and nights, twenty-four hours a day, without stopping. We found out that our three dollars was a lot of work! That was for a twenty-four-hour day. Pretty soon you'd fall asleep while playing. You just kept going and going and going. But after that three days of wedding, we had all those polkas memorized. We were playing them all perfect. Then someone wanted to hire us for another Lithuanian wedding. We told them, "That's too much work," and it was "gonna cost five dollars." They paid us five dollars. Then we had to . . . we thought we should get another two guys in the orchestra.

My dance band started out with just four of us, and we got up to a seven-piece band, and then twelve pieces. In those years, we listened to Glenn Miller and Tommy Dorsey, and sometimes we copied them. After a while we had a twenty-one-piece dance band.

When we decided to have a seven-piece band, we called it "The Rhythm Rockers."

I don't think we had a name for our first group. We just went and played. From three of us in the first band, we increased in size. We got a drum player, and a bass player, a trombone player. We practiced every week.

Now I can't remember the first sheet of music we bought, though I think it was "Little Old Lady," "Little old lady . . . catching everyone's eye . . ." I believe the first song for which we bought the music was "Diana." Next, we bought "My Wild Irish Rose." I think that was number three. A waltz. Then came "Alexander's Ragtime Band."

As I remember, Joe Hlodnicki played trumpet. Then there was "Toby," Alan Toby, who was first trombone. Toby was a real good trombone player, who played very mellow, beautiful music. Alan Stowder was second trombone. Bill Davis was the trumpet player who joined us as second trumpet, and Carl Bloomfield also played second trumpet.

For a while there, we had three trombones, and three trumpets. I played sax and clarinet. And I can't remember everybody's names. That was a long time ago. But Marietta Wagner, I think, was pianist.

We went around to different high schools playing for proms and sophomore hops. We played several cities all around Gary, even in Chicago a little, and Hammond, and I even played at Calumet City, in a striptease joint, once. How about that? It's "Cal City," they call it. See, half of the City's in Illinois and half in Indiana.

When we got up to being a twelve-piece band was when we named it "Mel Fisher's Orchestra." I was the one who was getting all the jobs, signing all the contracts. So I was paid about three times as much as the rest of the guys.

Finally, we had enough money for three trumpet players, three trombones, five saxophones, four singers, bass, drummer, piano player. I had a twenty-one-piece band! We started buying Glenn Miller orchestrations, and Harry James orchestrations, Cab Calloway's. I wasn't really the leader at first. It was really a democracy.

Probably those were my first contracts. And I didn't have any attorneys. I made my own contracts. I always do, though my attorneys really moan when I sign anything without them reading it first.

Mel Fisher's Orchestra played mainly in Gary and Glen Park, Indiana. But we also went other places, such as Flint Lake, Indiana, to other high schools all around that were twenty, thirty, or forty miles away. We played for the proms and the sophomore hops. Sometimes we played for weekend resort places where they'd have dancing. Every Wednesday night we played in Gary for the YMCA, where they had dances. That was more or less a steady job every week. We got paid—not a lot of money; I think it was $60 for the whole band—about a ten-piece band.

Our orchestra kept playing, even at the YMCA in Gary, after I got out of high school, and even when I was in college. We had an ongoing contract.

My college education started at Purdue University, and it was quite a few miles to Purdue. I had to drive back there and play every Wednesday night, then drive back to college. I was usually asleep in all my lectures and courses. I finally figured I just couldn't hack all this music and nightlife *and* college.

So I sold the band to Joe Hlodnicki. And I sold

him a whole trunkful of orchestrations. By that time, we had a couple thousand orchestrations. A lot of them were custom-made originals. But most of them were stock arrangements, like copies of Glenn Miller and all the other big bands. I sold him our public address system, with all the amplifiers and speakers and music stands, all the music and the business.

Joe kept on going with the band and I started studying engineering. I don't know how long he kept going. I really didn't keep track of it.

At Purdue University, I joined the Delta Chi fraternity. I was very much surprised because I had a good encounter with a man I'd been bucking, a man named Joe Petrillo, who was head of the musicians' union for several years.

He had been trying to get me to have my band become unionized, and that experience had made me antiunion for the first time. One night we were playing in the ballroom of the Gary Hotel, on the corner of Broadway and Fifth Avenue, and all the lights went out. They shut off all the electricity to keep us from playing. I think we were playing an Elks or Masons dance, ten or eleven stories up on the top floor—and the lights went out, the elevator stopped. Everybody kind of panicked. So we got some candles, lit the candles, and started playing music again. We kept going by candlelight until one o'clock in the morning. But then everybody had to walk down the stairs.

We came to find out that the head of the musicians' union had ordered that because we were a non-union band. Petrillo had told us we could never play there again and had to join the union.

But then, at Purdue, Petrillo made a compromise with me. He said, "I'll tell you what I'll do. If you'll quit playing music and quit competing with me—since you're a Delta Chi Fraternity brother, I'll give you a booking license. And you can book all the union bands into Purdue University. You don't have to do anything except line up the contracts and get them signed. And you'll make ten times as much as you did when you had your own band." So I did it.

Petrillo became my bosom buddy and gave me a booking license. Normally you had to pay $3,600 to become a booker. He gave it to me free because I was a fraternity brother, and told me to start booking the big bands in. So I booked in Glenn Miller, and all the top bands, into Purdue University. I did make ten times as much as I ever did, and instead of having to work, I could just go to the dance and have fun. That was a pretty good deal. I finally buckled in to the union. That's Joe Petrillo.

The band I was in during the Army, in an old photograph, shows an airplane with the bandstand in the foreground. I was third from the left on my row, playing the saxophone. Evidently, we had four or five saxes in that band. I believe that picture was taken at Tuscaloosa, Alabama, where I was going to engineering college in what was then known as the "ASTP" [Army Specialized Training Program]. We had a dance band there, and we also had a big orchestra, like a symphony orchestra. We practiced Ravel's "Bolero." For about eight months we played that same song over and over and over and over. There were about eighty of us musicians in the band, and we practiced Ravel's "Bolero" every day. Finally, we had a concert. The star of the show was a pianist who did a solo with the eighty-piece band as a background. It went off very successfully. There was a big audience, and a lot of clapping!

In 1941 I graduated from Lew Wallace High School in Glen Park, a suburb of Gary, Indiana. Right away I got my first job. The job was in the steel mills in Gary, at U.S. Steel.

The steel mills were always there on the horizon of Lake Michigan, but I had never been in them or knew how they operated. They never let kids go in there. I went down and filled out a long employment application. I was really proud of my education. I had graduated from high school and thought I was a pretty smart fellow. I believed I could get a good job because of my education and diploma.

They did give me a job. They gave me a job in the "lab," according to a paper they filled out. I followed this guy all through these gigantic buildings in the steel mills. It seemed we walked about a mile through these big buildings, by all these blast furnaces, rolling machines, all these steel beams and things.

Finally, we got to where I was supposed to be working, and the guy introduced me to my foreman. The foreman handed me this huge, gigantic sledgehammer. I had never seen one that big! I think it must have weighed about eighty pounds. I said, "What's this for?" He said, "Well, that 'LAB' on your job form there means 'laborer'." I said, "Oh, I thought I was going to be working in the 'lab.' So I had this big sledgehammer, and I could hardly even lift it. I was supposed to be knocking slag off the welded joints on the steel beams. I was in pretty good shape then. It's just that that hammer was so heavy. It was about like lifting one of the silver bars we found on the *Atocha*—it was about all you could do to lift it up.

After about three hours of that sledgehammer work, my arms and back were so tired that it was just impossible to lift it. My hands and fingers couldn't hold the handle anymore.

I thought, "Maybe my mother's right. Maybe I ought to get more education and go to college." That really convinced me, and so I actually only worked about a half a night. I told the foreman that I just couldn't lift that thing anymore and asked him if he had anything else to do. He said, "No, everything here is heavy, and we don't have any lightweight jobs."

That was the end of my steel mill work—I just quit.

Then I applied for a job with the city, and got a meter-reading job, which seemed somewhat below my stature and education level. But I thought, "Well, that's the only job I can get. I guess I'd better take it and make some money."

With some of the first money I got, I went and bought an automobile. I had heard of a good buy on the South Side of Chicago. A fire station was selling their cars and trucks and getting new ones. I bought a 1932 Model A Ford, a coupe. It had a rumble seat, and it was painted bright red, naturally, since that was the fire chief's car. The firemen had so much time to sit around and wait for a fire to start that they had to really take good care of that car, and it just shined everywhere. It looked beautiful, and it cost $35.

I kept the car for about three or four years and then finally sold it for $75. I thought that was a pretty good investment, but now as I look back on it, I wish I had kept it. Wish I still had it right now.

With the City of Gary, I then read meters for eight months—water meters, electric meters, and gas meters. They gave you a book with heavy covers on it. They also gave you a flashlight that was pretty tough that you could use to knock on doors, and to scare dogs away. You had to really walk fast and read the meters fast. You had to get the book done before the end of the day. If you didn't, then you didn't get a ride, and you had to catch a bus or walk. Or if you just did not get the book done, then all the other guys would ridicule you, kid you about being awful slow. It got to be a kind of a race. We would see who could finish reading all their meters in their book first. There was one old man who always got done first, and all of us young guys couldn't believe that he could read meters faster than us. But we finally figured it out. He had walked around the entire city of Gary, Indiana, about a hundred times. So he knew where every meter was hidden. He could remember from years previously when he was looking for meters and couldn't find where they were hidden. In the wintertime it got mighty cold there, so water meters all had to be in the basements or underneath, where it's warm. As a result, you were constantly going into warm places and then back out into the cold.

I remember one day I was in a blizzard. It was a blinding snow, and I was in the black area of town, walking around through the snowdrifts. The wind was blowing real hard, and it was snowing when I got to this little shanty and knocked on the door. I couldn't believe it. There were about a hundred people huddled around this great big pot-bellied stove, trying to keep warm. They invited me in. I was the only white person there—everybody else was black, and they offered me a cup of coffee. I told them I didn't drink coffee. They gave me some hot tea, and then I warmed up. They let me get right up next to the stove and get all warmed up, and then I headed out again.

Once in a while, you'd have to go down in the basement. There'd be mud, trash, and maybe two hundred or three hundred great big rats running all over the place. It was kind of frightening because some of them didn't run away from you. They'd attack you. It got to where the rats were worse than the dogs. I learned how to handle dogs on that job but not the rats. I didn't drink coffee or booze then, or smoke cigarettes, when I was young. I think my wife Deo's mother was the first one who talked me into having a cup of coffee, on the chicken ranch in California. I read meters for eight months, and then went off to Purdue University. I'd been playing with my band two or three nights a week while I was reading the meters too. I wanted to buy a car and put some money in the bank. I took a vacation too. I went by myself to Washington, DC, and New York City on vacation. That was quite an experience. I think I was only seventeen at the time; I guess I just skipped a grade.

In Washington, DC, I remember going into the Senate. I was disappointed about it, because it seemed that more than half of them didn't show up for the meeting. Of those who were there, one guy would be talking, and all the other guys would be reading newspapers, or talking to each other, or roaming around. It seemed like nobody was paying any attention to the guy who was talking about how many torpedo boats we should buy. That gave me a bad idea of the government. That's how it works? I thought all the Senate members would be listening to everything real close.

When I went to New York City—I guess I went by bus—I just walked down the street looking up at all the tall buildings. I went to Times Square and went up into the top of the Chrysler Building—that's the one with the point on the top of it. I also saw the Empire State Building. We went up there later with our children. That was quite a few years later. I remember when I was up there with the kids, I made an airplane out of a dollar bill—a paper airplane—and sailed it out. I thought it would sail way down to the streets of New York. Instead, it went way up, up, and went way up high out of sight in the sky. Instead of going down.

My first time in New York City, I went to the top of the New York Hotel. As I recall, Glenn Miller's band was playing, and Frank Sinatra was the star singer. That was when he first became famous. After just a couple of months of fun. There were thousands of girls crowded around him. The whole ballroom was crowded with women, and they were all swooning, screaming, even fainting. I couldn't believe all those women were screaming about every word he would say. Every time he would say a couple of words, they would all scream louder.

I had seen Glenn Miller's band before. But Glenn Miller was my favorite bandleader, so I would go see him whenever I could. Frank Sinatra was a new attraction too. I never did meet Glenn Miller. I was just another one of his fans. Also, my band buddies and I studied his music a lot and imitated everything that he did. We never did quite sound as good as he did, though.

Then I went off to Purdue.

Also, I still had my dance band. We had several contracts that went into the future, so I was doing some night traveling back and forth from Gary to Purdue. I had trouble falling asleep once in a while—whether driving or in a classroom. It was quite a drive, several hundred miles. I did enjoy it, though.

That first year I also joined the Delta Chi fraternity. What a bunch of treatment they put you through in these fraternities! All the paddles and the duties you do.

One guy who really inspired me, though, was Einstein. He wasn't one of my professors, but I gave him my bed when he came to my school.

I think he taught for a while at Princeton University in New Jersey. He came to Purdue University when I was a student—just now and then, I think—to play with a toy we had there. We had an atomic "atom-smasher." He would come there to do experiments, and now and then give a lecture. He belonged to the Delta Chi fraternity, of which I was a member. Whenever he came there, I would let him use my room, and I'd go up and sleep in the dormitory.

I remember him so well. It always amazed me, all the stuff he was talking about.

Einstein, of all the people I ever met or had for a teacher, has been my inspiration.

He seemed to have a very open mind, and he tried to encourage all of us to have an open mind. He encouraged us to think of things that other people don't think about, and not necessarily accept everything the way other people say it is. He wanted us to try and figure out new ways of doing things, new ideas and systems that nobody ever tried before. He always suggested things like that, so he was an inspiration to me.

He would not necessarily give us an answer, a solution, but he would show us that there was something wrong, that there was the possibility that it could be improved or changed, and that there is something else that we haven't figured out yet, and we've got to keep trying.

That's the main thing that he got across to me,

because all of these things we were learning, a lot of them we accepted—such as formulas. We accepted a logarithm, or we accepted something as a given. But he suggested you can later prove that it is questionable and search for new solutions.

In the years after, I always kept doing that all the time with new detection systems. Treasure is very hard to find, so you have to keep trying different search systems. All the different shipwrecks have different problems, different depths of water, different currents, different waves, different temperatures, different firmness of the bottom—some of it's like concrete and some of it's mud, and some sand, and some coral. There are all different conditions that you have to contend with. Sometimes all these different things will come up right on one wreck site. You have to be flexible.

I never did understand all of Einstein's advanced theories. I wasn't that smart. A lot of things he would be saying when I was in Purdue would seem to go in one ear and out the other, because I didn't understand it.

But at least he got the ideas out—and over the years I have thought about what he said and begun to understand more. That has really helped me search for treasure over all these years.

Then there was a teacher I got kind of angry at—my chemistry professor. I got angry because he knew that I didn't know the chemistry, that I hadn't taken high school chemistry when the other students had. So that professor would always ask me for the answer, and most of the time I didn't know the answer. He embarrassed me quite often, but I finally started to catch on. I did pretty well in the laboratory, and with some tutoring I got caught up and passed the course anyway. I just barely made that one. Later I took the same chemistry course over at Alabama University. This time I knew the basics of it, and the second time I took it at Alabama University, I got an "A." I don't mind doing something over if I need to. I knew I was weak in it, and so I took it again.

Engineering made you study hard. It seemed like you had about twenty-four hours of homework every night. They make you take all kinds of crazy courses that you know you are not ever going to need in life. You aren't ever going to do those things. They had me take a course in surveying. I thought "Geez, I'm not going to build any roads." But here I am, out here treasure hunting, and we are surveying every day out there!

We are constantly drawing up charts, drafting things. Of course, in drafting class, I knew I was never going to be a draftsman. But here I am drafting on a treasure hunt, you know.

They made me take English and do writing. I was never going to do that, and here I am writing a book. Also, I have to write contracts and other things.

I took economics. That was boring. "Supply and demand, or willing buyer–willing seller." I didn't want anything to do with that subject. Here I am doing it every day.

It is amazing. Every course that I took at Purdue University, I am using treasure hunting.

It's mind boggling. So when the kids come to me and ask me what to do, I tell them go to college. "You will be surprised, but every course you take, you are going to use through your life. It's very important to get your education behind you. That will help you succeed."

I enlisted in the US Army Reserves while I was in Purdue. They had stickers all over the halls that said, "Join the Army and stay in school."

They were drafting people then. I was on the list to be drafted, and at the time I was taking Reserve Officer Training Corps "ROTC" training, learning how to shoot field artillery and things like that.

I was also in the military band at Purdue and played at their football games. That was a real good big band. Excellent music. I played saxophone.

Through high school music, and his beginning with a saxophone as tall as he was, and a clarinet, Mel began his high school experience—then carried his music as well as his mind into college. There he continued learning at the higher education level, but with World War II looming, Mel moved into the Army's ASTP engineering program and was growing up in many ways. The handsome and intelligent young man was physically tall and strong, and yet sensitive enough to be a musician. And he was learning always about how to treat people, how to work with them. Out of high school, he was willing to work in the steel mills, he thought, but decided it was not for him, and he then tried working with the city of Gary, but that was also not for him. Still on a life quest that led him to Purdue University and higher education, and curious always about what's around the next corner, he met the man who really opened his eyes—Professor Albert Einstein, who, when at Purdue, would stay at his Delta Chi fraternity house. The great man would use Mel's bed (while Mel opted for the dorm) and greatly opened his mind to all possibilities. Quick to admit a lot that Professor Einstein said was beyond him, Mel said he would not necessarily provide answers but would show how there was the possibility that something could be improved or changed, something not yet figured out, and "We've got to keep trying."

Mel in the US Army. FISHER FAMILY COLLECTION

CHAPTER FIVE

Man of War: Across the Ocean

Y*ou're in the Army now! More seasoned now, after life in nature and then outside family and school buddies, but still the realistic optimist, Mel was rugged enough physically and mentally to deal with the realities of wartime and a journey into the heart of World War II and the Normandy invasion. He was a curious model of fearlessness and acceptance, but somehow the universe always contrived to keep him out of harm's way. Mel's higher education now moved to Georgia and continued in the Army.*

Probably early in 1943 they called all of the Army Reserves up into active duty. My second year at Purdue was when they took us out of college. I had been in the Reserves for about two months when, all of a sudden, they issued an order that all reservists in the US Army are "Hereby on Active Duty." They whisked us away. First, they sent me to Georgia to go through "basic training" in the Infantry. They sent us to Camp Wheeler, where we went through sixteen weeks of basic training for infantry. I learned how to do a fifteen-mile hike in the Georgia sunshine, how to dig foxholes, sleep in pup tents, and cut through swamps during the night. It was very interesting; I enjoyed it. A lot of the kids had never been in the outdoors. It was right down my alley.

So was the practical, "hands-on" training that was part of my time with the Army Corps of Engineers. One of our courses was carpentry, and a simple but important thing happened. I cut off a two-by-four; when I cut it off, the end was absolutely perpendicular. No matter which way you put a square on it, it was perfectly 90 degrees. I had cut it off without drawing any lines, just by eyeballing it and making it perpendicular. The teacher compared it with all the two-by-fours that everybody else in the class had cut off and explained to them why my two-by-four was better than anybody else's. Things like that—when somebody praises you—can really make you work harder and make you realize that there's a reason for trying to do your best on a project, instead of cutting that two-by-four off any old way. I was confident when I cut that section off without a lot of preparation. Some of the guys even would take a square and draw a line across, and then they'd take another square, and draw a line down. They'd try to line up the saw, and as they were sawing, to watch both lines and make sure they lined up everything. I just . . . cut it off. Mine was perfect, and everybody else's was off.

But then I had a little experience. As I mentioned earlier, way before I got in the Army, I had helped my dad build houses. My dad was a carpenter for many years. [As I said earlier], he took great pride in being able to cut stairsteps and roofs; cutting—designing and cutting gables, and different angles on the roofs on houses—is quite a skill. And he could figure all the angles—of a lot of mitered cuts.

After sixteen weeks of basic Army training, they gave us all a written test, an IQ test. Those of us who passed the test went back to college while in the Army. Those who passed could qualify to go into an Army Specialized Training Program—ASTP. I passed the test, and they sent me to the University of Alabama at Tuscaloosa. I went through about another one and a half years of engineering training at Tuscaloosa. That was three or four semesters. They expanded the ASTP, which was higher education. They decided on that while they were speeding
everything up, and they were going to call us all overseas. Instead of sending us directly overseas, they sent some of

us to different specialized training "quickie" schools. That was more relaxing than the Purdue atmosphere. The teachers weren't quite as strict, and they didn't give quite as much homework. I enjoyed it there at Alabama University. They had lots of pretty girls there too, and that made it interesting! I think I had my old coupe—I think it was a 1932 Chevrolet or Ford coupe with a rumble seat, and I learned a few card tricks there. That was in Tuscaloosa, Alabama.

I went back there in the 1980s, after I finally found the *Atocha*'s main treasure pile. They invited me back, and I had discussions there in some of the same classrooms that I'd been in when I was in the Army years ago.

By invitation, I gave a talk to the whole school there. I explained to them how important it was to study hard and complete their education. I explained how every course I'd studied at Alabama and Purdue I'm using now in treasure hunting. I told them that I hadn't had any idea I was going to be a treasure hunter. I told them that even though they can't realize right at the moment what they are going to gain from the knowledge they are learning, they will find out later in life they are going to use it all. Use everything they learn! When they invited me back there, they gave me an honorary degree.

I had gone from engineering studies at Alabama into the practical training of the Army Engineers. I went from Tuscaloosa to Alexandria, Louisiana, to an Army training school where we received the practical engineering. We actually physically built things and did things. I learned how to be a better carpenter. I already knew that, because my dad had been a carpenter, and I was pretty good at all kinds of constructions and repairs. Also, they gave us lessons in truck driving and maintenance, and repairs of trucks, air compressors, heavy equipment, air-operated jackhammers, and drills. Drills were for explosives. Then they had air-operated skill saws, chain saws, and all kinds of equipment there. They even had air-operated shovels—good for digging foxholes.

My experience with the Corps of Engineers at Alexandria brought me back to the kind of engineers who build things just as my grandfather built railroad bridges, and who are used in construction. They picked sixty-six of us to be in one outfit—carpenters, plumbers, other tradespeople who could take a bombed-out building and remake it into a usable building. Our mission was something like that, with a lot of Army baloney thrown in.

While I was there my girlfriend, Lillian, came down from Chicago and stayed for a while. We got married while I was in Louisiana. I had first met her three or four years earlier in Chicago at a hotel ballroom. That was before I went to college, when I was a meter reader. I asked her to dance. They had a big band there—I think it was Lawrence Welk who was playing. I was just there dancing and having fun listening to that good music. Anyway, she came down to Alexandria to be with me, and we decided to get married.

They decided to send us all overseas because it was almost D-Day. We didn't know there was going to be a "D-Day," but we knew they were sending us overseas.

First, they gave us a vacation, a furlough. They informed us that we were going overseas when we got back from our fifteen-day furlough.

I went home and had fun for two weeks.

To get back to Alexandria, you had to take a Zephyr train to St. Louis, Missouri, from Chicago. Something went wrong with the train that was going on from St. Louis to Camp Claiborne, Louisiana. I was stranded in St. Louis for a couple of days and decided to follow a bunch of people who were walking down the street. I wondered why all the people in town were walking in one direction, so I just turned and walked with them. We came to a big riverboat on the Mississippi River and went on the riverboat with them. It was really neat. They had a big band with music playing, and they cruised down the

Mississippi River and back again and had a lot of fun. But I was late getting back when we were supposed to be going overseas. My captain, the company commander, called me in. He told me that instead of reprimanding me for being late or "AWOL" [Absent Without Leave], he was going to reward me—promote me and give me a corporal's stripe. Then the next time I goofed up, he said, he was going to take the stripe away. So he had something to hold over my head, but I got a raise in pay and a little more authority—for going down the river!

I know the Army's pretty strict about AWOL, normally. But I learned a few lessons along the way. I still remember that company commander's surprise, and I have done that a few times with employees and kids and others in my life since—to do the opposite of punishment. In many ways it changes the other person's attitude and works really well psychologically. In the Army, just like in kindergarten art class when I was caught with my secret snowflake, I learned that it is good now and then to praise people for their good work instead of just criticizing all the time. When people do well, it pays to tell them so.

At that time I went to "PFC" (private first class), then to corporal. As a rating, I next earned a "Tech" insignia with a "T" under it, which means that it was some kind of specialized skill, and it was in construction. Now I was in engineering construction.

From corporal I went to "Corporal T5," and I stayed in that position all through the Army. I had several offers to go to Officers School, but I didn't want to do that. Probably one of the main reasons—probably the main reason—they made the offer to me so many times was that the first lieutenants and second lieutenants were dying off like flies at the front.

Somebody had to be the leader and say, "Follow me, men!"—and then head out. They were up against the Siegfried Line, where there was crossfire of machine guns.

In Louisiana, we were called the 1672nd Engineers.

We had sixty-five men in our outfit. Some were plumbers, some were electricians. Some were carpenters, some were roofers. There were many different specialized things. Our job was supposed to be to move into a bombed-out area and rebuild all the buildings, get all the plumbing and everything working.

I really don't think I have a genius IQ. I think my IQ test was about 134. But I believe all the schooling I got did give me a broad background to do almost anything I wanted to do. At least I had a touch of everything, so that helped me a lot.

About a week after my last furlough, my outfit boarded a train, and we went across the country to Baltimore, then on to Boston, Massachusetts. Along the way two of our main Army trainers—trainers who went all the way with us through engineering school—let us know they weren't going with us overseas. One old-timer and a top sergeant we had—I guess they were staff sergeants—came all the way through the train, saying goodbye to all of us.

We said, "What do you mean, 'goodbye'?" They said, "You guys are going overseas, but we're not. We are teachers and instructors, and you don't need us in France and Germany. We've got to go train some more of you guys and send another batch over there."

I said, "Well, how do you do that?" They said, "We think it is more important for us to teach more kids, so we're each going to eat a bar of soap, get sick, and get off the train." And they did. They each ate a bar of soap and got off the train. The rest of us all went to Boston and went overseas. Those guys got sent back to teach the next group of engineers. I think they had done that before; it was a staff sergeant and another sergeant who were our main instructors. Or, maybe they just said that, knowing they had to go back and train some more guys in construction work. They were good trainers, anyway.

I had KP [Kitchen Police] duty quite a few times in

the Infantry and in the Engineers. That was always a drag, peeling potatoes, washing kettles, getting food ready, and cleaning up the garbage. But I didn't really know what KP duty was until I got to Boston, where they had thousands and thousands of soldiers getting ready to go overseas and being loaded in these troop ships. They put me on KP duty there, and the pans were gigantic. They were about six feet high and six feet across. It just seemed like an endless supply of dirty dishes. You could never, ever get them done.

 The cooks were going twenty-four hours a day. Instead of peeling potatoes for sixty-five guys, you would be peeling tons and tons of potatoes, truckloads and truckloads and truckloads of potatoes! It really impressed me how much trouble it is just to feed an army. It is really something else.

Wendy: *Taffi Fisher Abt went into a little more detail about the "potatoes" lessons her dad learned, especially about cutting corners:*

Taffi: Dad told me an Army boot camp story with a lesson. Apparently, if they got caught making mischief, as a sort of punishment, they would have to work Kitchen Patrol, or KP. One time my dad and a buddy got caught doing something and got assigned to KP. The sergeant took them into a big empty room, and there was a rope hanging down from the ceiling. The sergeant pulled the rope and a big, six-by-six-foot hatch in the ceiling opened, and "zillions of potatoes dropped out of the hatch into a giant pile taller than me." Then the sergeant said, "Peel all of those potatoes, put them in that giant pot, sweep all the peels into a pile, and call me when you're done." Dad figured that would be a pretty easy job, and for the next several hours they sat and peeled potatoes, and peeled potatoes, and peeled potatoes, and after a while their hands were so raw and wet from peeling potatoes that they hurt. He and his buddy decided that the potato peels were so deep, you could throw whole potatoes into the peels, and they would be hidden, no one would ever notice, and the job would be done faster. When they finished that mountain of potatoes and called the sergeant back in, he walked in with a rake in his hand, looked in the pot, and started raking through the pile of the potato peels. When he found whole potatoes in the pile of peels, he shook his head, separated them into a new, small pile under the chute and pulled the chain again—and another giant pile of potatoes dumped out. Then he repeated, "I said peel all of the potatoes," and this time they peeled every potato. He never forgot that, cutting corners to save time usually ends up causing problems that take more time to fix than if you had just done it right the first time.

Mel resumes: I remember the Red Cross had some gals there when we were getting ready to get aboard the big ship, and they gave us coffee in mugs, and doughnuts.

Then I remember seeing the coast of the United States fading away as we left Boston Harbor. I remember seeing the land disappear.

Just after the land disappeared, I felt real strange. I had never been seasick in my life, and I didn't realize that I was getting seasick. The ocean seemed real calm, but there were these great big swells and the whole ship would go *uppp* and then *downnn*. That was the first time I ever got seasick. I didn't think you could get seasick on a big ship like that. I found out different. When we got over to England, we arrived at Liverpool.

When we got off the big ship, it was in the middle of the night. There was real heavy fog. You couldn't see anything, and there weren't any lights around. It was against the rules to have lights on, because they were having air raids and buzz bombs coming from Germany. They marched us for several hours through the streets all around Liverpool, and finally we got up to the docks again. We were also carrying all of our equipment.

Then they put us on an English ship. I think it was a fishing trawler that they had rigged up with two hundred or three hundred hammocks hanging in it. They didn't have any regular bunks or showers, toilets, or tables to eat on. But that was just a quickly made, temporary troop carrier.

We found out that the next morning was going to be D-Day, and we were going to attack the Germans in France. We took off and very quickly it was morning. We all wanted some coffee, but we found out that the British don't drink coffee. They only drink tea, so we all had tea. We also had some hard biscuits. They told us most people in Europe don't have bacon and eggs for breakfast. They just have tea and biscuits.

So my second day in Europe was D-Day. We were out in the middle of the English Channel; our boat was just waiting there. There were lots of boats out there. We were waiting in the channel for some landing craft that were supposed to take us in and dump us on the beach. The landing craft they had assigned to pick us up capsized because it was really rough. We had to spend another day and night at sea, and we missed out on D-Day. That was probably fortunate, because the first day there were many, many British and Americans who got killed.

We waited at sea off the coast of Normandy. Our destination was called the [Fox] Green Beach. They went by colors. I can't think of what city it was near, but there was no town there. It was just a deserted beach, fields, and a lot of mud up on top of the cliffs. We finally made it in. We got all wet getting out of the boats and onto the beach. All of our bedding, tents, guns—everything was wet. At least there weren't many people shooting. Just a few snipers. During the middle of the night again our captain told us to pitch camp "here," and it was in the middle of a huge mud field. The mud was about ankle-deep. We couldn't believe he wanted us to sleep in the mud there. A couple of guys griped, and he said this was where the convoy was going to pick us up, so this was where we got to sleep.

The captain gave me orders to build an outhouse. There weren't any toilets. So at about 2:30 in the morning, I built an outhouse. Then about an hour later, the convoy arrived, and everybody had to roll up their blankets and tents again, get in the trucks, and head out for Paris, France.

We went through a lot of little French villages along the way. They were all bombed out and shelled out. There were hardly any buildings left in any of those cities along our way.

I recall they had a Red Ball Highway and a Blue Ball Highway. One of them went to Paris, and the other one came back from Paris to the water. The highways were all blown up too, and all the bridges were blown up, so they had to have engineers, including our 1672nd, bulldoze their way through the cities and make roads. It was very dusty going through there. I thought I was getting dust in my eyes, and soon I could hardly see. So they let me go into the outskirts of Paris. They told me to ask until I found the Arch of Triumph, and that there was an emergency Army medical treatment place there. I went there, but I didn't know where my outfit was going to go. They told me just to check with Army headquarters in Paris to find out where my outfit went, so I could get back to them. After getting treated, I was to locate my outfit in the northern part of Paris—in the outskirts on the Seine River, where there was a big storage facility plus warehouses for military supplies. It had been a German camp, so the Americans had bombed and shelled it and ran the Germans out. Germans were still sniping around there too. They were using all kind of tricks they could to hurt American soldiers. Like booby traps—they had a girl with nice "boobies," and she would say, "Hey come on in here." If you went in there, they would shoot you. That was a real booby trap.

That was when we first got to Paris, the first night

there was when I first got on the subway. I had had some eye troubles for several years in the Army, and at times I couldn't see. It felt like I had gravel in my eyes, or sand in my eyes, when we got to Paris. So as soon as we got there—we hadn't gotten to any camp yet, we hadn't got to the place where we were going to be stationed—they just had me get off the truck. They told me to go to the Arch of Triumph, because that was where there was a US military clinic—across the street from the monument. They put me in a subway station. I didn't know how to speak French. Although I did have French in high school, I couldn't really speak it. People kept telling me which trains to get on and off of, and transfer to, and I finally got to the clinic.

I went to the Army clinic, and they put some kind of drops in my eyes that made me almost totally blind. I could just barely see blurs, and I was trying to go back across the Arch of Triumph, which is a huge traffic circle with hundreds of cars going around it. I was looking for the subway, but it was on the far side of the street. All the cars were honking at me and screeching their brakes, and I was walking along with my hands out in front of me across the traffic circle. It was actually a frightening experience. When I got to the Arch of Triumph—that's where the subway station was—I went down in the subway station, down these stairs. It was all white tile and bright lights, and I was crying. I couldn't see anything. I could hear all this giggling and laughing and screaming. All women, everywhere. Finally, this French lady who could speak some English came to my rescue. She explained to me in English that I was in the ladies' toilet and not in the subway. She helped move me out of the women's toilet, took me to another stairway down to the subway, and got me on the right train to go back to find my outfit. Then I got to where my outfit—by then it was called the 1655th Engineers—was supposed to be, but it was gone. For a short time, I didn't have anywhere to go. Then a pretty little

French girl took me under her wing. I remember she showed me the Eiffel Tower, and we walked for about three or four hours trying to find somewhere to go and finally gave up. I don't remember what happened then. I guess I went to a hospital. I didn't know where to go. I was completely lost in Paris. I didn't know where my outfit was. I didn't know where we were going. I finally found them out in the north part of Paris. I don't remember how I found them. I guess I just kept asking questions, and someone found out for me where they were.

I didn't know exactly what was wrong with my eyes then. It might have been more serious, but I don't think I ever found out. When I was discharged from the Army, they gave me a physical, and that was the first time that the medical officer put on my record that I had Horner syndrome. I guess there are several different things that can cause Horner syndrome. As a result, they did put me on the disability list. It has affected my vision some. I perspire on one side and not the other side, and one eyelid droops more than the other eyelid.

During my service years I was never shot, wounded, or hurt. I was often close. I could hear bullets whirring around, but I never got hit. Never got wounded.

That camp where I spent about eight months, in the northern part of Paris on the Seine River, had been blown up by the Germans as well as bombed by the Americans. When we got there, it was all wiped out. Our job was to get it back to being a supply camp again, to make sure the electricity and plumbing worked, rebuild all the buildings, and get everything usable again. We enjoyed ourselves and worked hard.

The closest to direct combat that I experienced was at that same camp about a year later, outside Paris on Christmas Eve 1944, just after the Battle of the Bulge. The Germans had captured quite a few American trucks, tanks, armored vehicles, uniforms, and weapons. Using what was captured, the Germans had a whole battalion in a convoy that was pretending it was an American convoy. They went right through the American lines and were crossing France.

On that Christmas Day we got word that our side had learned somehow that this battalion was going to come and let out the prisoners of our prison camp. They put us on alert, had us go out on Christmas Day and dig foxholes all around our place, set up some extra 50-caliber machine guns and 30-caliber ones. We put bazookas in place, and we had it rigged up for crossfire. We felt pretty secure. But it was a nervous feeling to know that the Germans were on their way. That night, just at midnight, an air raid warning went off, and the searchlights start going. We all went out to jump in our foxholes and get ready. Our foxholes were full of sleet and slush; it had been sleeting, halfway snowing, and raining. I thought, "Well, I will just sit down by my machine gun on the side of the foxhole." All of a sudden, they started bombing us. There were bombs landing all around us, so I just jumped right in the slosh. I didn't mind getting wet and cold. It was better than getting blown up.

The entire outfit didn't actually see anybody on land or shoot at them, because some other American troops stopped that convoy before it got to us. We did get to sleep on Christmas Day, to have Christmas dinner and celebrate.

After that the Germans went down pretty fast. Hitler got killed or killed himself. They never found him. I don't think they ever found all the gold either—the gold bars he had amassed. As his troops were going through the Netherlands, France, and Russia, they would stop at every city, raid the banks, take all the gold, melt it down into gold bars, and put swastikas on them with serial numbers. A lot of those went down in the oceans and seas of the world. Maybe I will go look for some of them sometime.

In Paris, when it got a little colder, we needed a fur collar on our jackets. I couldn't believe the cold that they had in Paris. I had always thought it was a warm place. We had eight inches of snow, and it was a blizzard. It was really miserable. At one point I was building a huge warehouse in the middle of this blizzard. I had forty German prisoners working for me. I was supposed to be guarding them, and I couldn't even see them in the blizzard. They could have taken off, but they didn't run away. Where were they going to go? On the back of their coats—and I have some pictures from then—it said "P.W." There was always a great big "P.W." on their back. But what was spooky was that sometimes in the morning we would go and pick up maybe two thousand of them. It'd be early in the morning in a real heavy fog. We'd be marching from a "P.W." camp to where we were going to work, and they'd all be marching in unison, Hitler-style, with their goose steps, and they'd be singing German military songs—in German, what we think of as "Home on the Range" songs. There'd be only about thirty or forty of us guarding all these prisoners walking through the fog, and you couldn't even see from one to the other. They had a lot of weapons, too, that they had handcrafted. You wondered how you could control all of that. But most of them didn't really want to go back into the war. They wanted to just sit it out there until the war was over. A few of them did disappear into the fog every now and then, and they'd capture them here and there around Paris.

    As part of my construction work, we had to make field toilets. Not very glorious, but necessary, like food, for a big army. So on pictures I'd send home, instead of words I would just mention things I built—for example, one stated, "A crapper I made." I was explaining to my mother what I was doing over there. I made lots of those "crappers" over there, lots of outhouses. The first one I made was the first night we got ashore in Europe. It was about 2 o'clock in a rainstorm, and my captain told me to go build an outhouse—"over there." It was *mud* all over the place, it was raining, and I guess the captain needed one. I drove a couple of two-by-four stakes into the ground with a sledgehammer and nailed another two-by-four on top of them. I drove a spike into that and hung a roll of toilet paper on it. Then I dug a little slit trench on one side of it, and I put a sign on it that said "Crapper." They'd sit on the two-by-four, do what they had to do, and then we covered up the slit trench.

That was my first toilet. I built some fancier ones later.

In Reims, France, we built some, only it wasn't easy to dig a slit trench there. Everything was solid rock. We had to dig a hole in the solid rock for these outdoor latrines. I built ones that would handle six thousand men a day. They were all waiting in line to admire my construction. Toilets were really in big demand. Lots of prisoners and no toilets.

Practice in practical problem-solving was what I got a lot of in France with the sewage situation. It was just getting to be too much. We couldn't dig the holes in the rocks fast enough. They kept filling up. I had to build a fleet of tank trucks and pump all the sewage out into these trucks. I didn't really know what to do with it. With the first truckload I just drove into the town of Marseille and opened up what looked like a drain on the corner of the street, in the gutter. I opened that up and dumped it all in there. Everybody was screaming at me in French and complaining. The next load I drove out in the country and dumped it somewhere. Again, everybody was screaming and complaining. Always I was asking, "Where am I going to take it?" They said, "Dump it in the ocean." I dumped it in the ocean, and everybody was bitching and complaining.

Finally, they told me to take it up to the so-and-so's winery or vineyards. I went up there, and they said, "Oh, we'll buy it! We'll buy your truckloads of sewage every week, and we'll pay you so much a truckload." Finally, I had found a place. I guess they just irrigated all their vineyards with this special fertilizer and made really good-tasting wine. Maybe that's the kind we are drinking these days! Maybe that's why French wine tastes so good.

. When I went to Germany, I missed the heavy combat there, fortunately. They didn't send me until a couple of days after our forces had broken through the Siegfried Line. When I got there all the pillboxes, cannons, and machine guns were silent.

They told us that the war with Germany was over, and we were in the Army of Occupation. I'm not really sure what that date was.

Then they sent us to a little village near Frankfurt am Main. That's "Frankfurt on the Main River." There apparently are two Frankfurts. I'm trying to think of the name of the little village [Frankfurt Oder]. They told us they wanted us to control that manufacturing facility and make it into a kind of Army camp and housing quarters. So we did. That took quite a while, a year or so.

From Germany we went back to France—Marseille, France. That's where they had big steamships that could take us home. I figured, "We're going home!" They took us into a nice place like a hotel, with a lot of cottages and trees around, and let us all bed down for the night. The next morning was the first time in several years that I didn't hear whistles blowing, and bugles blowing, and sergeants and people making you get up, yelling, "Chow Down," and "Time to Eat." Suddenly, we all realized that there weren't any officers or sergeants there, and we were all on our own. It was very much like a resort, and it was free time for a couple of weeks.

You could just go and come anytime you wanted to and eat whenever you wanted. You could go anywhere in Marseille, out in the country or out in the ocean, the Mediterranean. That was a really neat "Rest and Relaxation," as they call it. "R and R."

One time I went mountain climbing. We got halfway up a cliff and found a cave. It was on the outskirts of Marseille. There were some olive orchards there at the foot of the mountains. I remember eating the olives off the trees. They were really bitter. I had never eaten bitter olives before that.

We went in this cave, exploring or "spelunking," and we got lost in there. We had gone in through a tunnel. We didn't realize that there were so many beautiful things in front of us—all these stalagmites and stalactites. There were rooms filled with crystals. They were something like the emeralds we are finding out on the *Atocha*. But they were different colors. Some of them were violet, some blue, some pink. Some rooms were filled with different kinds of crystals. I wouldn't mind going back there someday with a gemologist and see if any of those are worth anything. They've got to be worth something, because they are so beautiful. I don't remember who they were, but I had a couple of other guys with me.

We almost didn't get out of there, because we couldn't find the tunnel to get out. It was hidden behind a big boulder, and there were other tunnels on either side of that. For a long time, we didn't see the one that went behind the big boulder. First, we went through about fifteen or twenty different tunnels trying to get out, and we just couldn't find a way. They were all dead ends. But we finally made it out all right. We just looked behind every rock and every square foot of everywhere until we found another tunnel that we hadn't explored.

I learned why they always use a string or a rope, or have chalk to mark a passage, or do something so that you know which way you went. Some of the tunnels went straight down. That impressed me too. You could throw a rock down. It was pitch black and you would just hear it going clink, clink, clink, and clink. Then the sound would fade away, and all of a sudden you would hear a splash. There was water way down there. That was pretty close to the Mediterranean and was probably the water level of the Mediterranean. These mountains must have been pretty close to the water.

This was not a tourist attraction. We just happened on the cave accidentally while we were mountain climbing. It was right in the side of a sheer cliff. There would be very few people who would ever go there. But I remember that there were some marks on the wall—marked with candle smoke. You can light a candle and let the smoke from it write on the ceiling of a cave. A lot of spelunkers do that, hold their candle near the ceiling, and the smoke from the candle will make a black mark on the ceiling. You can write your name and what date you were there. There were about a half dozen names and dates in there. Some of them were really old, although I don't remember the names and dates. I would like to go back there some time. I don't know if I could find it.

I remember seeing guys snorkeling in the sea there, in the Mediterranean. But I didn't ever go snorkeling myself. I went motorcycle riding.

We even tried ski jumping. I was mostly self-taught. But I also had some little kids teach me. I'd watch these little kids and do what they did. They'd tell me what I was doing wrong. I didn't hire any professional instructors. But what I particularly enjoyed was cross-country skiing. There's a place where you can go down the mountain, and it takes you three days and nights to get to the bottom. And as you're going, you're going through, I believe, it's Germany, France, Italy, and Austria. That corner right there is where all these countries abut. So as you're going around the mountain, you're going through all these different countries, skiing down. They have little places where you can stop, cabins and things where you can warm up and build a fire, rest or sleep or eat or drink—whatever you want to do. I enjoyed that. I was no real pro at it, but I could go down any of the runs. I enjoyed skiing and had a lot of fun, romance, and adventure in Garmisch Park.

When we left Germany, I couldn't believe the way they got us out of there. It was the first time in my life in the Army that they put us in a freight train. We got into boxcars in Garmisch, and they sent us to a port on the north end of Germany, where it was really cold and windy. Bremerhaven, Germany—that was one helluva trip! I can appreciate, now, the old French-American songs about "40 & 8" and riding the freight cars when they were in the Army in World War I, because these freight trains were antiquated, and there was no nothing in them. No beds, no washbasins, no toilets, no nothing. Empty boxcars, and you'd be freezing. The things jiggled so hard and fast sideways that they would shake your intestines back and forth, and your body so much, that you'd be trying to hold your arms around you in order to keep your guts from bouncing. Again, that was one helluva trip. I don't know why they ever did that. That was ridiculous. I decided they needed new trains there.

I don't know how long the trip was, a couple of days or something like that. One reason was because they would put us on sidings for other trains going by. We finally got out, gathered some wood and debris, and built a fire inside the boxcar. That was bad news too, with all the smoke and fumes.

Finally, we got to Bremerhaven, and I had that eye problem again. Again I had a lot of pain, and the weather didn't help. We stayed there for two and a half months, waiting for a troop ship to take us home. Everybody had been thinking about going home for about a year and a half or two years. They were impatiently waiting to go home, and it was very boring there, because the wind seemed to be blizzard-style all the time, about twenty or thirty knots. Always it was snowing or sleeting or raining, very cold. There was virtually no entertainment, or anywhere to go. They wouldn't let you go into town. Everybody had to stay right there in this military area. We were in barracks. They did have a recreation hall. So while I was waiting there, I learned how to play chess. That was enjoyable, something to keep my mind occupied besides just waiting around, with my eye ache, or sinus ache, or whatever it was that was hurting me. The weather was so cold and windy that it was a major effort just to walk half a mile to where the doctors were. A really miserable place.

Finally, we got on the ships and went home. We got out in the North Sea there, and boy—that place is rough! Big waves! Twenty-foot waves! Everybody on the ship got seasick. We just got out of the seasick North Sea and got out into the Atlantic Ocean—where there were only fifteen-foot waves, and it was Thanksgiving Day. They served everybody turkey dinner on the ship, and it had ptomaine poisoning in it. The entire ship, including officers, commanders, the guys who ran the engines, all the soldiers, everybody got deathly ill. They all had Thanksgiving turkey, and there was something wrong with it. So the ship was just kind of bouncing around like a cork out there, in this big storm, and there was nobody even capable of holding onto the wheel. They were all wiped out. People were just throwing up everywhere! Soldiers, at least, got more sick when they went to go to the latrine—the ship's heads have a section that comes up on each door, about a foot high, so that water can't come in, and it was full up to that level with puke. You had to wade through that to get to the toilet. There was nobody well enough to clean out the mess, and it was just horrible. That was one of the worst things I've ever seen in my life. I don't know how long that experience lasted, but it seemed like a long time. Probably about three days and nights.

The closest good things were rare enough to wait for in long, long lines. Ice cream sundaes. Like a hot fudge sundae, a strawberry sundae. It made me appreciate the little things. One day I was waiting in line in Reims, France, for an ice cream sundae, and there was a line about two miles long of GIs. The line made a big loop and came back next to itself, like an "e." There in the line across from me, I saw Joe Hlodnicki! He said, "Come on, cut in where I am, and it'll save you about an hour's wait." I did, and we talked a while. I asked him if he had his trumpet with him. He said, "Yeah." I said, "Well, I've got my saxophone with me, so let's get together and play some music." And we did. There at the Army camp. We got three or four other guys and did a little jazz.

We finally got across the big ocean!. They let us all loose in New York City. That was really something! We went out and had a chocolate malt, and a hamburger-cheeseburger. It was sure good to see the good old USA again. We sighted the Statue of Liberty as we came into New York City, and it was very exciting.

We just kept filling up on the goodies and desserts and walked around Times Square. I forget all we did.

I don't think they'd ever heard of chocolate malts over there when we were in Europe. And they'd never heard of cheeseburgers. They'd never heard of Pepsi-Colas and Coca-Colas. Dried eggs. We'd been on dried eggs for years—powdered eggs. You could get an egg in Paris; if you got a Class B Pass, you could go to Paris, and you could buy a fried egg for ten dollars. Whew! One fried egg.

Even in the hardships of war—real World War II—Mel Fisher found ways and time to enjoy what he was doing when doing it. And to keep an eye out for the ladies, even in the middle of the traffic around the busy Arch of Triumph and finding himself in a ladies' room. If his assignment was to peel potatoes, he at least learned one of his "life lessons." If it was an assignment to build a "crapper," he did it and did it well. If it was an assignment to get rid of sewage, he did it and did it well. He learned to get along with German POWs by using his human skills. And Mel learned about basic American values, food, and attitudes that would carry him on through life.

Mel with a speargun in the 1950s. Fisher Family Collection

CHAPTER SIX

Into the Sunshine:
Postwar Freedom and Florida Adventures

Strong of body and mind, a pioneering guy who was still young but nevertheless ragged from wartime challenges that bring each to his personal truth, Mel Fisher was facing what those who rise to great challenges must do on reentry to solid but different postwar American life. Independence of all kinds molds character but comes with a price.

Then I went back to Indiana and moved to the South Side of Chicago for a year with my wife Lillian and son Terry. Terry was born while I was overseas, I think when I was in Germany. We moved to the South Side of Chicago, near 63rd and Keeler.

There I went down to the carpenters union to see if I could join. They wanted to put me in as an "apprentice." Usually, you have to be an "apprentice" for a couple of years before you can become a "journeyman" in the union. I told them that I had all this experience in the Army, so they just let me take a test to get in as a journeyman. I passed the test, so I started.

As a journeyman, my first job was building forms for concrete foundations for a large building. They were building way down in a huge hole in the ground—a couple of stories below street level.

My second encounter with a union was worse than my experience as a musician. This one came when I was doing carpentry, and it really made me mad. After I got out of the Army, I joined the carpenters union. I was about twenty-two years old when I went to the first meeting. They said they wanted to have a four-day work week, and the guys who were running the union seemed awfully gruff, they couldn't speak very good English, and they were very brutal-speaking, commanding, unreasonable. They were bossing everybody around, and I didn't like that. So I stood up and said, "I don't want to work four days a week. I want to work five days a week. I wouldn't know what to do if I had every Friday off, because I'm used to just having Saturday and Sunday off. I want to work five days a week." Right away they had a great big guy come in on each side of me. They came down the aisle on each side of the middle section; I was right in the middle. They said, "Excuse me," "Excuse me," and they walked over toward me. They made the guys on each side of me get up and get out of their seats. They sat down next to me. When I went to stand, each one held a hand on my shoulder, on each side, and they wouldn't let me stand up. I started yelling out, anyway. That was one big hassle. I never went to another union meeting in my life—as a member.

I did go to other union meetings later—but not as a member. I went to one for the longshoremen. They had me there as a guest speaker because I was treasure hunting way back then. That was in the 1950s, and they brought me there as entertainment. I saw them pull the same thing on their people—the same kind of tactics. They were strictly organized labor, with powerful, gruff people telling everybody what they were going to do. For me, it was watching what happened to me before it happened again. I'd say it was like Mafia tactics. The guys who were talking seemed like they were very uneducated and very powerful. My conclusion was I didn't like the unions. I was going be an independent contractor, have my own business, and not be controlled by those kind of people.

I decided to move to Colorado. We started driving across the country, but we got out in Kansas somewhere, and it was really hot. We started having trouble with the tires on my car. At that time, they were rationing tires and inner tubes, and you couldn't get any. But the heat from the desert melted the patches off of the inner tubes. The glue wouldn't hold, so then I had blowouts. I had to put boots in the tires between the inner tube and the hole. I had some holes clear through the tire. So I put some little—they call them boots—a tough piece of rubber with cord in it between the inner tube and the hole.

We got to some little town, and I went all around town trying to buy a tire. We couldn't find one. Someone told me to go out to the city dump, and just go through all the old tires there, and see if I could find one the right size that was better than the one I had. I did that. I picked out about three tires, just in case. They kept going flat, going flat, and going flat. I was changing tires out in the desert quite a bit. Finally, I got to some city where I found a place that would sell me a tire.

We got to Denver and bought a home. We were a little low on money, so we rented out a couple of extra bedrooms. We took in thirty bucks a month to help make the payments.

I worked for a housing project where they were building about a hundred homes. For a while I was laying flooring, oak flooring. To do that you stand up and bend over and hammer the nails in, toenail them in, to get the boards to fit together real snug. It was backbreaking work. I got so I was very good at laying oak flooring. Then they put me on to hanging doors. I learned how to be an expert door hanger. After you do about a hundred houses, you know how to do it. Next, they put me on to doing trim work, and I learned how to do that.

Then I decided to put in an application to get a job with the government—the federal government—designing dams. Bureau of Reclamation? I worked on experiments making different kinds of concrete and cement out of different materials, and testing it under freezing conditions, under pressure conditions, steaming heat conditions, and different types of cooling.

Then it snowed. The snow got real deep. That was a surprise. It wasn't really wintertime, but suddenly it snowed and got real cold. I guess that was because Denver's up about a mile high. You never know at those altitudes about the weather.

My car wouldn't start. I thought it wouldn't start because it was so cold. It turned out that the water had frozen in the block and broke the block in two. That engine was shot. I got tired of the blizzards, the snow, and the slosh.

There was nowhere to swim out there. I liked the water a lot, so I decided to move to Florida and moved down to Tampa.

That was much nicer. It seemed like I was enjoying life. Instead of just rejoining the union or going to work for a contractor, I decided to put on a pair of carpenter's overalls, hang a hammer on my hip, and go door to door.

I'd knock on the door of these big old mansions in Tampa. I'd hand them a business card—"Fisher's Home Service." I told them if there was anything wrong with their house, I would fix it for them. Every one of those houses had a lot of things wrong. There is quite a bit of dry rot in Florida. Stairs, porches, and other things would start rotting away, or the termites would start getting them. They had me replacing the lumber and rebuilding everything. I changed a lot of sash cord. If someone had a window in the house that wouldn't go up or down, I could go in and take it apart. Most of them had cast iron weights inside the window frames that were on a piece of clothesline rope, cotton rope. I'd replace the rope with new rope, take paraffin, and wax the window up. I'd make it so they could open and close their windows real easy. I'd replace screens—rotten screens and rusted-out screens. I'd replace broken windows and cracked windows, patch roofs where they were leaking, and sometimes put on a whole new roof. The jobs kept getting bigger. I'd add on a carport, and then

I'd build a whole room on a house.

Finally, I built a whole house. It was the first time I had ever built an entire house, and it was fun just to see if I could do it. Some of it I learned just by going somewhere where they were building a house, sitting down and watching the guys to see how they did it. I had never laid concrete blocks. So I just went a couple of blocks away and watched these guys laying concrete blocks. I saw how they'd take a nail with a piece of string and stick it in, and then stick one on the other corner. That way they'd keep the layer of blocks straight. Then I watched to see what they did when they got to the top of the windows and the top of the doors. That's when it slowed down, when you had to put in reinforcing rods and cement over the doors and the windows.

I had never plastered before. So I went and watched some guys plastering. Then I plastered too. I built the house, and then worried that I might not be able to sell it. I put an ad in the paper and sold it right away. I made a profit. I did everything on that house. Just for the hell of it. I just wanted to see if I could do everything. I got it all done, the whole thing. Also, on the electrical and plumbing, I just watched other guys and then did it. At various jobsites, I asked some of them how to do it, or if they would show me how. They usually did. I told them that I was building my own house, and I wanted to build the whole thing myself. I asked them if they would show me how.

Then I decided, "I'll go big time and be a contractor." I started taking on a lot of big jobs and hired a bunch of guys. I had people on my payroll who did all this stuff—plumbers, electricians, carpenters, painters. I did that for about a year. At the end of the year, I did my accounting, and I made less money doing that than I had when I was just working by myself. I decided not to be a contractor. I guess I wasn't charging enough money. Or I was estimating how much a job would cost, and how long it would take—if I was doing the work. It seems like a lot of times other people goof off when you're paying them; it takes other people a lot longer to do something than it does you—if you are working for yourself. As a result, most of my estimates were not high enough to make a good profit.

Instead of making higher estimates, I just decided to do more skin diving and spearfishing, and less working, worrying, and payrolls. I went back to a one-man business. I would only work a couple of hours in the morning when it was cool, because it is hot in Tampa in the summertime. Then I would go diving and goofing off at the beach. I would work a couple of hours in the afternoon, and I had plenty of money to get along.

I was still in my twenties.

When I started goofing off was when my wife and I separated.

Then I decided, "To heck with all the goodness and trying to build up a big business."

My wife moved back to Chicago with her mother and our son. Then I just more or less quit being a hard worker. I started having fun and doing as little work as possible. For a couple of years I was a "beach bum."

I don't know how I felt about the marriage not working out. I think I was just having fun. I just did a complete turnabout. I was having fun and enjoying life instead of working so hard.

Postwar changes were occurring all over the world, including in the US, where a construction boom was underway while the nation was still digging out from wartime postures, with ramifications large and small, from union difficulties to finding a tire in a Kansas dumpsite. At that time, marital separation was a part of his lifestyle "breakout," at least for a time, then, from traditional American values, including family and hard work building a business.

Mel with a 438-pound fish he speared free-diving in 1952.
FISHER FAMILY COLLECTION

CHAPTER SEVEN

Diving In:
"Fearless Fisher" Spearfishing Sea Monsters

Willing to learn new things and unafraid to ask how to do them, postwar Mel Fisher was still young enough and strong enough to live only for the moment, to chase daily survival and adventure rather than "settle down" into any kind of long-range lifestyle. Independent people don't set out to be in history books as a "pioneer"; rather, they usually have the skills and courage to try new things and adapt what they know to work through failure for success.

My first skin diving and spearfishing experience is a Florida story. I started diving quickly. I was fishing with a fishing pole on Gandy Bridge—there's still a Gandy Bridge in Tampa. In fact, there is an old Gandy Bridge and a new one. But it was the old Gandy Bridge where I fished. I was on the St. Petersburg side of the Tampa Bay rather than the Tampa side. I couldn't catch any fish. They just weren't biting.

Here came a guy with a mask and fins and something like a Hawaiian sling. I was kidding around with him and told him there wasn't any use going in, that there weren't any fish in the ocean. He went down and came up in about a minute. He had this huge snook. It really impressed me that he got that great big fish. It seemed like it was so easy.

He did it again, and he came up with about an eighty-pound grouper. I couldn't believe that either. I couldn't believe there were those monsters right down there where I was fishing, and I wasn't catching anything.

That week I bought a mask and fins. I made myself a spear—something like the one the guy had. I went back to that same spot. I hadn't noticed it when he was diving, but there was a heck of a current going around there. The reason was that when he was diving it was slack tide, and when I got there the tide was moving like a real fast river.

I started to go down. It seemed like my eyes went cross-eyed, my ears hurt, my sinuses hurt. I couldn't get down more than about ten feet, and he was going way on down there. I didn't realize it, but he was holding his breath and going down about sixty or seventy feet to get those fish.

I couldn't even see any big fish—just a couple of little angelfish about two or three inches long. I would have to take off my fins and walk back down the bank because the current would move me so far so fast.

About the fourth time I decided, "Well, I am really going to go down deep." I had begun to catch on then. How to keep my ears from hurting. I still didn't know how. But I went down a little deeper, got pushed by the current, and I slammed into some iron rods that were sticking up. I cut myself all up when the current pushed me into them. I decided that it was harder than it looked to skin dive and spearfish.

The next Sunday I went back again, and he came back again—the guy who had been diving. I asked him if he would teach me how, and he said, "Yeah, but not here. Let's go over on the Tampa end of the bridge, go where it's shallow with no current, and I'll teach you there." That's what he did.

The first day in he speared a mullet. The water was about five or six feet deep, and I couldn't see how he ever speared that mullet. You can't catch mullet on a fishing pole, because they won't bite on anything. They won't bite on any kind of bait. They just eat the grass on the bottom, I guess. I'm not sure what they eat. Vegetarians? Then he taught me how to do it.

They're real fast; they take off every time they see you. You can't get near them. He'd go down and hide behind a big concrete abutment that was there. He'd just lay waiting, with the spear ready to let fly. When one would start to come around the corner, he would nail it. It was something like stalking a panther. It is harder than it looks. I caught on how to do that.

After a month or so, we finally went back to the other end of the bridge. There he taught me to take a cut of a sponge handball and cut it more to fit my nostrils. You'd take a rubber handball, a sponge ball, and you cut it into about four quarters. You cut it down to where two bumps fit into your nostrils. Then you shape the other side of it to fit inside your mask and glue it into your mask. The sections fit inside your nostrils.

Then you push the bottom of your mask up to your nose. That way you could build the pressure inside your mouth to equal the water pressure as you went down. The air would go through your Eustachian tubes to the inside of your ears so that your ears wouldn't hurt.

Also, the pressure would go from your mouth into your sinuses, so they didn't hurt or get ruptured. That way you could go down real fast, real deep. After I learned that, we went back to the other end of the bridge.

By then I also had learned how to use the fins better. I was going down eighty feet, then, spearing these huge fish and bringing them up. There were three or four guys who used to come out there every Sunday. I think most of them lived in Clearwater and St. Petersburg. We got to be pretty good friends, and even did some commercial spearfishing and selling snook to the restaurants.

Nobody—no restaurants, none of the tourists—had ever heard of snook. Nobody ever put snook on the menu. It was delicious white meat and tasted better than all the other fish, better than bass and snapper. The restaurants would buy it from me.

Each restaurant had a different name for it on the menu, but it was all snook. Some of them called it grouper, some called it snapper, and some called it pompano. They had all different kinds of names for it—fancy French names and German names.

One of the fellows wrote to me later. I think he was a judge over in the Tampa area by then. I think another one was an executive of a newspaper. One of them was called Deke, but I don't remember all of their names.

We kept designing new kinds of spears. They didn't manufacture any spearguns then, so we made our own guns.

At first we would make them out of a piece of wood about an inch by two inches and about five feet long. We would cut a notch in the end to hold three or four strands of surgical tubing. Then we would stretch it back to a notch in the spear shaft. We had a hole drilled in the shaft. Then we had something like a pin sticking up out of the gun wood. The hole in the shaft sat on that pin—something like a nail sticking out without a head on it. Then we cut a little slot just forward of that through the wood. We had a piece of strap iron about an inch by a quarter of an inch by six inches long. It was like a great big trigger. We'd pull on that, and it would push the shaft up off the nail. That would fire the spear.

With our own spearguns and shafts, we would go after these big fish and big sharks. We had a contest going to see who could get the biggest fish. We set certain qualifications, such as that you could only have twelve feet of line on your spear shaft, and you couldn't have any ripcord on it. For a while they were using a ripcord, so that if a big fish took your gun away from you, you'd grab this handle and swim up with about seventy feet of parachute cord, real tough nylon. That way you could go up and get some air, come back, and try to pull on the fish some more.

Usually, the fish would wrap around some pilings

or wreckage down there. You would have to go down and untangle him or swim around the pilings a couple of times to get him out in the open again. We made quite a bit of spending money selling fish.

We used to go diving all over Florida.

One time we took a trip. I had an old car; I think it was a 1935 Chevrolet sedan. I cut the back end out of it so that it was like a truck, and I hung ladders on the side of it. I loaded in a bunch of roofing, roofing supplies, and roofing repair materials. This guy and I took off around Florida. We would stop at every bridge that we came to as we were going around the coast of Florida and dive under the bridge, spearing fish.

Then we'd sell the fish, and if we needed some more money, we'd do a roofing job. We'd repair somebody's roof and then go drive some more. We ended up going all the way around both coasts of Florida and diving under every bridge there was or every place where you could get to the water.

The biggest fish were usually under the bridges. There were always jewfish and lot of other big fish, a lot of big tarpon. There was a drumfish that would make a noise like hitting a drum, and snook, which they also called "robalo." I think that's a Spanish name for snook, "robalo." If we had to, we would wrestle the fish until we just wore them out.

Mainly, what we did was for sport. But sometimes we got more than we could eat, so we would sell them. We didn't waste fish. I enjoyed that sport for a long, long time—several years, both in Florida and California.

Finally, I think I had speared about everything that you could spear. I decided to start feeding them and petting them instead of spearing them. Then I started taking pictures of them underwater—stills. I also started taking underwater movies of them.

I speared another crazy fish in California. It was the most god-awful-looking fish I'd ever seen, and I've never seen once since. That monster was about fifteen feet in diameter. I speared it, got it, and brought it in by myself. I couldn't believe that thing. I forget what they call them. It was a great big fish!

The biggest thing I ever landed in Florida, when we were going around that state, was a 350-pounder.

My first adult trip across the country to California was when I drove out and bought my first Aqua-Lung.

When I was first diving and spearfishing, we didn't have any dive equipment. At first, we didn't even have snorkels.

At last, somebody started making snorkels. There weren't very many people making masks, snorkels, or fins back then. I don't think there was such a thing as a snorkel for quite a while.

When I bought that Aqua-Lung, it was from Rene Bussoz. He had a sporting goods store in Los Angeles. Rene's Sporting Goods. He had imported six Aqua-Lungs. I saw a tiny ad in the paper in Tampa noting that.

So I drove out to California and bought one of the first six that he got in. I asked him if I could be a distributor for him in Florida. He said, "Yes." But I didn't know anything about business at all at that time. I couldn't get anybody interested in selling them. I went to some drugstores, a department store, and a sporting goods store. They'd never seen one before.

Nobody'd ever heard of scuba diving. Nobody wanted to buy them or sell them.

I was the only one who had one in Florida!

When I used the Aqua-Lung the first time, it was a little frightening. They didn't have any instruction book. There were no instructors. I didn't know anything about it. I didn't know anything about air embolism or "bends" or anything like that.

So I just put it on my back, turned it on, and went down.

But I picked a very treacherous place to try it. It

was at the very center of Gandy Bridge, underneath the drawbridge that they raised up for the ships that went through. There's a channel, so the water runs through there very rapidly, and the water's very murky.

Many sharks and big fish are there. I went down behind one of the huge concrete pilings so I'd be out of the current. I was just slowly settling down, and I couldn't see but about a foot. If I looked toward the sun, I could see shadows of all these big fish swimming between me and the sun. It was spooky.

I sat down on top of a gigantic jewfish. He pumped his tail, took off, and rode me around a little bit. Then I just sat still and watched those shadows going by. For about half an hour I didn't go anywhere. I just sat suspended there behind that post. I knew if I swam out, the current would sweep me away. So I just remained there, watching all those big shadows going by in front of me. Then I came up safely.

Unfortunately, there wasn't any place to get my underwater "lung" refilled with air. Nobody had any high-pressure air compressors. The only place I finally found where I could get my air tank filled was where they made oxygen for welding. But the guy wouldn't shut down his equipment for making oxygen just to fill a tank for me, because it was a lot of expense and trouble for him. I had to wait until he shut it down regularly to clean everything up, change the oil in the compressors and things. Then he would fill my tank and go back to pumping oxygen again. As a result, only about once a month could I get one more tankful of air.

I knew I was the first one to use an Aqua-Lung in Florida, though I only got to use it once a month. At the time there were only six in the country. They were made in France by a company started by Emile Gagnan and Jacques-Yves Cousteau. Cousteau did the public relations, "PR," and Gagnan was the inventor. They formed a company. Then Rene Bussoz started a new company that was called U.S. Divers.

"Fearless Fisher" was a name my buddies gave me, first in Florida and then in California, mainly because I was always looking for sharks and trying to get them to come in instead of running away from them.

The name stuck everywhere I went. I was a shark fanatic. The name started in the Tampa area.

When I got to California, I started the first skin diving club, I believe, in the United States. It was called the "Sharks."

We made a list of things that everyone had to do to get their special "Sharks" arm patch. One of them was catch a shark with your bare hands. It had to weigh more than thirty pounds.

Everybody thought I was nuts. So I showed them how easy it was.

But the darned things do have a special trick. If you grab one by the tail, it's a big mistake, because they can make a U-turn with their body and bend around and bite their tail. So they can turn around and bite you too.

At the old Gandy Bridge in Tampa, Florida, Mel had his first experiences with skin diving and spearfishing. He finally decided that he would go in the water with a mask and fins. Then he decided it was harder than it looked, and because it was hard and challenging, he was "hooked" forever. He learned about the need for equipment that didn't exist until he developed it. He went to California to get the first Aqua-Lung from Rene Bussoz, an associate of Emile Gagnan and Jacques Cousteau, then he became the first distributor in Florida, but had a hard time finding a compressor to actually provide tankfuls of air. He then also became known for the first time as "Fearless Fisher," starting in California, in the first skin diving club, called by him, naturally, the "Sharks."

Above: Mel with a raft full of lobster. Below: Mel and Deo caught lobster to sell to local restaurants in order to buy building supplies for what would become the world's first dive shop, "Mel's Aqua Shop." FISHER FAMILY COLLECTION

CHAPTER EIGHT

Fun, Romance, and Adventure: The World's First Dive Shop

*P**ioneer of the sea, Mel Fisher was also postwar and looking for what he always called "fun, romance, and adventure." That would become a lifelong siren call, as Mel followed his own wondering and wandering. He still carried his little boy imaginative thinking, though it was now in a young man's body as he followed adventure around the coastal waters of Florida and then along those of California. From the Atlantic to the Pacific oceans, a mechanically-savvy but free-spirited Mel spent time working in salt water and on underwater equipment for swimming, fishing, and diving. He worked on spears and spearguns, swimwear, cameras, and movie possibilities.*

Note to readers: There are several additional voices in this chapter, which add to the rich tapestry of Mel Fisher's life—his daughter, Taffi Fisher Abt, and most importantly, Dolores "Deo" Fisher, his wife and business partner. I interviewed both of them. These interviews are important to Mel's story.

I did not really use the Aqua-Lung until I got out to California, because there was no way to fill it with air, and that was it. I had done maintenance work, home service work, and spearfished for a couple of years in Florida. But diving was now my main interest.

Starting while I was in Florida, I also did make and sell a few spearguns. We were losing quite a few spears and guns to the big fish when we were commercial fishing. So we'd make up about a dozen of them at a time.

Then other guys would say, "Hey, I want to buy

one of those," so we'd sell them one.

In Florida, I also started making gas guns. I'd take the valve from a fire extinguisher. That's one way. I'd put a small tank on instead of a big one, so you could swim around with it.

Then I put a stainless-steel barrel on it. Stainless steel shaft and spearhead. I think we were the first ones who ever had detachable heads that came off, instead of barbed heads that opened up. I also started selling gas guns, at thirty-five bucks apiece.

I bought some Schroeder valves from war surplus. They're stainless-steel snap-on valves and hoses, "heartbreaker" hoses. We'd hook that hose up to a big fire extinguisher bottle. Then I'd snap the snap-on onto the gas gun and open the valve on the big tank; that would fill the gas gun, recharge it with carbon dioxide (CO_2) gas, which is liquid. It was liquid CO_2. Then you'd pop off the snap-on from the hose, and the liquid would stay in the small cylinder. They have a little valve core in them, something like a valve core on an automobile, except it was better, to withstand high pressure. There are three different ways that CO_2 can be, and it depends on the pressure, the temperature. It comes in solid blocks, like ice, it comes in liquid, and it comes in gas. It's all the same thing. It's all CO_2.

Starting with my buddies in Florida, and later out in California, it just seemed like we were all interested in the same things—water and women.

I don't think we had a club per se, and a formal name and all that. But we did have a group. About fifteen of us enjoyed diving and spearfishing together. We'd go chasing women, too, and enjoyed dancing and drinking and having fun at the beaches.

We didn't go to the Keys on my first round trip around Florida with my buddies. We went straight across from Tampa to Miami and up. I remember diving in Government Cut. Government Cut at Miami was interesting, because there was such a tremendous current. The water was very clear. You'd just go underwater, and you'd be moving along really fast without having to use your fins. You could hold your breath longer, since you didn't have to exercise.

On that trip I believe we did spear one of the biggest fish that we had ever speared. I've got a photograph of that. I recall it was 350 pounds.

Later, I speared a bigger one with Nelson "Doc" Mathison down in Baja California; it was 438 pounds. It took two of us to get him. Usually, we tried to make it that one guy had to do it all by himself, without a boat, without an inner tube, without a ripcord.

Just man against fish, so to speak.

One of the most ridiculous situations I got into was when Kenny Bridgeford and I jumped in the water in California. We had very powerful CO_2 gas guns that I had made out of fire extinguishers. We also had heavy-duty, half-inch stainless-steel shafts, big Brown's lily iron arrowheads, spearheads. Lily iron spearheads are the kind they use for whales. This was out in the middle of the channel between Catalina Island and Los Angeles. The water was very clear.

Both of us came up to this thing that was about sixty feet long. I came up to a monster. My buddy and I were looking at each other, and we signaled that we were both going to shoot at the same time. I aimed at his spine, right behind the head; hit him in the spine back toward the tail. Instead of taking off real fast like most fish do when they get speared, this thing just didn't move at all, and just started quivering. I thought, "Wow, we must have got him. We hit him in the spine, and he can't move."

We had two truck inner tubes tied in a ripcord to our guns. Next thing, he very nonchalantly tilted his head down, lifted his tail up out of the water—the tail was about ten feet across—and he just started going straight down.

The inner tubes went down, too—great big inner

tubes! When he got way down, what really surprised me was that when the inner tubes got down about ten or fifteen feet, they went *plaaat* and flat. It was the first time I'd ever seen anything pull an inner tube underwater. Great big truck tire tubes!

About ten minutes later, the inner tubes came back up, but we lost our guns; we never saw them again. I think it was a whale shark—a huge shark that looks like a whale.

The first experience I ever had of anything in the ocean fighting back was during an underwater movie I made of Chuck Peterson spearing about a hundred-pound grouper near La Paz, Mexico.

He speared the grouper. Then it turned around, came up, and bit him on the knee. He had his leg bent, and it took his whole knee, thigh, and calf into its mouth, then spit it back out again.

I got a movie of that; I've still got that film. But that was the grouper acting in self-defense, I think.

Also, a big ray that got me was a case of self-defense too.

I really think it's very unlikely that anything in the ocean would attack anybody without provocation—except sharks.

***

Taffi: As a child, I remember my father telling me the story of how he helped his parents in their move from Indiana to California. My grandfather was a talented carpenter and builder and had taught my father the same skills.

After WWII ended, my dad spent almost a year in Colorado and a few years down in Florida. About that time the federal government approved some program where substantial federal financial support would be allotted to states who were updating/maintaining and/or constructing the Interstate Highway System. My dad's parents decided to go into the "real estate" business for a while, and Dad went along to help. My grandmother got the plans of the routes and went ahead of the highway construction crews, researching—by looking at the property tax records—who owned vacant lots and houses not too far from the planned highways. They would purchase the empty lots, and my grandfather and Dad would build solid wood foundations on them. Then they went door to door to homeowners whose homes were being purchased in the "right of way" or "condemnation" process, and they would offer to buy their houses. Usually, the owner would sell cheap, because the government had already paid them to move on out of the way, and they had to leave soon anyway, since the houses were going to be demolished. Most of them had already sold their houses to the government for enough to go buy a new one. Sometimes the houses had already been completely abandoned.

Then my dad and grandpa would put the whole house on a huge, extra-wide trailer, using some sort of logs as rollers, and move the whole house—lock, stock, and barrel—to the foundations they had recently constructed on the vacant lots, hook up the electric and plumbing, and put a "for sale" sign up.

They did this from Indiana all the way to California. They made quite a bit of money and were pretty tired of the business by the time they got to California. Then they decided to set some roots and stay put for a while, so they bought a chicken ranch business. And that was that for a few years.

***

Mel resumes: I moved out to California a couple two or three years after I made my spearfishing trek around Florida from Tampa.

My parents, Earl and Grace, wanted to make a new start in California, and I was ready to try some new business endeavor.

This was to be a chicken ranch, not in Indiana, but California, with its seacoast and its golden hills.

For the Fisher family chicken ranch, we bought a house at an auction, a public auction in Los Angeles where they were building a freeway through town. The government condemned all the houses and auctioned them off. We got one for a low price and moved it out to the chicken ranch. It was a big, old, wood frame house. We built a footing under it and let it down on the footing.

The first time I laid eyes on Deo, she was a cute little teenage redhead! My family and I had decided to sell them the chicken ranch, and they didn't know anything about eggs—what created them, why chickens lay eggs, or what you do with the eggs.

I had to stay on and teach Deo, her mother, and sister how to run a chicken ranch. I had to teach Deo about "The Egg and I." Most people think chickens have to make love to make an egg, but really they don't. They just keep poopin' 'em out every day regardless. She learned that in a hurry. Every day I would go in, and there would be thousands of eggs. So I'd tell her, "I thought you cleaned all those eggs yesterday! Thought you weighed those eggs yesterday. Didn't you put those all in the cartons yesterday?" She began to learn that a chicken ranch is a twenty-four-hour-a-day job, seven days a week. Chickens lay eggs on Christmas and New Year's morning, and you never get a day off.

Then we built a feed shed, about twenty by forty feet. Half of it ended up being for feed storage, and the other half was where I started my skin-diving shop. I made the first showcase.

Instead of buying a showcase, I just made it out of an extra window that came with the house.

I had been seriously taking up this sport/business of scuba diving, spearfishing, manufacturing special gas guns, inventing power heads, and things.

When I later got into making underwater movies, I also developed some camera housings and related equipment. I was pursuing the sport and business originally in one of the feed sheds. I finally built several counters, like store counters, out of extra house windows. I put in some fins, masks, and regulators. I believe that was actually the first skin divers' store in the world, the first one selling strictly skin-diving equipment.

I did that for two or three years there at the chicken ranch.

My dive shop work hours would be just part time, from 6 to 8 o'clock at night, so when they got off work, people could come down and buy some equipment. I found out I was making more money in those two hours with the scuba diving equipment than I was in the other twenty-two hours with the chickens.

Deo and I got married and got a little boy and decided to build a store on our own location. That would become Mel's Aqua Shop at Redondo Beach, California.

***

Wendy: *Dolores "Deo" Fisher was more than a wife—she was also a mother of four children, a full partner with her husband Mel in the "family" business, and she was also a movie star, starring in his underwater movies.*

With focus on the early years of Mel's California and Caribbean adventures and his pioneering underwater equipment, dive suit, and other underwater and dive developments, Deo sat with me and looked randomly at old news clippings, little reminders of a long and wonderful life together. Below are some of her comments during our interview:

Deo: Here was an article which was in March of 1957. The write-up was about a month-long trip that we took down through Mexico and Yucatan. We dove in six "cenotes"— they are those old ancient wells of Mexico. Some of them were sacrificial wells. That's part of the Mayan civilization.

The caption says:

"Redondo Beach diver welcomes the risks involved in his underwater profession. 'That's what makes life interesting,' he said with a smile."

He was shooting a movie on *Life in the Sea* for *Encyclopedia Britannica*. Here the clipping talks about all the millions of dollars' worth of gold and jewels in some of the cenotes. Mel said that it would take months to dig under the mud, silt, and rocks covering the skeletons and jewels. He reported, "We didn't have time on this trip, although we did find many bones. But we know the treasure is there, and we may go back."

That was the way it was every time we took a trip. We had to come back before we discovered what we were really looking for.

Here, by this clipping, we found a shipwreck then.

"Transferring activities to Cozumel Island in the Caribbean, the party discovered an old shipwreck encrusted with coral. 'Thousands of beautiful fish were milling around it,' Mel Fisher recalled."

This one doesn't have a date caption with it, but it says:

"Next stop buried treasure. Mel Fisher holds up a sheepshead. That's a California sheepshead, and it's different from the ones here. During an afternoon skin diving, Mel Fisher is headed on an expedition for buried treasure."

Here's another clipping without a date:

"Sunken treasure goal of skin-diving party. The man who found a fifteen-foot ancient anchor off Catalina Island last week is leading the expedition tomorrow to see if the kelp-covered relic can lead him to the burial place of four million, five hundred thousand dollars in sunken treasure which went down with the frigate sunk off the island in 1802.

"Mel Fisher and a friend spotted the anchor last

Sunday. The trail of the anchor chain was resting on the bottom of the steep undersea cliff. They had to go up because their air was running low."

The frigate went down near Ship Rock, near Catalina. That's where the anchor was found. We always thought there was one of the Manila Spanish galleons out there around Ship Rock somewhere. Maybe this anchor led us to believe that. At that time, we didn't know ancient shipwrecks like the galleon didn't have anchor chain.

Underwater cameras were taken along. Here's some of the other ones we were on that you could [reference]:

"Point Arguello, forty-five miles northwest of Santa Barbara, known as the 'Graveyard of the Pacific.' A large number of ships sunk there."

"Skin divers after the '*Yankee Blade*,' a clipper ship which went down in the 1850s with five million dollars in gold."

I remember we went out there. We had an experience at Point Arguello where the boat that we were on—we were looking for shipwrecks then—the boat we were on was almost sunk itself.

We got in a real bad storm, and it was sinking. A hatch came off the bow, and water was pouring in there. I remember I had to go underneath and hold a thing up over the bow until they were able to get it. Two divers had to go out in this really rough, rough sea and put another cover on top.

Auntie Marion (Unger, family friend who cared for the Fisher children) can tell you about that, because they had us reported as sinking. She heard it on the radio that the boat had disappeared. 'They' had heard a loud noise, and then the boat had disappeared.

She had the kids, and she was crying. We managed to get back to the coast. But the captain of the boat said that he wasn't moving the boat from there if it took a week for the water to calm down.

So we got in our wet suits and went ashore.

Mel and I, and another couple, went on shore, walked up a cliff and over some fields to a lighthouse up there.

When we saw that lighthouse at sea, we were so comforted because we thought, "God, at last, safety." We are in sight of land and these people in the lighthouse will see us, even if we sink before we get there. We will be saved.

Then we got up to the lighthouse—after going through a field that was full of bulls, and Mel had this bright red jacket—these people were flabbergasted to see us. They hadn't seen our boat. There were no people around this area at all, just the people who were caretakers of the lighthouse. They were just flabbergasted to see us. They were very friendly because, I guess, they don't get to see people very much. They took us in and fed us pancakes, coffee, and tea. They even took us into a little town nearby called Lompoc. We caught a bus from there and went back to where we lived in Redondo Beach. We got there very late at night and went to pick up our kids.

When Auntie Marion opened the door, she saw Mel and said, "You're supposed to be dead!" She started crying. Then she told us what they had been saying on the radio. That was not on a marine radio. This was just on regular radio.

That was more training. That was preliminary training for this treasure hunt down here. I'm sure that all of this, in the big master plan, was training for us.

(Mel joins by listening in.)

Here're some ads for Mel's shop in 1954: "Mel's Aqua Shop." So I guess it was in full swing by then. Dirk was born in December of 1953. I remember taking him for walks down to the shop before I went back to work.

I think Mel was just building the shop then, so his

shop actually must have opened up the early part of 1954.

This is advertising an underwater camera unit or a speargun. Oh, this is 1955. OK, 1954, Cornelius portable air compressors. Desco line. Hope and Page. Boy, these were really some of the early developments in the equipment line.

Somebody invented a nonreturn valve for the Aqua-Lung, so that when you blew the water out of the hose, it wouldn't come back into your mouth.

Up to that point, if you got water in your hose, you had to roll over on your left side and blow it out the exhaust. Otherwise, water was always in your hose mouthpiece there. That was one of the first—Hope and Page—nonreturn valves.

Then the Scott Hydropack was a full face mask unit. Scott Hydropack makes a lot of equipment for firefighting, and they had decided to go into the underwater area. They invented a full face mask for use with tanks underwater, also spring guns and CO_2 guns.

Wendy: *So Mel actually came along with his developments at about the time that equipment was beginning to be developed?*

Deo: Well, he developed a lot of it before this point.

Here's the Arbalete—that's a French-made speargun. This is 1954, but he had been making spearguns for, I would say, four years before that.

So about 1950, he was into developing equipment. Spearguns and spear tips.

I don't know if he actually worked on developing power heads or not. I know there were some other guys developing power heads—you know, to shoot fish with.

Let's see, what else did he work on? He also developed a breathing apparatus himself. Unfortunately, some of these brochures are not dated. This one has to be later, because it says, "Learn to dive with certified county instructors."

Wendy: *So that would be after Los Angeles County began certifying divers?*

Deo: Yeah, and we are advertising our boat, the *Golden Doubloon*. That's because we took our boat on that first trip, then came back and started using it to take divers out.

Wendy: *So you took the* Golden Doubloon *to Silver Shoals first?*

Deo: We tried. But we never actually got that far.

Wendy: *You came around and got as far as Panama, right?*

Deo: Yeah, the other side of Panama.

Wendy: *Then brought it back? Through the canal and back up the coast?*

Deo: Yeah. We may have gone through there before, when we were down in the Virgin Islands and Haiti.

Wendy: *I don't remember your saying anything about Haiti.*

Deo: Yeah, we were there because Pan American Airways was one of the sponsors.

Wendy: *You know that Pan Am was born in Key West?*

Deo: Yeah. They were making some—let's see, this is June 1955. We went to Haiti then. We were looking at shipwrecks then, in 1955, off the coast of Haiti. We were making some films over and under the Caribbean, and Jantzen Swimsuits and Pan American Airways were paying for the expenses of the trip.

That's also when Mel had decided to go into 35mm movie shooting. That was 1955. Then 35mm film was very expensive, but it offered much better quality for television. He had developed several camera cases in which to use 16mm movie film.

Then he built something about this big—about three and a half feet tall, and it held reels, four-hundred-foot magazines of 35mm movie film. What he built had its own little breathing unit, so that when it went down, that whole case would be pressurized, and when it came up, there was an exhaust valve so that the compressed air could come out of it. It was really something. I even learned to use it.

Wendy: *He had developed this himself?*

Deo: Yeah, he built it all himself.

Wendy: *Did anyone ever make use of it beyond you guys? Did he ever market any of his inventions?*

Deo: That he didn't. He finally ended up selling that big 35mm unit. I think he sold it when we decided to come treasure hunting. He had it for years. But it didn't take long for him to realize that he couldn't afford to shoot 35mm movie film. It was just too expensive.

We had an old movie projector. We set it up in one of our back bedroom closets. We cut a hole in that wall into the hall, then another hole in the living room wall. We then projected pictures and movies across the living room on a big screen.

When we got through with that 1955 trip to Haiti where we were shooting that movie, there was a guy named Homer Groening, who was with Jantzen Swimsuit Company. He sent Mel a telegram after he had seen the footage that Mel had shot.

The telegram said, "Your film better than *20,000 Leagues Under the Sea.*"

Wendy: *Do you think that Mel was more of a pioneer in a lot of ways, in a lot of these things? Was it just that he chose not to go forward with marketing or selling inventions or developments once he had developed them?*

Deo: He was a pioneer. He wasn't into manufacturing and selling the stuff as much. Since what he needed was not what was available, that's why he invented and developed things. His pioneering was usually because he wanted something and it wasn't there, so he had to build it.

Wendy: *What I'm wondering is if, in the long haul of things, it's going to be shown that he was the first developer of certain things that you might not even be aware of now. Developments in the field that we might make clear. I don't know. What areas he is a real pioneer in, I guess, are what I am trying to nail down.*

Deo: Well, he was a pioneer in the underwater field, period. In general. Scuba diving, spearfishing. Probably, I think that the spear tips that he developed—probably the design that he developed—is being used now, and I don't know if they were actually unique then.

You know that it is awfully hard to find something new that you invented that really is new. Maybe the Polynesians had been using them two hundred years before.

Wendy: *But he never researched that.*

Deo: He developed what he needed. Maybe he was in another life on the Polynesian Islands, fishing for a living, who knows?

But the spear fishing was what got him into the underwater world, definitely.

He was in Tampa; he was fishing with a fishing pole. A diver came up who had—just a skin diver—and he said this diver had some huge fish that he had gotten spearfishing. I think that was the turning point in Mel's life that took him into the water, where he has been ever since.

He has gone through phases in the underwater world.

First, he was interested in spearfishing. Then people wouldn't believe his fish stories, is the way he told it to me.

So he started developing and building cases for underwater cameras, so that he could take pictures and movies, and that he could prove what he was saying was true.

That took him into the field of underwater photography from spearfishing.

He eventually lost most of his interest in spearing fish. It was a challenge and a sportsman type of thing to do when it was first introduced, but he lost interest when he started taking underwater movies, and then he became more interested in the movies.

Then taking the underwater movies took him to shipwrecks.

They were a photographer's dream because of the beauty of growth on shipwrecks and the sea life that surrounded them.

So he progressed from one phase to another, on into the shipwrecks.

Actually, the movie business took him into exploring other types of past history in addition to shipwrecks. Movies took us back to the time of the Mayans, exploring some of the cenotes, sacrificial wells, and some of the ruins down in Yucatan. Making movies took him to looking for a shipwreck off of Acapulco, Mexico, and then he found some shipwrecks down off of Cozumel.

Wendy: *OK, you go from the Mayan exploration to the shipwreck off of Acapulco and the Yucatan area.*

Deo: There are still a lot of shipwrecks down off of there in Mexican waters.

Wendy: *So the movies took him to the land-based Mayan explorations, the well diving.*

Deo: And into caves. I remember exploring caves on Tortuga Island off of Haiti, where there were reports that there was a lot of caves.

Wendy: *Underwater caves?*

Deo: No, on land, because there was reportedly a lot of pirate treasure that had been secreted away in these caves. We also looked for shipwrecks there, on our first trip, whenever it was. 1957? Or 1955? There were some shipwrecks off of Haiti. People at that time had told us that there was a belief that one of Columbus's ships was wrecked in that area.

Wendy: *Did that prove true?*

Deo: Well, I don't know. It is still questionable. They haven't proven it yet.

Wendy: *But would it be the same area where they are working now; Have you compared notes?*

Deo: Yeah, I think it would be the same area. It was not off the capital. It was off of the side of the island near Tortuga—Cap-Haïtien. Off of Cap-Haïtien. The year that we got down there, they had had a terrible storm. It was probably a hurricane gone through there and had ruined most of the boats. The government actually provided us with a boat, because we were doing this filming. It was amazing to us how the people lived on this island. The storm had washed their homes away because they just lived in these little grass shacks. They were really devastated by it.

Wendy: *Here you are "home safely" from something—December of 1954. But to continue this line of thinking, because it is going to help me with the overall outline. So Mel's experience direction was spearfishing to spearguns to camera cases to movies, into shipwrecks and simultaneously into some land-based exploration of wells?*

Deo: Later developments—I guess it was a challenge to him—included gold diving in the rivers. It was never a really serious profession with us, though. It was more of a hobby that would get us away from our business and take our family up into the "Mother Lode" country around Sacramento and the San Francisco area, back in the mountains, streams, and rivers.

That was more or less for fun. But this was also part of the big plan, because the equipment that we developed for use in the rivers, we used later in the sea—adapting some of the gold miners' equipment with sluice boxes, taking different tables—shaker tables—and adapting them to underwater, and developing an underwater venturi dredge, which we used to vacuum the crevices in the river. We actually brought the material up and over these, and through these different refining and separating processes.

That was some of the first equipment that we used when we started treasure hunting in Vero Beach in 1963, 1964. Some of that was further training.

Wendy: *Indeed, it's been a long time developing! Backing up to spearfishing, which was first in Tampa. Then Mel goes from Tampa to California, does he not?*

Deo: Yeah, that's part of his life that is a little bit foggy to me. Where did we get to with this developing, 1950?

Wendy: *Timing-wise, we skipped backward. Dirk was born in December 1953, so it was early 1954 that Mel opened "Mel's Aqua Shop."*

Deo: What's this 1950 here?

Wendy: *By 1950 he was into developing equipment—spearguns, spear tips, etc.*

Deo: He had also developed a breathing apparatus himself. June of 1955.

He graduated in 1941. He was in the service until 1946.

So there is a period off about four years that is foggy to me, because I don't know—Tampa, I think he lived in Chicago, or he went to a hospital in Chicago after he got back. Then he lived in Denver for two years with his wife. Yet he was in Tampa when he first started this spearfishing.

Wendy: *You guys were married in?*

Deo: 1953.

Wendy: *By 1950 he was developing equipment already, you say. So by 1950 he was in California and doing this equipment developing.*

Deo: I think he was in California, probably.

Well, this picture is 1951, when he was going down to Baja California and spearing fish. Here's a picture marked "Sarasota, April 9, 1950"—Mel's mother has a note down here: "Note hand-carved wooden guns. They were making their own hand-carved."

So April in 1950—here's what this clipping says:

"A Los Angeles, California, resident and two Tampa men are shown with 395-pound jewfish they speared under New Pass Bridge."

Wendy: *So Mel had gone to California and come back to Tampa.*

Deo: But I think he had just come back for a visit. Look at the little round weights. They had iron weights—round, one-pound iron weights with a hole through them, and they were painted this kind of a jet navy black. He'd just have to wear so many of them.

This is 1950. These are some of the guns that he developed. A tarpon gun, Fisher's CO_2 gun, the "Shark."

He also invented another one that—oh, yes, this is what the business was called then—"Fisher's Sporting Goods."

He invented another one called the "Peewee."

Wendy: *So he was in business?*

Deo: Yeah, "Fisher's Sporting Goods."

This address is at the chicken ranch, 4135 W. 182nd St., Torrance, California. That was the chicken ranch. We let him use one of the feed sheds. He had made a little workshop there for developing things. They were all living together at the chicken ranch.

Wendy: *So he had rejoined his parents then.*

Deo: The scrapbooks start there at 1950—that's thirty-seven years of scrapbooks. That's neat. That's a devoted mother, right.

Wendy: *So let's go from 1950. He was developing these units, so you come into the picture as a movie star of sorts?*

Deo: Me? Oh, no. I was a little farm girl from Montana.

Wendy: *I understand that, but what I am asking—developmentally, in his life, Mel has done the equipment developing, but he's into the underwater movies as you come along?*

Deo: Right.

Wendy: *So you became his movie star.*

Deo: That's right, I did. He taught me how to use the snorkel, and masks, and fins. I'm trying to remember—I got my first dry suit, I think, before we got married. A friend of his was making them with him. These are dry suits that they just made of flat rubber, and they made one up for me.

Wendy: *What's the difference between a wet suit and a dry suit? The point is that with a dry suit you stay dry?*

Deo: You stayed dry inside, and you had to wear long underwear underneath for insulation.

Wendy: *And a wet suit does what?*

Deo: A wet suit is made of intercellular neoprene. This suit has air cells throughout, so it keeps you insulated. It doesn't absorb water like a sponge, but it is much more comfortable, because it doesn't have to be so tight around the extremities and the neck to keep the water out.

Wendy: *So it's a later development than the dry suits.*

Deo: We could probably tell by some of these ads in here, but they probably started about 1954 into the wet suits.

Wendy: *What about the moviemaking? Were you his movie star?*

Deo: Yes, in most of his underwater films from the time that I met him through the period when he decided that we were going to be doing full-time treasure hunting, and nobody was going to take any pictures, movies; then we weren't going to go for fish or lobsters, we were going to put our blinders on, and we were going to treasure hunt. We were not going for seashells or anything else. But, yeah, I guess that up until that point I was his movie star. It's amazing to me now, when I think back to the things that I did, because I heard that camera switch go on, and I knew the film was running, and I knew how much the film cost, and I knew how much the whole process cost.

***

This is a family business because it is also a family life, and in fact, it is also an "extended" family, because so many people have been a part of Mel Fisher's "family" of people who share Mel's own views of life—extended into business and, most importantly, the freedom and excitement of the open sea.

Mel is not only a pioneer, but a leader of people who believe in what he did—"fun, romance, and adventure," and "today's the day," while also engineering daily against the everchanging ways of the ocean. Mel and Deo, and for a time Mel's parents, started farming chickens, and moved toward their goal, a skin-diving business, first at the chicken ranch and then on their own site in Redondo Beach, California, built one wall at a time with sales from the sea. Together Mel and Deo had four children. Meanwhile, they were focused on fun and adventure—off the coast of California, and then places like Panama and "Silver Shoals" in the Caribbean. They were also developing things of the sea, from power heads for spearfishing to dry and then wet suits. And as a matter of course, Mel moved on to underwater pictures and television, and treasure of both monetary and historic values, moving with the tides and times.

From left: Dirk, Kim, Kane, Deo, and Mel Fisher. The children are wearing wet suits custom-made at Mel's Aqua Shop.
FISHER FAMILY COLLECTION

CHAPTER NINE

The Other End of the Line: Making Underwater Movies

M*el chased adventure first in company with other buddies and eventually with wife and family, who were his true "partners." Amazingly true, Mel and Deo were actually married in the all-glass Wayfarers' Chapel, set high on a cliff in California, looking out over the ocean that was to be the beginning of their life together. He always had a sense of fair play with adversary fish and sea creatures, whether hunting them, or later filming them for motion pictures. If he hunted creatures for movies or television, those they caught were given as food to jails, churches, or other places where they were eaten. Mel found his ways to mix work and pleasure, in an environment he chose and to sustain himself, his family, and associates, in ways that would amaze and entertain his audiences, all the while educating them to the real lives underwater. For his educational dive trips out of California, Mel used the* Golden Doubloon, *his sixty-five-foot former fishing boat, skippered by his much-appreciated skipper, Captain Eddie Tsukimura. But for working "vacation" trips, Mel and Deo would use the captains where they were, including on their first real "honeymoon."*

One of the most spectacular spearfishing films I have ever seen is one I made with Deo when we went on our honeymoon out at sea from Key West in June of 1953.

We chartered a boat from Captain Ed Ciesinski. He had a pretty big boat, and I had quite a group of divers with me from California. We told him that we wanted to go to shipwrecks. He took us out to the area near where the *Atocha* is.

He took us to another shipwreck out there, and we got movies of that. Then he took us out to the wreck *Valbanera*, which is about twenty miles farther out than where we later determined the *Atocha* had ended up.

That place was just loaded with fish. At one end of it, in the current, there were about a thousand barracuda schooling, just sitting there and slowly swimming into the current and staying. They weren't going anywhere. I had never seen so many barracuda.

Usually, you'll only see one. Once in a while, you see two barracuda. But at this place, there must have been a thousand of them. Just a wall of barracuda, with all their eyeballs glaring at you. They were staying right next to the shipwreck, even though they were swimming fast—the current was very fast, so they were just standing still, more or less. Like treading water, underwater.

The jewfish down there reminded me of cows in a barn, where cows are being milked while their heads calmly look out the stall windows. The jewfish had all their heads sticking out, just like a barn scene. I went down holding my breath, without a gun or camera.

While Deo was loading film in my camera that morning, I grabbed an eighty-pound jewfish with my hands, brought him up, and threw him into the boat. He was flopping all over that boat.

Everybody was really surprised; they wondered how I ever speared the fish without a spear. There was no spear in him. But they couldn't believe I'd just grabbed him and brought him up.

After a lot of years of messing with fish, I found out that if you put your thumb and middle finger in their eyeballs and squeeze, they stiffen out like a board. They don't fight a bit. When I got that big fish up on the boat and let go of him, he started flopping all over the boat, almost kicking people overboard.

That first morning out there, I wanted to get into

the water very early to get some movies with a bright yellow camera case I had built and a 16mm movie camera. I grabbed the camera, jumped in, and started to take movies of the barracuda on the end of the shipwreck there.

This was at the *Valbanera* shipwreck on what is called Halfmoon Shoal. That's where we later built our first "Eiffel Tower" to keep track of where we were going and coming from on our *Atocha* search—with a theodolite and a marine radio. Those darned barracuda came right up and started biting on my bright yellow camera case. I was holding the camera to my face. I was taking movies of them as they were coming up and biting the camera. Usually, I handled my camera equipment very tenderly. But this time, I swam up fast, momentarily leaving the camera suspended underwater. I had a cord on the camera that I used like a ripcord in case I dropped it or wanted to have somebody pull it up on the boat. I pulled the ripcord and came up, then used no gentleness when I pulled the camera up.

I dived into the boat fast, because I wasn't sure that the barracuda weren't chasing me. Actually, they just stayed by the camera.

The film I made that day we called *The Other End of the Line*, and it was made for the Voit Rubber Company.

At some time that day, I went down and speared a giant tarpon with my CO_2 gas gun. He weighed about 150 pounds. That tarpon towed me around for about four hours before he finally tuckered out. He was a powerful, powerful fish.

Usually, I didn't use scuba gear while spearfishing; it just didn't seem fair to the fish. When you're just holding your breath, it seems like a more even contest.

We had some rules like that as early as when my buddies and I, all single then, traveled around the Florida coast. We had to bring up the fish without using scuba gear, and we limited the length of line we could use.

In one shot, I had the movie camera bolted to my gas gun when I speared a huge shark. The shark came up and tried to eat the camera. That was a really good shot!

That morning in 1953, I remember feeling a little like Paul Bunyan, with all the big fish I did catch. That was a string of fish that were huge! That day I caught about—I can't exaggerate on this, because I took movies of it—I got about six or eight huge jewfish, a tarpon that weighed about 150 pounds, a big shark, and, I think, a barracuda. "Doc" Mathison, who was with me, got underwater movies as I was swimming along, towing this huge stringer of fish that I had caught. It is amazing that a shark didn't come in to go after that huge string of fish. "Doc" Mathison and I went on trips together all around the Caribbean and California, taking underwater movies together.

Finally, I believe when I went East to go treasure hunting, we divided up all the film fifty-fifty. I wish I could find his wife out in California—because he has passed away—to see if I could buy that film from her. She's got half of the movies that we shot.

I think the Voit Rubber Company still has got the original of that film, *The Other End of the Line*. I don't know if they are still making prints of that or not.

Deo remembers how Captain Eddie Ciesinski " . . . took us out when we were down here in 1953, and again when we moved down to Key West to look for the *Atocha*. Our children went to school here eventually, and Kim had his son as a teacher in wood shop in school here." Eddie was a famous skipper way back then.

My interest in shipwrecks was big even then, because I asked him to take us to shipwrecks. I couldn't believe how he could find a shipwreck way out in the middle of the ocean, where you couldn't see land in any direction.

He just took us to one. We'd make some movies, he'd take us to another one, and we'd make some more movies. Then he'd take us to another one, way, way out in the ocean.

Deo read an article in recent years in which somebody had asked him about our trips, and he supposedly was a little upset at all the fish that we had killed during that trip. But as I remember, when we came back, we gave the fish away, some to the hospital, some to the prison, and some to the jail. So the fish were all eaten up. We didn't sell any of them. We could have, I guess, sold them at the fish market.

But we just figured we'd let people have them for nothing. We made our movies—that was what we were "into" at that time.

For Voit Rubber Company, we did something like a promotional film. Another film we made was for Jantzen swimsuits. That film was made when we later went down to the Virgin Islands. Deo remembers how we had some swimsuits in international orange and fluorescent green for another film, this one for Gantner swimsuits.

From our 1953 footage, Voit made an advertising film out of it. I think it was only a fifteen-minute film, and I believe it's still available.

Probably it was pioneering, at least in the US, for us to have a group of guys who made up rules for themselves that were more or less a code of ethics under the water, such as no tanks when spearfishing.

In the beginning, I think I was probably the only one making underwater movies in the United States. Cousteau was making underwater movies in Europe; his classic film was *The Silent World*. Then there was Hans Hass, who made a movie for the theaters called *Under the Red Sea*. He made some movies in the Red Sea while I was making them in the US. We all knew each other existed, because we would look at each other's movies, but we hadn't really met at that time.

I remember that Hass had movies of one of his guys coming up to a leopard shark—or a leopard ray. The creature was about forty feet long, and the guy would go up, stick his head up in the shark's mouth, and then come out again. That really amazed me.

The films I did were all for different companies, different sponsors. That was like having a paid vacation. My moviemaking was done during the years while we had our dive shop.

For about twelve years, until 1964, we operated our dive shop, and we were mass-producing scuba divers! That was when scuba diving was really young, in the early 1950s. We were the only ones in the United States teaching people at first.

We gave the lessons free at first—we didn't require anything. Then it got to be where we'd say, "If you buy a mask, fins, and snorkel, we'll give you free scuba lessons." Most people would go ahead and buy scuba gear from us too. About ten years later, discount houses started coming out, and they were selling scuba gear at cut rates, so when people had bought their gear somewhere else, we would have to charge them $35 for a scuba lesson.

The sport grew fast, and finally, by 1964, there were about five hundred scuba diving stores in Los Angeles instead of just one—which was mine—and a lot of discount houses and discount stores.

I announced at a meeting of all the scuba diving stores that I was going to tell them "the good news": I was going to retire, sell out my business, and go treasure hunting. They wouldn't have me as competition anymore.

They all laughed and cheered, because I was a pretty fanatic kind of competitor to everybody.
Then I said, "The bad news is I'm going to take six months before I retire. I'm going to have a six-months sale and give everybody a bigger discount than they can get at any discount store or any dive shop." I did that, so everybody got 30, or 40, or 50 percent off on everything. I sold a lot of thousands of dollars' worth of equipment in that last six months.

***

As fate would have it, it was about twenty years after our honeymoon trip that we came back out to the same shipwreck, the *Valbanera*, and that is where we started our treasure hunt for the *Nuestra Señora de Atocha*. Amazing.

After I had started my dive business in the feed shed of the chicken farm, I soon bought my own air compressor. Rene Bussoz—from whom I had bought the first Aqua-Lung—and I both had air compressors then, and many people started coming to my chicken ranch to get their tanks filled. That saved them an hour or two driving up to Rene's place in Westwood Village. I made many, many trips up there with my station wagon, loaded it completely to the ceiling with dive equipment, even tied stuff on the roof. I would get lots of spear guns, tanks, all kinds of equipment. That wagon also hauled an awful lot of diving equipment to Mel's Aqua Shop, which I opened in Redondo Beach, near Torrance.

I bought a high-pressure compressor, one that could pump two thousand pounds. That was about what we used in air tanks back then, two thousand pounds psi (per square inch). I built up some filters for it to keep the oil from getting into the air.

I started getting a lot of business.

This was not a specialized dive compressor. I'm not sure what they were made for; I think they were war surplus. The government used them, but I don't know for what. There was still only one other place in the Los Angeles area that had an air compressor, and that was Rene Bussoz.

Every time I went up to buy diving gear from him—another station wagon full of spear guns, fins, and things—he would have me bring a dozen fresh eggs. He would sit there and eat them in front of me while we were talking. He just broke a hole in both ends of the egg and would *schlurrrp* it down raw. I never tried that. I don't know how it would taste. But he really liked them. I like eggnogs, and an egg beat up in a chocolate milkshake. So I imagine it wouldn't taste too bad.

Rene had an exclusive import license for the United States on all of the French diving equipment. The French were the first ones to come out with the Aqua-Lung. There were no other types being manufactured in the United States for quite a while.

Finally, Dive Air came into business. They made a regulator out of aluminum. But that didn't work out too well, because it corroded. Our guys were making homemade regulators from war surplus oxygen breathing equipment. I made some too.

There were two different types of war surplus equipment that it was possible for people to convert, for those who didn't have any money and wanted to dive. It would cost $80 for a new Aqua-Lung and regulator, but they could get one of these surplus rigs for about ten bucks. They could build a new unit out of it, and then take fire extinguisher tanks and use them to hold compressed air. They could make their own harness out of straps. I had a riveting machine, bought strapping, and made a few hundred or few thousand harnesses.

When I was first in business out on my chicken farm, I also invented another kind of gas gun. What I made reminds me of handling dynamite.

I made a stainless-steel cylinder, like a piece of pipe, that was threaded on one end, with an O-ring seal. Then I'd buy CO_2 in blocks, like ice. I'd drop a block of CO_2 in there, and I'd start screwing the pipe onto the gun.

But it's melting and turning into volatile liquid very fast—if you don't have the pressure there. Sometimes it would blow back off before I could get the pipe screwed back in. I remember the first time I got it screwed in. Then I took off and ran.

I laid it down in the field and ran, because I was afraid it was going to blow up.

It leaked. I came back, and the gun was just all covered with frost, the whole gun was frozen. I decided that blocks were too dangerous for the average guy to load. So I went back to using liquid CO_2.

A friend of mine later began using liquid nitrogen for a magnetometer that was to be more like a gradiometer. It was supposed to detect gold and silver at long range.

Once we decided to relocate our dive activities, we bought a business lot in Hollywood-Riviera, near Redondo Beach, California. We didn't have enough money to build a store, so we went out lobster diving. Back then we were the only ones going out diving, so there were jillions of lobsters all over the ocean. We'd bring in about a ton of lobsters and sell them to the restaurants, then build a wall.

Then we'd go out and catch another ton of lobsters, sell 'em, build another wall to the store. Another ton of lobsters put a roof on.

Pretty soon we had Mel's Aqua Shop, the first real scuba diving business in the world.

We started at ten in the morning so we could sleep in, because we worked to midnight every night. We were teaching people at night how to dive and ended up with a very successful business.

We made a lot of money and taught sixty-five thousand people how to dive out in California.

We had fifteen instructors working with us and had a TV show every week.

We'd shoot movies each weekend about expeditions that we made, diving up in the rivers in California for gold, diving at Jade Cove for jade, diving on shipwrecks to see what we could find, or going for lobsters.

Every week we would have a different kind of underwater television show. This brought in a lot of new customers.

I remember one night I dumped out about twenty ounces of gold dust on TV, and then I had a five-gallon can of black dirt, and I dumped it out. I told the audience that there were all kinds of valuable things in this dirt, and if they wanted to come down and learn about black sands and gold diving, to "come on down" to the Biltmore Hotel, Los Angeles.

I got down there the next night, and there were thousands of people. The parking lot was jammed, the hotel was full of people, and the hotel manager told me that they were all there waiting for me to give my talk on how to find gold in the rivers.

I asked him if the ballroom was for rent. He said, "Yes." We filled the ballroom, and it was still overflowing.

I got a lot of customers from my television shows. Every week, for four and a half years, I would make a new television show.

When we first started diving out in California, the water was really cold. One time I remember we put lard all over our bodies because somebody told us that would keep us warm. It really stunk and was really greasy and messy. We all put lard all over us. It didn't work, and our complete boat and everything aboard was all grease! It was quite a mess to clean up.

Then we drank honey. We were told honey would keep us warm, but it really didn't do any good either.

Making dry suits was the product of a new company that started up, Bel-Aqua. They would buy sheet rubber, cut it out with patterns. They would make up a suit that had a crawl hole, so you could crawl in with your feet, and then stretch it up over your head. We wore long underwear underneath it. The crawl hole where you got into the suit was under your belly, so you just wadded it all up, and wrapped a piece of rubber around it to keep it from leaking. They had special anklets, cuffs, and neck pieces that were real thin, that would seal and keep the water from leaking down your neck or onto your wrists or your ankles. Most of them had feet; your feet were inside of them too.

Then the Pirelli Company in Italy came out with a new dry suit that was pretty good; it fit better. They had a system where pants and shirt were separate, with a hard neoprene rail that went around your waist. They had a large O-ring that fit into that waist groove, and the pants and shirt sealed together. It was a little easier to get in and out of. It worked pretty well.

Finally, somebody dreamed up using foam neoprene. It turned out to be much more practical. The whole suit was made of foam neoprene. There was no rubber at all.

The suit would just let you go ahead and get wet. That's why they called them wet suits. But the material had thousands of tiny air bubbles in it, the foam. Those bubbles wouldn't soak up moisture; it wasn't like a sponge. They stayed dry. The air bubbles were what really insulated us from the cold. That worked pretty well.

I don't think there were any suit companies at that time, so we made our own. I had friends and relatives who would help me make the suits.

We sold a lot of jackets to the surfers too. The suits sold for $27, and now they're $200 and more for the same suit.

I was the first business to make a wet suit, as far as I know. However, there were a couple of other dive shops that were in business by that time, and they began making them too. It's possible that one of the other dive shops might have started making them before I did.

I do know mine was the first dive shop in California, and possibly the country or world. Bussoz had a sporting goods store. I was the only one who sold only diving equipment. Rene didn't handle any other dive equipment except the French kind that he was importing.

But I handled different brands of everything that was made. Also, I carried spare parts for everything that all the different companies in the world were making. So a lot of customers came to me, because I had everything there was. If they ever needed a part, or anything repaired, I could repair it and sell them the parts.

I built up a real good business, especially after I opened Mel's Aqua Shop in Redondo Beach. There were people waiting in line every morning when I got there.

The feed shed where I started my dive shop business was just a plywood building painted dark green. It didn't look like a store at all. It had just a regular wooden house door and no windows.

When it was time, I decided to build my own building, or store, in a business section. I was low on money, so I went down to a section of Torrance that was near the ocean, on the main drive that went up to Palos Verdes.

Palos Verdes is a big mountainous bluff that juts out into the ocean. There are big rocky cliffs going down to the ocean. A lot of people in Los Angeles like to go there to dive, because there are big kelp beds all around it, lots of fish, abalone, and lobsters. It was the closest place to this mass population of Los Angeles.

So that's where I built my store, at the entrance to Palos Verdes. I wrote down the addresses of all the vacant lots in the business area there; they call this business area Hollywood-Riviera Village. Then I wrote a postcard to all of the owners.

I went down to the county courthouse and looked up the names and addresses of the people who owned all the vacant lots. I wrote to them and asked if their property was for sale, and for how much.

Most of them wanted high prices just for one lot. For example, there was one lot, thirty feet by one hundred feet, that was priced about $10,000!

Finally, a lady answered a card—from Indiana. She said she owned one of those lots there, and another one about a block away, where there was just a field, nothing there but sand dunes. That second lot was between where my store was and the ocean.

She said she'd sell, but that she wouldn't just sell the store lot by itself—that I had to buy the other one too.

The price would be $5,000 for both lots.

I had $1,000. So I sent her the $1,000, and told her I'd raise the rest of it. I put an ad in the paper and sold the other lot for $5,000. That was because lots in the second area were also selling for about $10,000. So I could sell it real quick at half price.

That way, I got my lot free, and got my $1,000 back. That's how to do the real estate business—or how it could be done in the past. People who lived out of town, who lived a long ways from these places, always pictured it the way it was when they were there. They didn't realize that the place was booming, and that there were big apartment buildings going up all over the place.

The sand dunes were changing into condominiums—"condos"—even then.

I never did like money, but it took money to do what I wanted to do. So I had to figure out ways to make it.

Then I had the land. I wanted to build the business myself, because I knew I could build it. I didn't have enough money to pay a contractor to build it. The city building code and inspectors were quite strict. I didn't have a California building contractor's license.

But the city official was helpful. He explained that there was one way I could get around it, which was to have a homeowner's loan and be an owner-builder. However, I had to have architectural plans that were done by a licensed architect. I checked around with a couple of architects. They wanted about $5,000 or more just to draw up the plans.

So I went into the store down the street and asked the owner if he still had the plans for his store building. I asked him if he would sell them to me, because I couldn't afford to hire an architect. He said, "Oh, I'll just give them to you. I don't need them anymore."

He just gave me his plans. I took the plans down to the building inspector, and he said, "OK. They'll pass the building code."

So I started building. But I didn't have much money. The money ran out right away.

I still had the business in the feed shed, and I stayed open there from about 5–8 p.m. every night. When the guys would get off work, they could come there and fill up their dive tanks, get whatever they needed, rent some equipment from me, or whatever.

Deo and I were married at around that time.

We would go out in the boat together, to one of the outlying islands where nobody ever went, to Santa Cruz Island. We found some areas where there were big pockets, or potholes, in the bottom of the ocean, with ledges all around. Each ledge would have maybe a hundred lobsters in it. There would be a circular underwater hole, with a ledge all around it. There would be solid lobsters in a circle.

I would have a tank on, and I would grab a lobster or two, and hold one up in my left hand. Deo would dive down snorkeling from the surface, and grab the lobster from me, then throw it in a dinghy that a kid was rowing up above us.

I'd go all around that circle catching lobsters, and the ones I missed would just scoot over to the other side and go back under the ledge. But they couldn't run away. So by the time I went around twice, I had them all.

We went from pothole to pothole, and we caught more than a ton of lobsters in one day!

We took them to the commercial fish market in San Pedro. They were only paying fifteen cents per pound for the lobsters from the lobster trappers.

So I went to a fancy restaurant on the highway up in Los Angeles. That's one advantage of being near a big metropolitan area—there's a big demand for everything. At that restaurant, I asked the owner how much he'd pay for lobsters. He said seventy-five cents a pound. So I sold them to him. But he wanted them live.

I learned that lobsters that die put out some kind

of a poison sometimes that can make people ill. So they all had to be live lobsters. We made enough money then to buy a couple of truckloads of concrete blocks, and some cement, mortar. I wore leather gloves.

At that time, we didn't have wet suits yet. I was using a dry suit with long underwear under it. I had two pair of long underwear under it.

I also had a pair of coveralls on the outside of my dry suit, because lobsters have stickers all over them, and spines, and when one of those spines brushed against a rubber dive suit, it would tear it, or punch a hole in it.

Then you got wet, and you got cold. We never did get through a whole trip of commercial diving without our suit flooding out and us nearly freezing to death. It was cold there all year round, although in the wintertime it was about 55 degrees, and in the summer time it would get up to 70. But it was still cold underwater. Even at 70 degrees on the surface, you'll start shaking after a few minutes.

With the lobster money, we built the retaining walls for the shop.

Deo would hold her breath. She would dive down fifteen or twenty feet and grab the lobster from my left hand, take it up and throw it in the dinghy. By that time I'd have another one, and I'd change it from my right hand to my left hand, and I'd hand it up to her.

She kept going up and down, up and down, all day long, while I kept catching them. That was the first time she did anything like that. Nobody else had ever done it either.

We'd build, and then we'd run out of money again, go out and get another ton of lobsters, build a wall. We'd go out and get another ton and build another wall. Get another ton and put a roof on. Another time we put a front on the store.

After about six months, we had it all done.

We painted a big underwater mural on the side of the building. (There was no store next to us.) It said, "Go underwater and really live!" The mural showed a diver down with a tank on, fish swimming around, a mermaid, and a treasure chest.

Soon we started to teach scuba diving. There was no civilian school anywhere to learn how to dive.

We started the first school, where we gave out certificates, cards showing that people had completed their lessons, passed their written tests.

Over the next several years, we built up the school to where we had about fifteen instructors working for us. We were really cranking out students. We had classes every night of the week, until midnight, and on weekends too.

We ended up giving out more than sixty-five thousand dive certificates to students. Every now and then, even now, people come in and show me their "Mel's Aqua Shop" Diving Card with my autograph on it.

Mel's Aqua Shop, as we called it from day one, was at 1911 South Catalina Avenue, officially in what was called Hollywood-Riviera, California, near Torrance. There's still a dive shop there right now. I think now they call it "See the Sea." The mural is gone, though. They built a store next to it. As I remember, I traded some fellow a tank and regulator for it. I did a lot of trading for my business—still do today.

I always enjoyed swapping things. I'd swap a plumber to do the plumbing, and diving gear to a glass man for the windows. There were two big windows in the front of the store. I traded a cement man for doing the sidewalks. I traded a roofer for the roofing. I knew how to do all that stuff at that time, but I got to where it was easier just to sell some equipment or trade some equipment than it was to do it myself.

All of a sudden scuba diving became really popular. I helped it quite a bit, because I had the television show in Los Angeles, and it was always about scuba diving or snorkeling. Several hundred new customers would come in every week, and I made a lot of money. I'd teach them to dive and sell them all their equipment.

I'd take them out on organized dive trips. We would make up a calendar for one year in advance and have a trip planned for every Sunday to somewhere.

Sometimes we'd make a three-day trip down to Mexico, or somewhere far away, up in the mountains in California, or to Jade Cove, where we'd go diving for jade underwater, under the ocean.

There's one "chimney" that's probably still there, a beautiful thing. You're diving about thirty feet down, and it's a pillar of jade sticking up that reminds you of a fireplace after a house has burned down. There's a cave, and when you go inside, it's all beautiful, smooth, green jade inside that chimney, going up. I bet it's still there, unless somebody dynamited it to get the jade.

With our diving course, at first we'd just teach people in one night. We had a three-hour "quickie" course and would teach students how to blow water out of a mask and blow the water out of their mouthpiece. We'd teach you how to switch over from the snorkel to the regulator, and from the regulator to the snorkel, so you could get back to the boat when you ran out of air.

In three hours, we could teach a lot of people a lot of the basics. If they didn't do well, we'd have them come back the next night, and keep trying until they learned everything.

We found out that it was more practical, money-wise, to conduct the first night of the school in my store, to have a lecture, and show a movie that I made about how to dive. I made a twenty-minute film called *The Blue Continent* for U.S. Divers Company. It's an instruction film, and they're still using that film in the commercial diving schools today.

In the course, I'd explain all the different brands of equipment, the different manufacturers and types, and suggest what kind of snorkel people should buy, what kind of fins, masks, tanks, regulators, suits, weight belts. I'd explain to them about the buoyancy factors, equalizing their ears and sinuses, about air embolism, and the "bends."

I'd just touch everything lightly the first night, then get students in the pool the next night. Soon, we were giving three night classes—nine hours of training. Then we started giving twelve-hour courses, and fifteen-hour courses. They kept getting longer.

I always gave free lessons if people bought twenty-five bucks or more worth of equipment. I furnished the tanks, regulators, the air, the instructors.

If people didn't want to buy any equipment, I'd charge them $35 for a full course. At that price we made a lot of money. Nearly all the outfits ended up at about $250 by the time they bought a complete outfit. Of course, back then you could buy a lot more with a dollar than you can now.

After a while in the chicken and egg business, my dad had decided he'd like to retire. That was when Deo and her mother came from Montana and bought the chicken ranch from my mother and dad.

My folks, Grace and Earl, bought a house near the highway in Rolling Hills, California, and retired. As agreed, I stayed and worked at the chicken ranch, teaching Deo's mother how to run the business. I would take care of the chickens, feed them, vaccinate them, raise them. I would take care of the chickens when they got sick.

While I was there working on the chicken ranch, I had a "GI Bill" that I hadn't taken advantage of, so I attended El Camino College in Torrance, California, and earned enough credits to get a degree in Agriculture, Poultry Husbandry. I completed my four years there. I already had a lot of college credits, but they were in engineering, from Purdue and Alabama.

So my actual college degree is in Agriculture; I never did get a degree in engineering. Well, I did get a degree at the University of Alabama. Last year they invited me to give a lecture there, and they gave me an honorary degree. I also have one from Purdue University. But I don't know if they count. I guess they do.

Originally, I had enlisted in the Reserves to stay in school at Purdue University. Then about three or four weeks later, they whisked us all away anyway.

After finishing my college time in California, I bought a boat, a sixty-five-foot boat that had been used in San Pedro, California, to haul passengers for hire. It was a Coast Guard-approved vessel for taking people out sports fishing, and it could haul sixty-five fishermen.

The boat was in pretty bad shape when I got it. I paid $20,000 for it at a sheriff's auction. My payments on it were $1,000 a month. I remember I really had to work hard to make the payments on that boat. I swore I'd never buy anything again where I had to make $1,000-a-month payments.

(Now, on the building I bought to house the Mel Fisher Maritime Heritage Society, I'm paying twice that amount of money, just for the interest.)

The boat was called the *Golden Doubloon*, the same name I later put on the old Swedish lumber ship I found in Europe, converted into a replica galleon [museum], and moved along the Florida coast to Key West.

In California, on the first *Golden Doubloon*, I built a long aluminum boom, something like a crane boom, and had it sticking out from the stern of the boat, up into the air. I put a war-surplus magnetometer on the end of the boom to look for shipwrecks.

For quite a while In California, I had been chartering boats every Sunday. I'd charter different vessels to take my students out.

Finally, with my own boat, the *Doubloon*, I started hauling people every week.

I didn't operate it all the time. I hired a skipper, a licensed skipper. He was Eddie Tsukimura, a little Japanese guy, very hardworking, conscientious, and after some years

I ended up selling the boat to him—for $29,000. He faithfully made the payments, and he's now the proud owner.

He's still hauling scuba divers out of San Pedro, California, and still hauling albacore fishermen out to catch fish on a fishing pole.

***

Wendy: *In June 1989, with Deo also on the phone, I called and interviewed Eddie Tsukimura, who said he was looking for his maps and books, but would talk with us anyway, since I also had a tape recorder going. For Eddie, the time was twenty-nine years earlier, in 1960:*

Eddie: OK, this is how it started. I was running my boat. The first time I carried divers to Catalina, and they were testing underwater equipment. When I saw that underwater activity, I said, "I've got to start diving instead of fishing on the surface." So toward the end of 1959, I came to the shop [Mel's] and Massa [Eddie's wife] and I enrolled in the scuba class. Both of us. Then Mel said, "Hey, I bought a boat, and I'm looking for a skipper." So I told him, "I've got my own boat. I'm running fishing trips. But for weekends, I'll have my brother-in-law run my boat, and I could run it for you." That's how it started. And then I went over to see what kind of boat it was that Mel bought; I was pretty shocked, because that was the boat I used to own, and that—with my wife and her brother—we used to go all the way to San Diego to go fishing on. So that was quite a coincidence.

Then in the beginning of 1960, I got certified and then, officially, when we ran a charter, [there was] me as your captain. But that day, I was a student diver to be checked out. So first-day skipper and first-day student! That's how we started. January 1960. So I did start taking the class, and I talked to Mel, at the end of 1959.

Wendy: *By then, Mel was a husband, father, businessman, and dive instructor in California. What was he like?*

Eddie: Well, I tell you, he was different than any person I used to know. He's a pretty bighearted man. He won't let little bitty things bother you or worry you. So he just smiles and laughs and says, "Yeah, we'll teach you how to dive and this and that." I said, "My wife can't swim. How about that?" He says, "That's more better, you know, for scuba diving. Better you don't swim." (*Eddie laughs heartily.*) That's the first time I talked to Mel. That's how he was. I said, "Wow. This man is all right." So when he said he's looking for a skipper, I said, "Well, I don't mind trying it."

That was the turning point in my life, I tell you, when I started working for Deo and Mel. I was still working for Douglas Aircraft, but the time came that the boat was going for treasure hunting. Then I had to decide whether to stay with the aircraft, or I give that up and go with Mel. And you know what happened. Ever since then, I've turned into "boat people."

Those days there weren't many diving shops to begin with. He was kind of a pioneer. He was a pioneer. He was the first to be doing scuba diving, one of the first. And he was the first to be teaching [diving]. I was participating early, you know, diving boat skipper too. There were more fishing boats, but not too many diving boats.

I started working for Mel just on weekends, and then it got to be going toward full time, because Mel wanted to practice dragging the magnetometer for getting ready for the treasure hunt. So I started to spend a little bit more time other than weekends with Mel.

Wendy: *Eddie jokes about being a "Kamikaze pilot," but it was actually very close, as was his "almost" being a mariner in the Japanese Navy, although he really grew up in Hawaii. He was temporarily in Japan and going to go to school there. He applied for* *aviator school, but his mother would not sign permission.*

Eddie: It's a joke to me, but it was a pretty close call.

Wendy: *And a year later, while you still in high school, you applied for the Merchant Marine school.*

Eddie: And that, too, my mother turned me down. If she didn't, I would have been in the Japanese Navy, and I would have been on the bottom of the ocean.

Wendy: *Eddie went on the two Caribbean expeditions from California, and on many adventures with Mel and Deo, well before Mel and others of his comrades headed east to Florida and to history.*

Eddie: I always was looking for shipwrecks. Whenever any of my customers would come in, we'd be talking about lobsters, abalone, fishing, and once in a while one of them would mention they saw some wreck, wreckage here or there. I was always checking out those spots.

***

Mel resumes: One customer said one day he had found some cannons, and I couldn't believe it. We were all excited. It was right out of Palos Verdes Estates, California, near where my store was. The newspapers heard about it. We went out and checked. Sure enough, there they were, all covered with seaweed and coral.

So I chartered a boat to go lift a couple of them and told the boat to pick me up at Redondo Beach Pier. There were television news crews there and reporters.

They wanted to know if they could go with me. I said, "No, we're keeping it secret." We didn't want anybody to know where the wreck was, what we'd found. We thought maybe we'd find some gold or something, a Spanish galleon!

So we went offshore and lifted two of the cannon to the surface. Instead of coming back to Redondo Beach Pier, we went all the way around to San Pedro Harbor. We were very secretively coming into this dock and going to quietly unload the cannon.

But, whoa! There were all the television crews waiting for us, newspaper and radio reporters. They had me on TV that night, with the cannons, and all the newspapers and radios had stories.

We put what we'd found on a truck and took them out on the end of Redondo Beach Pier. Thousands and thousands of people came down to look at those cannons. So they started charging a dollar admission for everybody to go out on the pier to look at the cannons, and they made a bunch of money.

Some guys came from the Smithsonian Institution to check them out. They measured them and inspected them. Then they said the "cannon" were "circa 1894" sewage pumps. I don't know how they got there, but we'd found sewage pumps. They had me on TV again, to talk about the sewage pumps. And they had more stories in the papers and on the radio, naturally, about the sewage pumps. They really looked like cannons.

Nobody tipped the press off that we were going the other direction; I think they just saw us. They went up on the cliff, and they watched us bringing them out. I think they saw us heading around the other way and just followed us all the way around.

We checked out other shipwrecks around Palos Verdes, Catalina, Santa Cruz Island, Anacapa Island. We'd learned that right along Anacapa Island, on the land side, there was a side-wheeler.

I'd usually take my students to that side-wheeler and let them look at it, pick up some old pieces of glass, nails, or something for souvenirs. About fifteen years ago, some guys found a "mess o' gold coins" there, on that side-wheeler. I wouldn't doubt but what there's a lot more still there right now. It's just that nobody has made a professional effort to check out the area.

I've got a lot of research on that. In fact, I've got a thick file on hundreds of shipwrecks along the California coast. One way I researched was to go down to the Los Angeles Library, and they had all the ancient newspapers on microfilm. I'd sit on a microfilm reader, and I'd go through every newspaper every day, all through the years.

Whenever I'd see any articles about shipwrecks, I'd make a copy of the article. Or just make notes on it. It's easy to get sidetracked when you're doing that, because you find so many interesting and exciting stories that went on through the years.

Especially during the war, they sank a lot of ships out there.

One of the ships we dove on became virtually a public showplace dive spot. It was right near the dance pavilion in Avalon-Catalina where all the tourists go every week. The *Valiant* was its name. I know I took some primer cord down and wrapped it around the nut—the big, big, giant nut that screws on to hold the propeller in place. I spun the nut off with the primer cord.

There's usually a cotter key behind that, so the propeller can't come off. We knocked off the cotter key, but we couldn't move the nut. We had giant wrenches, but we couldn't move it. Then I wrapped primer cord around. Depending on the direction you wrap the primer cord, that's the way it spins. Then I fastened a rope around the propeller, and up to the stern of my boat. The propeller was about ninety feet deep, and it was about 120 feet deep on the bow end—the wreck was on a slope. Then I put some more primer cord behind the propeller. I exploded it, and the force kicked the prop off of the shaft. That big shaft was just hanging on a rope, under our boat.

With it, we drove the boat over to Avalon Harbor. There I got a small boat, a little workboat that had an A-frame on it. We brought the propeller up, took it back, and sold it for scrap brass. I was going to go get the other one, but I had made a mistake. Before I left, I put another spin of primer cord on the other prop. It was a twin-screw ship. But I wasn't very moxie at that time, and I didn't realize that with twin screw boats, usually one prop goes one direction, and one prop goes the other direction. Some boats, they don't; they go the same direction. But with most boats, the props oppose each other. When I put the primer cord on the second prop, I wrapped it the same direction as I did the other one. Instead of spinning the nut off, it tightened it.

There was a newspaper article done about it, with a picture of us with that propeller. Before I got out there the next weekend, some other guys went over and got the other prop off. They beat me to it.

I was getting famous out there at that time too. I had a lot of press stories and television stories.

At a conference in Las Vegas, Nevada, a few years ago, one of the wreck divers out there gave me a coin, and on it, it said *Valiant*. I think the coin also said something like, "With this token, a beer is five cents." I remember I got underwater movies on the *Valiant* of Deo sitting in the bathtub, scrubbing her back. That was about a hundred feet down.

We also thought we'd found a safe in there. It was way down underneath a bunch of iron wreckage. Somebody else beat me to that too.

We found another wreck, one we'd found first in the newspapers. That wreck had belonged to Al Capone. He had it anchored three miles off of Seal Beach, California. The vessel was a gambling casino, nightclub, with booze. In the old newspaper, I remember seeing one picture of the governor of California out there trying to board Capone's boat to give him a court order or something to stop gambling.

The newspaper also shows a cargo net over the governor and his police boat. Al Capone's group threw a cargo net over everybody, and they left and gave up trying to arrest him. They were shooting fire hoses at him too, from the ship.

There was another gangster who also had a gambling ship three miles offshore. I've got research on both vessels. On Capone's boat I found a cash register, a chuck-a-luck machine, a slot machine, and a roulette wheel. Those are the things that I brought up. There were a lot more slot machines there, but I didn't bring them up. The cash register still had money in it. I've still got the brass spindle of the roulette wheel here somewhere in the building, and the center of the chuck-a-luck machine. That's a dice machine where there are two cages, and you flip it upside down, it rolls the dice without shaking them.

The other gangster who had a ship in Santa Monica Bay went out at about 2:30 in the morning, blew up Al Capone's boat—and sank it. The next night, Al Capone and his group went and blew up the other guy's ship.

I've been diving on both of them; I found them years later. I believe it was 1929 when the boats were blown up. Just before the Depression, when everybody was spending a bunch of money, living it up!

There was supposed to be a Spanish galleon near the isthmus of Catalina Island. I took quite a few trips out there with my students. We scouted the entire area—around, and around, and around. Way down deep, the bottom drops off quickly. We never did find any signs of wreckage there. Also, there was supposed to have been a galleon hit on the north end of Catalina Island. We searched around there, visually and with detectors, but we never found anything.

We found a lot of shipwrecks off California and other places. We were looking for just anything. Unfortunately, that boom I built for the *Doubloon* didn't work very well.

The first magnetometer was war surplus and not waterproof. These "mags" were hung in the tail-stinger on a PBY [a seaplane], or some kind of a Navy airplane, to look for submarines. They would fly with them. Because they were not waterproof was why we had ours on the boom. But it didn't work well. I tried waterproofing several war-surplus "mags," and it worked a little. But it was a hassle, and they were too cumbersome.

The first wreck we ever found with my associate Fay Feild's magnetometer was Al Capone's gambling ship. After that, we started looking for wrecks every week, for a long time—several years.

The magnetometer that Fay Feild built was small and handy, more dependable. We started using his "mag" all the time. I think Fay was self-taught in scuba. He came into my dive shop to get equipment now and then, or maybe fill up his dive tank. Sometimes he'd go out lobster diving with us.

We had fun every year when lobster season opened up, just as we do now. The lobster season opens up, and all the scuba divers get all their equipment out and go catch lobsters.

There was supposed to be another shipwreck on the eastern point of San Miguel Island. We went out there, looking around and taking underwater movies. There was a school of seals, and a school of "sea elephants," I think. Or they were big walruses, or something. Big things! There were a couple of thousand seals and a couple thousand of those other big things.

I remember the movies I took down there were kind of frightening, because they were very curious, and they circled all around us real close. There were just solid bodies, all around us, in all directions.

And we were making movies of that! They didn't actually ever touch me, but they sure came close. Real close. All around us.

It just seemed like solid bodies above us and below us and around us. They never touched us. At first, they were quite a distance away. But they kept getting closer and closer, until they just balled all around us. That was off the east end of San Miguel Island.

We had problems that time, too. A huge storm came up. Lightning hit and burnt out our radio.

A big wave broke the window in, and Deo was sharp enough to take the chess board, put it up against the window, and lean her back against the chess board to keep more waves from pouring in through the window.

As fate would have it, she got valuable experience then. About ten years later, when we got in a big storm headed for Silver Shoals in the Caribbean, the same thing happened.

That time, a big wave broke out the window on the bow of our shrimp boat, and we were taking green water over the bow. These huge waves! So she took a table and put it against the window space and leaned up against the table with her feet pressed against the other side of the hallway to keep the waves from filling the boat up.

We made it through that storm off California, but we couldn't tell anybody on the radio.

The waves were so high and the troughs so deep that we couldn't turn the boat. We couldn't go sideways to the waves, because it would flip us right over. And we couldn't turn around.

So we had to keep heading into the waves on an angle toward shore, and we ended up way north of civilization.

I think we were somewhere near Port Hueneme. It was right about the same area where one of the presidents had his home. There's a lighthouse not too far from there.

When we finally got in to shore, we went into a huge kelp bed and anchored inside there. The kelp broke the breakers of the big waves. So it was relatively calm inside, although there were big swells.

We were very low on food and water, so Deo and I and another couple decided to swim to shore. The other guys were going to take the boat back down south when the water was more calm.

A guy named Harry Wham was on that trip. He later became a well-known dive shop owner in Las Vegas, and he was a talented musician. He was also a treasure hunter.

We swam in. We put a few pieces of clothes in a little water-tight rubber bag we had, and made it through the breakers, then we climbed up a cliff. After we made the top, we were walking through a field there.

I had on a bright red plastic jacket, and suddenly, here came a bull chasing me! I took off my jacket. I was going to turn it inside out. But it was red inside too. So I rolled it up and hid it. We got to a creek, and we jumped over just in time. The bull decided not to jump over the creek.

Then we got to a dirt road and walked up to the lighthouse, where a guy and his wife were living. They were the only people for miles around. They gave us some coffee and a peanut butter sandwich. Then they gave us a lift into Lompoc, California. That was a little tiny village in the mountains. From there, we got a ride out to the highway.

Then we hitchhiked and got a ride back to Los Angeles, California. We didn't know until we returned that they had put on the radio that our boat had been struck by lightning and sunk. And that we were all dead.

Our babysitter, Marion Unger, thought we were all dead.

When all of a sudden we arrived and walked in the door, she couldn't believe it. She had been crying. She had all our four kids and was wondering what she was going to do with all of them.

She said something like, "What are you doing here? You're supposed to be dead!" I still have to chuckle at that.

It was really dangerous. Big storm! I think what caused the "death" story was that we were talking on the radio, telling how dangerous it was, and how big the waves were, and the lightning flashes all around us. Then they heard the power of the lightning flash on the radio, and the radio went out.

They sent a boat out to look for us, and we were gone. They saw some driftwood floating in the water, so they figured we had sunk.

In the meantime, we had gone way up north and gotten stuck up there in the boondocks. I don't think they had a telephone at the lighthouse.

I guess we could have called from Lompoc. But we didn't know that anybody thought we were dead.

We knew we weren't dead.

I taught Marion how to dive enough to go with us down into the kelp beds, which she really enjoyed. I also taught both of my parents to dive.

My dad's face was quite wrinkled, so the water always leaked into his mask. We couldn't find any mask that would work on him. So he said, "The heck with it." But he helped me at the dive shop. He must have filled ten thousand diving tanks full of air. He kept them in good shape.

My mother was helpful as a model too. I made a movie every week; in at least one of them, my mother was a model. She was kind of shapely, a good-looking woman. So she was one of the actors in the movie.

***

I taught a different system from what they teach today. Now they teach the "buddy" system. I didn't believe in that. I taught everybody to take care of themselves and be able to "handle it," no matter what the occasion was. I still believe in that system.

More people get in trouble with their buddies! There's one advantage of the buddy system: when a big shark comes in, you can keep your buddy between you and the shark.

(Note to divers: Follow the directions of your individual dive instructors. Mel was an experienced professional.)

***

To do whatever I decided to, I developed or improved upon all kinds of equipment—spear guns, power heads, spear tips. I even built a complete regulator for breathing. Underwater dredges, gold dredges. Underwater cameras.

Several of us worked together on power siphons for slurping gold out of the cracks in rivers. Rupe Gates invented the power siphon, but I manufactured and sold them for him. Deo remembers how we used to have a little hand gold "slurper," something like they used to use for collecting tropical fish, only this was really small for getting gold out of the creeks.

Then I invented a gold "magnet." Everybody said, "A gold magnet? What's that?" What it was, was I took a magnet and made something that resembled a hypodermic needle with a magnet in it. You'd push the syringe down, and it would pick up everything in the gold pan or in a sluice box of an underwater gold dredge. It would pick up all the iron, black sand—everything that was magnetic would be picked up by the magnet. Then you would pick it up, pull the plunger, and what it did was pull the magnet away from the iron.

The iron would all fall out, and everything that was left in the gold pan or the sluice box was gold. I called it a "gold magnet." It was painted gold, and I sold them for $5. I sold a jillion of them. It was a gimmick, but it worked. You have all this black sand mixed in with gold. That would take all the iron out of it and just leave the goodies.

We also started building the first wet suits that were available—customized wet suits. We used to drive out to Rubatex Corporation, about forty miles inland, and buy rolls of neoprene foam material. We would measure everybody, cut all the foam up into suits, glue it all together, and make wet suits.

Deo remembers the first ladies' wet suit that I ever made. I think I goofed a little bit on that suit. I had one boob higher than the other one. One was playing up and one playing down. I was experimenting. I hadn't had much practice at making wet suits at that time. Making wet suits and patterns, we had everybody enlisted in making these wet suits. Auntie Marion, who was taking care of our kids full time, and Deo's mother, her sister, her brother-in-law, everybody was making wet suits.

Deo: Everybody was making wet suits, and my mom was real good at making patterns, my sister also. Eventually we figured out how to cut the patterns to make the suits fit, how to make a woman's suit so that it had bumps in it.

Mel: At first when we first started making them, they were all just like men's suits. Women needed some incentive to get into scuba diving, because it was a very unglamorous sport. It was fun measuring the boobs. You had to measure from tip to tip, and from tip to body, shoulder to tip, armpit to tip, tip to tip, waist to tip. We had to make sure we didn't have one pointing up and one pointing down. We had to get them just right, so they fit perfect. We had to have about thirty-six measurements on women and only about twenty-eight on men. This was all developed after much strenuous practice and a lot of mistakes.

Deo: But we were the first ones who were custom-building wet suits. After that, some other companies, such as Bel-Aqua, went into wet suits. They were first making dry suits, with which you had to wear long underwear. Those dry suits were real tight at the wrist, real tight at the legs, or they had boots in them, and tight at the neck.

Mel: We did sell a lot of them. They sold at about $30,

$29.95, in the beginning. Then we sold them for $40, $60. When we sold out in 1963, they were about up to $60 or $75. We usually had sales, and we'd sell them for "39 bucks." That would be a custom-tailored wet suit. Now they're selling them for about $250 or $300. More or less, they're the same thing, except they have improved the materials a lot.

A dry suit is what everybody wore at first. I think some of the first dry suits came from France. They were made by Pirelli Rubber Company [actually from Italy]. They were black, and they were excellent. Some real good suits. Then when Rubatex Corporation came out with this intercellular neoprene material, it was much better.

Deo: At first there were some plastic materials that were invented, but they were pretty fragile. They were in pretty colors, and in whites, but they ripped up easily.

"Then this company—Rubatex—I believe they developed foam neoprene, though I don't think it was just for the underwater world. I am not sure what the material was developed for in the first place; I think they made it for other things. But all these developments of yours enhanced the sport of skin diving or scuba diving, as they call it now, everything from snorkeling all the way to scuba diving."

***

Mel resumes: In the development of self-contained underwater breathing apparatus for sport divers, it was a follow-up from the war period, when they used oxygen rebreathers a lot because they didn't make bubbles. You would rebreathe the oxygen. Momsen lung was the name of one of the early rebreather systems.

I guess I popularized the sport a lot because, for one thing, I was the only one who had an underwater television show every week in Los Angeles, California.

There would be about five million people watching every week, and so we really had a booming business. I had several different names for the show. *Skin Diver* was one of them; *High Road to Danger* was another. Then there was *Blue Continent*. I used different names for my show, and I didn't always go to the same station. I would do a series of thirteen for one channel, then I'd do a series of twenty-six for another, and thirteen for another. They usually went in increments of thirteen. I think I did fifty-two shows. Then I ran out of stories and started repeating some of it. I couldn't think of any more story lines.

Each one was a half-hour show. It wasn't a dramatization; it was real life. It was always an adventure, taking viewers down to Acapulco, wreck diving, gold diving, or going out for jade off of Jade Cove, California. Diving on a gambling ship that had sunk and finding slot machines, or night diving for lobsters.

I also started making a training film—that became *Blue Continent*. The idea was to intersperse training film with adventure, so viewers would get both. They are still using my training film now in the commercial diving schools. I made that about forty years ago, and they are still using it as a training film. Even my mom was a model in the training film which I made for U.S. Divers.

With my mother and all my students, I taught them to take care of themselves, be independent, and not rely on anybody else. That was one of the basic differences that I have had with the different dive program leaders. The different dive programs now, NAUI [National Association of Underwater Instructors], PADI [Professional Association of Dive Instructors], and the others that are in business, promote buddy diving, buddy breathing, and depending on your buddy.

But in my view and my experience, it really doesn't work.

That was proven for me again in recent years when I was out diving on a new Spanish galleon that we had just found down in the Caribbean. My attorney John [Dougherty] and a surgeon went down. They were buddies. They both overextended themselves and their air supply. They ran out of air, and the current was sweeping them away from the boat. John is a very intelligent, high "IQ" type of guy who doesn't panic; so is the surgeon. John was figuring, "Well, by golly, I'm drowning." He grabbed the leg of the surgeon to help him. But the guy shook him off and said, "Well, to hell with you John, take care of yourself!" Then John decided, "To hell with all this equipment. I'm taking it off."

He finally got his tank halfway off. Then he couldn't figure out the highfalutin' buckle on the other half. But he finally figured it out and got the tank off. Then he thought, "Oh, boy, I can take a breath." All of a sudden, he was going down fast and he realized that he had not dropped his weight belt. He dropped his weight belt, got up, and finally got a breath of air. Then he felt free, and he was snorkeling back to the boat. He went past the surgeon who was his buddy. The surgeon was in trouble too, and he dropped his weight belt. John said, "Well, I really should help you get back to the boat. But I think it would be more prudent if I swam back to the boat real fast, and had the boat come back and save you."

So much for the buddy system. When you are really drowning, you can't depend on your buddy!

In many circumstances, if you are underwater and especially if you are trying to buddy-breathe, to take turns breathing on a regulator, it doesn't work. People panic, they want air for themselves. And if they're drowning, they aren't going to share.

That's why I tried to teach everybody that no matter what went wrong, they could take care of themselves. They knew how to get up by themselves, and they knew how to get back to the boat by themselves on their own power. That's the way I taught them. I taught sixty-five thousand of them using that system with fifteen instructors working for me at Mel's Aqua Shop.

Later on, after the county—Los Angeles County— was the first more or less organized outfit that was getting into the instruction business, that began certifying divers, Deo and I went down and took the county instructor's course. We started issuing Los Angeles County certificates as well as our own certificates from Mel's Aqua Shop.

Before that there was only Mel's Aqua Shop certificates. They said: "You are, hereby, a Certified SCUBA Diver."

They were pretty fancy certificates, and people had to pass a water test and a written test. There was no specific amount of number of hours of training.

If one person did a lot to popularize a sport for millions of people worldwide, it was Mel Fisher, starting in California. He knew a lot about the new environment that was calling them, more than most. And he had the engineering skills and mechanical savvy to produce what was needed for this wondrous new sport in the sea. Also, he had a family to focus on helping him accomplish his goals, even a pretty, "mermaid" wife. He was a showman, too, and knew intuitively how to maximize his presence in the new mode of television. Right, as one would say, up his "sea" alley, from a chicken feed building to his own store, built one lobster at a time, the first skin diving–and–scuba–only store, and then the first private dive instruction classes.

Mel on the rocks, holding his self-designed, self-built underwater movie camera housing—and getting ready to jump back in.
FISHER FAMILY COLLECTION

CHAPTER TEN

High Road to Danger: Attack of the Leopard Ray

Marriage only enhanced Mel's spirit of adventure and accomplishment in company with his beloved lady Deo. Together, they launched farther expeditions that carried them from California to the Caribbean and in amazing loops of history to the waters of Florida and the Florida Keys. But his motto for most of his years leading up to, and including, the Atocha, *was "Don't go deep."*

The main rule of thumb I have used over many years was: "Don't go deep. Don't go deep. There's no reason, even for treasure."

Nowadays that has changed for me some. But it was my personal rule for those I dove with over the years. Normally, there is nothing down in deep water that is worth messing with. All the beautiful fish, wrecked galleons—all the neat things—are in shallow water.

Those early ships were very strong and sturdy. They wouldn't sink in deep water. Normally it was only in a hurricane, when they hit a shallow reef that was twelve feet or less that they would break up, tumble, and roll, and spill out their treasures. Most of the treasures are in shallow water.

First of all, I have lost a lot of friends to deep water. It is very, very dangerous, extremely dangerous. Even with modern science and technology, there are still many unanswered questions.

Regardless of all modern systems and technology,

divers who go down deep are permanently disabled and get gases in bone marrow. They haven't figured out how to counter these deep diving elements. People should not go down under these pressures. Let the robots do it.

If I'm talking about doing a salvage job in eleven hundred feet of water, I'm not going to have people down there subjected to that pressure. We'll do it with robots, submarines, or something, so people don't take the pressure.

Another wreck I first dived on many years ago, before it became so well-known in the diving world, was the *Rhone*, a huge shipwreck in the Virgin Islands. That shipwreck was used for the movie *The Deep*. I didn't know what the ship's name was originally, but that was also where I got hit, and was seriously hurt, by a giant ray.

We had been diving there before. It was a known wreck—though not by name—and diving spot in the Virgin Islands.

I recall we went to the "Baths," as they call it, first, which is a tourist spot now. Near there was the *Rhone*, which is also a popular dive spot now. In fact, I still dive there. Years after the first dives, I was surprised to learn that the *Rhone* was the exact same wreck that I had originally been diving on years ago.

It was before breakfast, about 6:30 in the morning, the first time I went down to the *Rhone*. That was a huge shipwreck.

One of us went way down. There were tons of fish there, all different sizes, lots of huge, giant tuna. There were varied turtles, barracuda, sharks, angelfish, every kind of fish we could think of, just swarming all over that shipwreck.

There was also this huge leopard ray, the biggest one I've ever seen. I yelled at my pal "Doc" Mathison to get his camera, come in the water, and take movies of me. I told him I was going to go down and spear this giant ray, to be sure and not take his finger off the trigger of the camera. I alerted him because I was going to hang on, and I wasn't going to let go, and wanted him to shoot the whole roll up. I went down and I speared it.

This monster took off. I couldn't get back up, so I pulled a ripcord I had on the handle of my CO_2 gas gun, a homemade gun I'd put together. I think I had seventy-five feet of ripcord on it. I finally got up, and I got some air.

Then the thing started towing me out to sea. It kept going and going and going for a couple hours or more. It just towed me way out in the ocean. There was a Frenchman who was running the boat. He and somebody else, I think Deo, who got in the boat with him, came and got me. They were rowing. They were trying to catch up with me. I was getting towed very fast out into the ocean. They finally caught up with me, and I got back in the boat. The ray almost pulled the back end of the boat under. So I put my ripcord up at the front end of the boat. Then he turned around, and started heading back to where our boat was, where the *Rhone* shipwreck was. He towed us back very fast, right to where we had started from.

We got there, and I was all rested up. We reloaded our movie cameras.

We were shooting 35mm underwater movie film. I don't think I had ever done that before—at that time. This meant we were using a real big film frame, expensive, professional stock. "Doc" got in the water with the camera. I jumped in and went down.

I was riding on the ray's back. I think it was about nine hundred pounds, real wide—about ten feet wide—and he had a long tail on him. There were five stingers near the base of the tail. The stingers were about five or six inches long, and they were serrated, like arrowheads, saw-toothed. They were all slanted in one direction, so that when they went into you, they wouldn't come out. They would stay in. They had little poison glands at the base of each stinger. The rays kill their prey that way—from the poison, paralyze them and kill them.

That big leopard ray kept trying to hit me with those stingers, but I would always be to one side or the other. I knew he couldn't hit me when I was off to the side. Every time he tried to hit me he'd squirt poison out. Fortunately, he had used up most of his poison in the poison glands from trying to hit me.

The ray finally outfoxed me. He made a dive and turned real fast. That swung me over to the middle of him, and he whopped me with two of his stingers underneath the arm, in my armpit.

He didn't just put 'em in the muscle. They went right into the bone of my arm, and they were in there solid. I couldn't get loose from him.

I was holding my breath—I was just snorkeling.

I tried to get away from him, but he was real slippery.

Finally, I got my fins between me and him. I gave a big push with my legs. Instead of pulling the barbs out of my bones, it pulled the barbs out of the ray by the roots. I finally got up and got air. I was really starved for air. I don't know how long I was down—probably about three minutes, holding my breath.

I came up and yelled at the Frenchman. I said, "Poulez les barbs!" I couldn't think of my French. I couldn't think of how to say, "Pull out the barbs." I just said, "Poulez les barbs!"—and "Poulez" means chicken, I think. We were in the boat *Moeme* that we chartered from another well-known treasure hunter, Peter Gimbel. The yacht was owned by Gimbels Department Store, I think. It was his yacht we were using.

I asked the Frenchman to find the pliers. I couldn't think of the word for pliers in French either. I was a little shook up. (*Deo recalls: "Everybody else was. He was shook up, but everybody else was in shock!"*)

"Where is it, where is the pliers?" I said. They looked all over the boat; they couldn't find the pliers. The crewman said, "I think I threw 'em in the dinghy." He looked in the dinghy, but they weren't there.

I said, "How 'bout, maybe, under the floorboards?" He finally found them under the floorboards. He was all shaken. He went to pull one out, and he broke it off—down inside of me. It was still in my bone. I said, "Well, let's go up in the big boat instead of the dinghy, where it's not so rocky and rolly." The second one he pulled out without breaking it off.

The first barb still was down inside of me. "Doc" Mathison was a surgeon, and he happened to have his scalpel with him. He didn't have any kind of anesthetic, so he took a bottle of rum and poured it on the wound, the wounds. He dug in with the scalpel, then he took the pliers and put 'em in there. He got hold of the start of the barb, and he got it out.

Then I drank some rum—quite a bit of rum—for my anesthesia. I really didn't feel any pain, because the poison had made my arm all numb.

Then we went full speed into Saint Thomas and went to the hospital. They gave me a tetanus shot and some morphine. I don't know what else they gave me, three or four shots. I told 'em I was OK, that I felt fine. We were supposed to go to a dinner party that night. I started to walk out of the hospital, and I fainted. I just collapsed. They said, "You'd better stay here tonight." I said, "No, I don't want to stay here; I've got a hotel."

I wasn't worried about footage. We weren't on a real job that trip, although we may have been taking movies for Jantzen swimsuits and Pan American.

Looking back, I sure could have been killed in that encounter and in lots of others. All that stuff's dangerous—messing with sharks and sea monsters. But I enjoyed it, and it was adventurous. Also, we got nice vacations in faraway places, and we were paid money too!

I just did it because I wanted to.

Now, as I look back, I think I was kind of crazy, doing all that—stabbing sharks, shooting sharks, wrestling with 'em and hitting 'em on the head with hammers.

As I got older, I got smarter, I guess. Besides, it wasn't worth all that messing around with those monsters that eat people up sometimes!

Now, whenever sharks come around, I just tell all my guys and gals to just, "Get out of the water, and don't mess with 'em. Let 'em have lunch and go have lunch yourselves. Then go back in the water." That usually works pretty well. Wait about an hour, and they're all gone. You never see 'em again for another two or three months. Then you might see another one or two, and we'd yell to get out of the water again.

I believe that leopard ray was really one of my toughest opponents. At least, he's the one that wanted me the worst.

That same trip, I was wounded by sea urchins. So were Deo and all of us. We were shooting pictures of sharks eating fish and each other. Then the sharks ate up all the fish.

They decided they were going to eat us too. We all had to scramble up a cliff and get out of the water. We were all covered with sea urchins; there were broken off spines all over us. We were like porcupines.

***

My first organized, serious treasure hunt was looking for a Spanish galleon at Cortes Banks off the coast of California, about 125 miles offshore from the mainland. I was paid some of my expense money by the television producer for a show named *High Road to Danger*. It was a series of thirteen television shows.

The producer wanted me to make a film of this treasure hunt, and I did, topside and underwater. Looking at that film in recent years, it amazed me how well equipped we were way back then. I think it was around 1950.

We not only had underwater movie cameras and still cameras, but we had a huge underwater sled, sixteen feet long, with a windshield on the front of it.

We had a watertight panel in front of the diver that held metal detector electronics. It could actually discriminate ferrous from nonferrous objects. Also, it had a depth gauge, a watch, and a few other things that we needed to keep dry.

Most of these things were homemade—I guess all of them were. I had other people helping me, like a fellow named Dave, who was working on that sled, and some other guys were too.

Then we had a dome for the electronics that I made in my oven at home. I took a flat sheet of Lucite or something similar to that—plexiglass—and set it on top of a dishpan in the oven. When it got hot, it melted down to the shape of the dishpan. Then we bolted it onto the sled and that kept our equipment dry—up to a point.

Then on the back end of the sled we had a gigantic metal detecting loop, four feet in diameter. We don't even use loops that big right now to detect metal. I wouldn't mind having that sled right now. Maybe I'll build another one.

We were searching an area out there about a hundred feet deep, with that sled being towed behind the main ship by rope.

While I was down there the case for the equipment imploded. It sucked my face right into it, broke my mask, and cut me up a little.

It knocked my mouthpiece out of my mouth and scared the heck out of me! I got water up my nose. Then I held it so I wouldn't get any more water up my nose. I found my mask, but it was all ruined. I gave up with that and decided to just go up and stay alive.

I got my mouthpiece back in, got the water cleared out of it. Then I just held my nose and swam back up to the surface.

That was a pretty long haul. You could get the bends in a situation like that.

We had made some little, battery-powered, propeller-driven underwater gizmos that dragged the diver around underwater.

We also had hand detectors.

We made a big search line. I remember we had a piece of rope about six hundred feet long, with a knot every fifty feet. We had a diver get on each knot and make a big, long line. Then we started out doing visual searches with that line. I figured we'd cover a six-hundred-foot-wide path, and anybody who saw anything different would holler, and everybody could come check out that area.

We also had our magnetometer with us—an underwater magnetometer that Dave built. It didn't work too well out there, because there were quite a few highly magnetic rocks that stuck up on the bottom. Evidently there was a high magnetic volcanic mountain peak underwater there.

Then we got to a real shallow area. It's called Bishop Rock, and we found out why it was named that—for a sunken ship called the *Stillwell S. Bishop*. I think it sank in 1812 and probably does have some good artifacts and treasures on it. But we were only there for three days. All we brought up was the binnacle and, I think, the compass, and some of the controls of the ship.

So probably, Bishop Rock was named after the *Stillwell S. Bishop*, and Cortes Banks was named for the Spanish galleon that we were looking for.

We never did find any signs of the Spanish galleon, but I think it's still there. It just takes somebody to go looking for it. I forget where I got the research on it. I'd have to check my files. I'm pretty sure it's a Manila galleon that came across the Pacific up to about Canada and then down the California coast.

It was heading for Acapulco, but it hit that rock out in the middle of the ocean. Nobody would think there'd be anything, any water that shallow, way out that far offshore. There's no islands or anything anywhere around there.

We made a very good film of it, showed it on television. I received royalties and residuals on that film for several years. The guy paid me every time he used it—a very honest and capable guy. I recall his name was Sterns.

***

I'm not sure of the year, but Deo and I were in the living room of our new house at 117 Via Pasqual in Torrance, California.

We had invited over Al Corbett and his wife, Carol. It must have been right after we moved into our house, because I don't think we had the furniture yet. We were talking about going on a treasure hunt.

Deo got out this world atlas book by F.L. Coffman that has treasure maps throughout. There were maps of different countries and places, and little red "X's" showing where there are treasures, giving the names of the ships, when they sank, how much treasure was on them. After talking and talking and talking, we couldn't figure out where to go on our treasure hunt vacation.

We finally decided that I would be blindfolded, Al would open up the book, and wherever my finger came down—that was where we would go on a treasure hunt. That's real professional research!

So he opened the book, I put my finger down, and it landed on Silver Shoals.

That's a place way out in the Atlantic Ocean, east of the Dominican Republic and Haiti. It's about seventy miles offshore.

There's no land in sight out there. But there are deadly reefs that are just a couple of feet under the surface of the water.

When the ocean's calm, you can't see these reefs. That's why there are a lot of wrecks that happened there, I understand.

Then we picked a date to go. We decided to write to England to try to get some better charts of Silver Shoals. I didn't have a boat then, so we decided I would go a week ahead of time and find a boat to charter or rent so we could go on this trip from Miami.

On the map it didn't look like all that much distance to go from Miami through the Bahamas, to Haiti, and then on out to Silver Shoals. But it turned out it was quite a long trip.

We got four or five other couples to agree to go with us to share expenses. One of them was Deo's former classmate in high school, I believe, from Billings, Montana, and her doctor husband. She had just gotten married. Another one was an electronics guy who had been developing and helping me build magnetometers that we had taken from war-surplus airplanes. We'd make them waterproof, and we used them to find shipwrecks. I believe his name was Lew Black. A couple of guys from Florida went on that trip too.

For our Silver Shoals adventure, I went from California a week ahead to find a boat to rent, as I said. I found one; it was about a sixty-five-footer. I helped the guy do the shopping, get all the food, supplies, extra rope, anchors, injectors for his engine, spare parts for anything he thought he would need for this trip. We got extra life jackets and all kinds of stuff.

I'm trying to think of the name of the boat. I remember we called the captain of the boat "Captain Tuna." He thought that was a pretty nice name, but he didn't know that the girls had picked that name for him because he was so scared all the time. It was like "Chicken of the Sea," you know. Every time something would come up, a storm or a reef, he would really get scared.

Anyway, we went across the channel, the Gulf Stream.

I forget where we went through the reef on the Bahamas side, but I remember it was spooky. It was night. I remember it was real nice to get out of the rough weather and get in behind the reef onto the Bahama Bank. Everything was fine until we came to the Tongue of the Ocean.

When you look at the chart, the deep blue water looks like the shape of a person's tongue. As soon as we got to the deep water, I couldn't believe how rough it got. There were great big waves and swells. It made you feel seasick and wonder if you were ever going to get there.

When we got into Nassau, we weren't sure where to stop and dock the boat. We went through most of the town, and just when we went to dock, trouble occurred. There was a real strong current there in the channel. I don't believe the captain, myself, or anybody realized how strong the current was. When the captain got lined up to back into the dock, somehow he killed the engines. The current took the boat and smashed it into the dock and also put a big dent in a real plush yacht that was tied up alongside. That caused a little hassle.

We had just gotten our land legs back for a day or two and gotten some last-minute supplies for the next haul, which would take us as far as Haiti. If we ran low on fuel, we were going to stop at Great Inagua, although we couldn't see any place marked on the chart where they had a harbor or fuel docks. So we put as much fuel on board as we could at Nassau and headed south, staying on the banks.

Earlier, we had planned to go out in the ocean the whole length of the trip. But after crossing the Tongue of the Ocean and seeing how rough that ocean could be, we decided to stay on the flats and go down the inside of the reefs as far as we could.

That worked out quite well. We didn't have any problem. We passed several pretty islands in the Bahamas, and finally the coral reefs got so thick that we had to head out into the ocean.

That's quite a big jump of open ocean to Inagua. We got there and decided we'd better get fuel. It didn't look like we were going to make it to Haiti, so we pulled in as close as we could. There wasn't any harbor, but some of the natives there brought out fuel to us in fifty-gallon drums. We bought enough fuel to make sure we got to Haiti. I would have to measure the distance we traveled on the chart; it's a long way. When we were on our way from Inagua to Haiti, I remember all the engines stopped. I don't know if it was water from the fuel we got at Inagua, clogged filters, or what, but all the engines stopped.

We were trying to figure out how to get them running again. None of us were really diesel mechanics, but somehow, we got the engines running again. We made it on into a port in Haiti, though I can't recall the name.

On our sixty-five-foot boat, there were five or six couples, about twelve people on board. There were more guys than there were gals, though.

We refueled at Haiti, left right away, and went to Tortuga Island. That was very nice. We anchored in the lee on the west side of the island. The big, rough ocean breaks on the other side of the island, so it was very calm where we were and a pretty island. There were lots of mountains and jungle, and the water was really clear. We found a little wreck and did some work on it.

We were getting ready to go out to Silver Shoals, which was the next big jump, and then the captain said he was scared to go out there.

We tried for two or three days to talk him into going out there, but he just flat-out refused to go. He also wouldn't let us go and leave him there, so we just resigned ourselves to staying at Tortuga.

We learned a lot about the history of that island. It had been pirates' headquarters for about two or three hundred years. Pirates of all different nationalities had stayed there. They even had built their own fort to keep the Spanish and British governments from coming in and raiding their hideaway.

That was like a complete pirate nation. They even had their own government. They would make raids and bring the loot back in there.

In high school, I had read about the "buccans." They are the guys who went out in the jungle and got hogs. I guess they called them "buccans," like "bacon," and then they changed their name to "buccaneers," and then that's where they got the name buccaneers.

They started, I think, on that island and on the coast of Haiti where we had stopped for fuel.

So some of the group went and explored some big caves up on the island. I don't think we went on that trip. I can't remember why, but I would have remembered the caves if I had been in there.

The voodoo drums were playing all the time when we were there. On that island they were heavy into voodoo and very serious about it. It surprised me, because they had Catholic symbols. I thought first that it was Catholicism, and then I found out it was voodoo. They had these different rituals.

One night, I remember they had what seemed like a big religious ceremony.

They had a lot of drums; some of them were huge, gigantic drums, about ten or twelve feet in diameter. I wouldn't doubt but what they still have them there now. They had a dwarf-sized guy who was like a gymnast, and he used the drums like a trampoline. He would bounce from one drum to another and play voodoo music.

They had a lot of smaller drums too.

There were huge throbbing drum sounds. They also used their drums for talking back and forth and sending signals. It became spooky, frightening.

The people there are very, very poor. For them it is all right to swipe anything they want. So they would come over to our boat, sometimes with several canoes full of people. They would be very friendly; they would offer us coconut or pineapple. Then we would give them some clothes or candy. But, while we were looking at stuff, there would be other people all over the boat picking up stuff, looking at stuff, and putting it in their bags. They'd be swiping everything in sight that they could get their hands on.

We decided not to let them on the boat anymore, because they took some of our tools and things that we couldn't get along without, then pretended they couldn't understand what we were saying. They'd come squirming on the boat anyway.

Finally, the captain got a pistol out and fired a few shots.

Then we knew for sure that they understood that language.

That night it was real pitch dark. I think a group of four of us had gone to look for treasure in these caves. They were supposed to be back the same day, and they didn't get back. We were worried about them. Then we heard another one of these voodoo things starting up, and we could hear these drums coming out towards us.

All the throbbing drums. And we could hear *splash*, *splash*, *splash*, like they're paddling with their hands or paddles. They had a whole mess of the drums in their canoes, and they were coming out around our boat. It was so black we couldn't see anything.

Everybody got all their weapons out. Spear guns, other guns, and things. We were afraid they were going to mob all over the boat.

It was very quiet, and the first thing we realized was that we were drifting out to sea. They had cut the bow line off our boat and taken the line and the anchor. I guess they needed the anchor for one of their boats. Either that, or they were just trying to give us a hint to leave.

We couldn't leave, because four of our people were

still on the island. We didn't know if they had gotten kidnapped or what.

The next day, about 2 o'clock, the people came back, and we were glad to see them. One of them was Deo's classmate from high school. She said that on the way back from the cave they had stopped at a monastery, a Catholic monastery. A monk there spoke English; he was studying zombies, and there are a lot of zombies on the island. We learned they had about a hundred of them in this place they had built there—a big stone house or clinic. He was trying to figure out what caused the zombies and how to cure them. The classmate's husband was a doctor, and he got interested in that. They were talking about zombies until dark, then they figured they couldn't get down the mountain in the dark. So they had stayed at the monastery overnight.

The next day we started a systematic magnetometer survey going the length of the entire coast of the island. Every time we would get an anomaly, which means something different, we would throw a buoy. We were so interested in watching the magnetometer and getting the buoys in that we hadn't looked backward.

Finally, we stopped and looked back. The first buoy we had thrown was about a mile behind us. We could see a dugout canoe going back into the beach. At the next buoy toward us we could see a canoe there, and guys pulling the buoy up. At the next buoy, we could see a guy on the way out to get it. They were hard up for line for their lobster traps.

There's no "road to danger" that Mel Fisher was not willing to take. Why? Because he enjoyed it, and it was adventurous, and he and his family got to take vacations in faraway places—and get paid too. Probably his greatest natural adversary in the ocean was the giant leopard ray he challenged (with the camera rolling) in the Virgin Islands. He was able to survive his encounter because he fortunately had a surgeon for a friend—on that adventure. Also, he was younger then. And Mel had great faith in himself and the universe, always believing that somehow, he would get on through the problems of the moment. Which meant—he had a higher calling.

Deo Fisher and Captain Ed Tsukimura on the Golden Doubloon.
FISHER FAMILY COLLECTION

CHAPTER ELEVEN

Hunting for Gold on Silver Shoals

He *always wanted to find a gold doubloon. Treasure, especially Spanish gold, was in Mel Fisher's consciousness, back to reading* Treasure Island *in high school library period. The more he studied and learned about lost treasures, the more he was inspired to tackle the difficult (nothing was impossible). Few in the world could merge practical reality with the possibilities in dreams like Mel Fisher. He had a sense of "fair" from life experiences and did not like to be regimented. He was unafraid to ask for help or guidance, given his open and persuasive personality. He was also a smart-enough leader and businessman to get others who shared his dreams to partner with him and invest in risking much for a great goal. Mel just didn't know how hard such treasures could be to find, or how long it would take. Along the way he would find many who chose to share his adventures—and "keep on a-goin'."*

Our second try for Silver Shoals came after Deo and I went down to San Diego to a boat auction. We bought a second-hand sport-fishing boat that was licensed to haul sixty-five people for hire out in the ocean. The price was twenty grand—a thousand dollars a month for twenty months.

Those were the hardest payments I ever had to make in my life.

We named the boat *Golden Doubloon*. I wanted to go find a gold doubloon. That was my goal in life—one gold doubloon. I found out they're very hard to find. It took me about ten years to find a gold doubloon.

We thought we'd find it right away. We used the

boat for taking out skin diving charter groups from San Pedro, California. We went to Catalina, Santa Barbara, San Clemente Island, and Santa Cruz Island, Anacapa, and other islands out there, out to Cortes Banks.

Then in the late 1950s, we got ready for the "big one," to take a trip from San Pedro, California, to Puerto Vallarta, Mexico; from there to Acapulco, Mexico; from Acapulco to San José, Costa Rica; and from Costa Rica to Panama, through the Canal, on out across the Caribbean to Silver Shoals!

But this was my first long voyage on a motor vessel. I didn't realize what a big, big ocean it is, how often-dangerous it is, and what all the storms, currents, and winds can do.

We got together twenty-two people who wanted to go on a treasure-hunting vacation, each paying a thousand bucks. I put up the rest of the money. Without me, they got on the *Golden Doubloon* and headed south from San Pedro. I stayed in my shop to keep making money so I could pay for our total expenses. Just before reaching Acapulco, they got in a big storm. They took on water in the bow and almost sank the ship. But they bailed it out and, still floating, limped into Acapulco. I flew to Acapulco and met them.

In the bow we had all the dynamite that we had been going to take with us. We took it all out and threw it away. When dynamite gets wet, the glycerin settles to the bottom, and it's very delicate. A jar will set it off.

We wanted to test some new diesel outboard motors, and so we launched our search boat in Acapulco Harbor. They didn't work. These were the first diesel outboard engines I'd ever seen. We decided to buy some regular gasoline engines.

The *Doubloon* was equipped with one of Fay Feild's magnetometers. We also had some of the hand detectors that Fay had built, and some hand detectors that another friend of mine, Lew Black, had built. We were going to go to Silver Shoals to look for the shipwreck *Concepción* and anything else we could find out there. I wanted to try to find a gold doubloon!

After we got the ship and expedition equipment organized in Acapulco, where I got on board, we went from there to Costa Rica.

Along the way we saw millions of sea snakes swimming in the water. These things are deadly poisonous. All sea snakes in the ocean are deadly, like cobras. Some of my guys insisted on snagging a few of them, bringing them on board, and putting them in bottles. I tried to explain to them that they shouldn't be messing with those things.

Then we got to a famous bay down there called Tehuantepec off the coast of Costa Rica that always has storms that sweep down it. You can't just sail along by the coast. You have to cut across the area out in the open ocean. Sure enough, a big storm hit us there.

While we were in the storm, something else happened. There was so much rain that something shorted out with our electrical system. Anything we touched would give us an electrical shock. Not only iron and copper things, but even wood things, plastic things shocked us. No matter what we touched, we received electrical shocks. We were all constantly getting electrical shocks—all day and all night—until we got into Costa Rica. By then we were all dead tired, our nerves were all frazzled, we were hungry and dirty. It was really good to get into civilization there, to pull up to the dock and get off where we weren't getting shocks.

It was very hot, and we hadn't had a shower for a week. All of us, about twenty-five people, got in one big circle. In that circle, we all sprayed each other with a garden hose. Then we all scrubbed each other's backs and hosed everybody off.

That was very relaxing, and it was good not to be shocking!

We took a little stroll through town and the park

and shopped for bicycles and fruits. We had our electrical system checked out and repaired so we wouldn't get any more shocks. I forget exactly what caused that, it was just a short somewhere.

After rest, we started on down to Panama. We would travel a long, long way, across a big, big ocean!

We arrived at Panama and found out they had a waiting line to get through the Canal, with several dozen huge ships ahead of us. The transit involves great rigmarole. You don't just go through the Panama Canal. You have to register with all the proper authorities, put up a bond. You have to have an agent. Then you have to wait in line, and, finally, they schedule you to go through.

In the middle of the night, we arrived. A harbor pilot came out in a pilot boat to tell us where to go to anchor, to wait our turn in line. The pilot got on board and told our crew where to go. It happened that Deo and I had already gone in another small pilot boat to find out about food and supplies. We went to the area where the boat was supposed to anchor, but it wasn't there. We waited, and waited, and waited. Finally, we rented another pilot boat and went searching for the *Doubloon*. We couldn't believe our eyes.

The *Golden Doubloon* was sitting about ten feet up in the air, on land, out in the middle of the harbor. We didn't know that they had about a twenty-eight-foot tidal drop there. The Panamanian pilot who was telling our captain where to go had put him right on top of a mud hill. The *Doubloon* was stuck there when the tide dropped. Our boat was sitting way up in the air. It was all mud, all the way around. Worse, it looked like the boat was starting to capsize in the mud. I had everybody on board gather up a bunch of two-by-fours we had on board and jump out in the mud. They all were walking around in mud, knee-deep and thigh-deep, trying to prop the *Doubloon* up with these two-by-fours so it wouldn't tip over. We had to dig the mud out from under the propellers so it wouldn't bend the shafts and propellers when the boat settled down in the mud. Boats aren't supposed to be sitting in mud. But there we were—in the middle of the night, in the mud!

Everybody had to help. They thought it was fun. They were even throwing mud balls at each other. Everything worked out all right. Daylight came, the tide rose—and twelve hours after we were stuck, it just floated the boat again. We took off and finally got our turn through the Canal.

We got in there, and it was impressive. It's a big old canal. The first lock we got into, we learned a hard lesson, because we were unfamiliar with their system. We had some nylon lines that, as I recall, had to be 150 feet long, of one-inch nylon. There was a loop in the end of the nylon, so we put that loop on the cleat on the bow of our ship and threw the line up to the guys on the side of the canal. They pulled the line in tight, and tied us up, and then they let the water out of the canal.

The water went down, but our boat couldn't go down—because they had it tied up short. Before we knew what was happening, the bow of the boat was pulled out of the water. The cleat was pulled clear out of the deck, and half of the deck was torn out. We wised up not to depend on the people who worked at the Canal—and never to have a tied-down line again.

We would always have our line so we could let it out when we wanted to.

We went on through the Canal. There's a big lake in the middle of it, Gatun Lake. That was an enjoyable cruise. At the last lock, just before you come out into the Caribbean, there is quite a drop. I think the guys who run the locks get a kick out of watching the entire little neophyte boats. When the little boats get to that last lock, they suddenly open the gates wide, and it's like you're going over a waterfall. You just go flying down out of that thing.

Through the Panama Canal, we tied up at the yacht club there in Colón, Panama, on the Caribbean side. I think we moored at the American Yacht Club, planned for tourists.

One night when we had a nice dinner at the yacht club, we got a little tipsy and were walking back down the dock to go to the boat. Deo just walked right off the end of the dock—and kept going.

She disappeared, so I jumped in to look for her. They had told us not to go swimming there, because it was full of alligators, sawfish, and sharks. But all of the rest of the people started pushing each other in. There were about ten of us who didn't want to go swimming in that dark place with all those alligators and sawfish. They got in the boat to go back to the *Doubloon*. But the rest of us who were swimming tipped that boat over. Then everybody was in the water—at about 2 o'clock in the morning.

Fortunately, nobody "got ate up." That story they'd told us was just a myth.

Also, while we were at the yacht club in Colón, we visited a nearby vessel that turned out to be the same boat that we had taken years before on the earlier treasure hunt from Miami bound for Silver Shoals.

We headed out this time for Silver Shoals, full of enthusiasm. Aboard, however, we also carried trouble. In Colón the day before, I had told this young boy about sixteen or seventeen years old to change the oil in the engines. He thought he did. The trouble would be that it wasn't oil, but fiberglass resin the boy put in the engines. Fortunately, he didn't put any catalyst in, only the resin. The engines seemed to run "OK" when we started out the next day. We got out of the harbor and through the breakwater. A couple of miles out, one of the engines stopped. Then the other engine stopped. Everything got quiet, and we wondered, "What's wrong?"

We were checking the oil. Somebody tasted the oil, because it didn't look just right. We discovered it was really fiberglass resin. We got a tow back into port and went into a native place that rebuilt engines. They came down and tore the engines completely apart, cleaned out all the fiberglass resin, and gave it a valve-polishing job.

I looked down in the engine room, and there was Demostines "Mo" Molinar. He was replacing the valve seats. They didn't have modern equipment there, so Mo had something that looked like an arrow such as I had with my bow and arrow set, with a suction cup on the end. He had the suction cup on top of the valve. He'd roll that arrow in the palms of his hands, back and forth, to make the valves go round, to seat them in.

We didn't have a mechanic on board, and I thought, "We need a diesel mechanic." I asked Mo if he'd like to go treasure hunting. He said, "Sure, Mon." I said, "I'll double your salary—whatever you're making, I'll pay you double." The next day I said, "By the way, how much are you making?" He said, "I make $18 a week." I couldn't believe it. So I said, "OK, from now on, you get $36 a week." He thought that was a real good deal, and I did too.

When we left again for Silver Shoals, after I had hired Mo, I didn't tell Eddie Tsukimura, the skipper, because he would have wanted to go through all the Immigration and Customs, and all that paperwork again. So Mo just stowed away. We got out about ten miles. At sea, I opened the hatch, and I'll be darned, there was Mo. I yelled "Stowaway! Stowaway!" Mo had to go up and tell Eddie that he had stowed away, and put it on the ship's log, so Eddie wouldn't get in trouble.

We traveled way out to sea on the *Golden Doubloon*, our sixty-five-foot sport-fishing boat. We were again on our way to Silver Shoals from Panama, and we found out again how that's a big, big ocean. On a map, the Caribbean Sea looks awfully little—about six inches across. When we got out there, it was lots of miles.

We didn't know until it arrived, but "here came a hurricane." The darned hurricane was off to the side of us. We didn't get right in the middle of it. But the waves from the wind were going one direction, and the swells from the hurricane were going the other direction. So there'd be huge swells, and then about four or five waves on each swell that were going the other way, with big whitecaps. That was all-mixed-up water.

The waves were going clear over the bow of our ship, over the wheelhouse, then coming down on deck, and knocking everybody over. Waves were just destroying everything and going down into the bilges. It was really serious weather. They didn't have any satellites back then, so we didn't know the hurricane was going to happen.

That was just the kind of storm that made all those Spanish galleons sink, and we didn't know one was going to happen either. I told Mo the stern looked awfully low, to go check the bilges. He lifted up the hatch, then came back forward and said, "That's full, Mon!"

The bilge was full of water all the way up to the hatch. I mean, that's about six or seven feet of water. We had watertight compartments, thank God. But they weren't absolutely, positively waterproof. The water started overflowing into the next compartment, where the fuel tanks were.

Then it started going over that wall into the engine room, which was really serious. We tried to use the bilge pumps, but they got all clogged up with toilet paper. That was because we had stored away a bunch of toilet paper in the lazarette. The toilet paper was floating all around, the water was sloshing back and forth, and the bilge pumps were clogged up.

I had everybody start bailing water with buckets. We got all the buckets we could, and had all these twenty-two people rotating, giving buckets to each other, and throwing water. Then a big wave would come up over the front of the boat and fill it all up again. I had another idea, because the stern was underwater by that time, about six inches underwater.

It looked like we were sinking. Capt. Eddie Tsukimura called out a "Mayday," which means, "We're sinking." Thirty years later he would still be the captain of the *Golden Doubloon*, and by then, owner, still going from the same dock in San Pedro, California, taking out scuba divers, and albacore fishermen.

But we didn't know that, so Eddie called a "Mayday! We're going under." We were only about one-third of the way across the Caribbean when that hurricane hit us. I had some sheets of plywood I'd brought along to build a box for a magnetometer head. Mo and I tied some ropes around our waist and tied them to the mast, so those waves wouldn't wash us overboard. We went out on the stern of the ship and made a box there with plywood that would stick up out of the water.

Then we started bailing on deck to get the water off the deck. Next, we opened a hatch to get down in there and start bailing water from down below. The boat started to slowly float again. Then some of the other people tied ropes on themselves, came back, and started helping us. One gal was a psychiatrist.

She was running around talking to everybody, and writing it down fast, like Wendy Tucker: "How does it feel to be drowning?" "What are your emotions at this time?" She'd say, "With death imminent, and, since we're sinking, what do you think about this?" So I gave her a job. I said, "Look, forget the writing. You go get the emergency food rations out. Put some of them in the dinghy, and some in the lifeboat—I mean our search boat—so we won't starve to death if we have to abandon ship." That got her out of our hair. We got the wall built around the stern.

Then a huge wave came over the bow and washed away the whole wall, tore it all to pieces. We started to go down again—deeper this time.

The stern was about a foot and a half underwater. The engines were still going. I had another team bailing water out of the engine room. I told them if the engine room got full, "we're in deep trouble." We had three different crews bailing—with buckets and everything they could find. Mo and I built another wall on the stern with plywood. This time we used more nails and made more braces. We started bailing off the deck again, started bailing out the stern again.

Gradually, with all these people in action, the boat started to float again. One team was working on the stern, one in the middle of the boat, and one in the engine room. At last, the boat actually started floating.

I told Eddie, "Let's turn around." He said, "We can't turn around." I said, "We've gotta turn around. We've gotta head back to Panama. We've gotta turn around!" We started counting these big waves—about every seventh wave would be a monster. Right after one of those big monsters—which came over the wheelhouse—went past us, we made the turn and started going back, which meant we were moving with the swells instead of with the waves.

It was like surf-riding. Our whole sixty-five-foot ship was a big surfboard, surfing down these huge swells. The seas would tend to make you turn sideways and capsize. You really had to goose the throttles when you were going to turn sideways, straighten the boat out, and make sure you went perpendicular to the waves. We were really making a lot of speed then.

But that was good, because we were heading away from the hurricane. We made it back to Panama, surfing all the way.

There we licked our wounds. We went back to the yacht club, had another steak, another party.

I said, "To hell with Silver Shoals. That Gulf of Mexico is too darned big. Let's go to Seranilla Bank." Everybody said, "Where's that?" I said, "Well, it's only right up the road a piece. Just up toward Yucatán. It's a lot closer, and the ocean's getting calm now. This is hurricane season, and in hurricane season the ocean's real calm—when you don't have a hurricane." The hurricane had gone by, and the ocean got really flat and calm. We all decided, "The heck with Silver Shoals. We'll go there some other year. We'll go up to Seranilla Reef, Seranilla Bank, where [I told them] there's a 'whole mess o' Spanish galleons and treasure'!"

We started heading up there, and something else happened. One of the engines quit. Then another engine quit. Only this time it wasn't rough; there was nothing wrong—so it seemed. Except the engines quit. Then the generator quit. It got real quiet. The ocean was just flat calm and slick. Nothing would run. Eddie was trying to start the engines and start the generator. None of them would start, and soon the batteries all went dead. There we were, just sitting out there. In this great big, peaceful, beautiful Caribbean. Just drifting, very quiet and calm, peaceful, blissful.

There we sat with the batteries dead, and none of the engines would run. No wind. It didn't seem there was even any current, although there probably was. All the batteries on the boat were dead. All of them. I don't remember what was wrong, but I remember everything stopped. All I can think is that we must have gotten some bad fuel, or maybe some salt water had gotten into our fuel tanks from the previous storm, got into the fuel and made the engines quit. For some reason they wouldn't run.

The batteries went dead because Eddie was trying to start the engines. If you have a dead car engine, and you try to make it start, pretty soon the thing goes *Weoooow, weoowwww, weooww*. Then it goes *Enhhhhh*. Everything went that way on the boat.

We agreed, "We've got to figure out something." The next day we were still just floating there, very calm and everything. We discovered one of the extra batteries, just a little automobile battery, had a partial charge in it. We were testing all the batteries with battery hydrometers. First, we got a little, teeny, gas-fired generator working. Just a little portable emergency unit. That made everybody happy.

At last there was some noise, and something was running. I think it was just a small Briggs & Stratton lawnmower type of engine. We hooked the battery charger up to that, and got a big battery charged up for the ship's generator.

In the meantime, we were cleaning out all the filters on the generators, all the filters on the engines, and trying to vacuum salt water, or any kind of water, out of the fuel tanks. We were bleeding all the fuel lines and clearing everything we could think of to make the engines run again.

We finally got the bigger generator to start. That was a big plus. Several hours later, that generator charged up batteries for the main engines, and we got one of the main engines started.

We got underway, and I said, "Well, why don't we forget Seranilla Bank, and go treasure hunting in Panama?"

So we turned around. After we got part way back, and we got the other engine started, we went on to Panama, because our vacation time was running out.

We returned to Panama, and Mo said he thought he could get me a treasure hunting permit in Panama.

About that time, they put an article in the Colón newspaper with a headline that resembled: "Crazy gringos arrive in Colón." I don't know how they heard about us, but they wrote a story about the crazy treasure hunters. At about that time, Mo said, "I know the Captain of the Port," and that he probably could get us a permit for treasure hunting there. I said, "Yeah, but I haven't got all that much money." He said, "Ah, let's go talk to him."

So we went to the Captain of the Port, they talked, and Mo told me, "This guy says if you give him fifty bucks, he'll give you an exclusive salvage contract on all the wrecks in Panama." I said, "OK, here's the fifty bucks." I gave him $50, and the Captain of the Port wrote out a permit saying I could search for and salvage treasure anywhere in Panama. I said, "OK, let's go." He wrote it out, and so we were legal in Panama.

We took off and went to Portobelo. That's a

beautiful harbor where the Spaniards used to send in a whole fleet every year. They would have a fair there for thirty days each year, trading treasure for things from the Old World. By the time we arrived, there was a nice little village there, just a few buildings. There was a great big church, which is now collapsed and in ruins. I remember I bought a sword from a guy, one of the natives there, an old Spanish sword. I also bought a few coins from them.

When we got back out on the boat, I looked up on the side of the hill. It looked like a pyramid there, all overgrown with jungle. I said, "Wow, look at that! It looks like a pyramid!" Everybody agreed. I said, "Let's go up there and check it out tomorrow." We did. We brought some machetes; we had some shovels and picks. We hacked our way through the jungle and got up to the pyramid. It was all clearly covered with jungle.

But we found an entrance that had had a cave-in, was buried and sealed off. We started digging to see if we could get inside the pyramid. We figured we were just about inside of it when along came a guy wearing what looked like a general's costume, with a big hat, and bars and gold braid all over him. He explained to Mo that this was a national park, that we couldn't mess around in this national park, and we'd have to cover this doorway back up again.

I said, "Mo, why don't you ask him if he'll give us a treasure hunting permit for $50 for pyramids?" Mo is a pretty happy, funny guy. He told the fellow, "For $50, we want to buy a treasure hunting permit for pyramids." The guy was very happy too, enjoyable, a nice guy, big smile. But he said he was coming up for election in November to be the "Minister" of the entire area, that he was going to get twice as much pay, and he wanted to not accept the $50, because they might not give him this big promotion.

I told Mo, "Try $100." But it didn't work.

The guy said, "No, I've got this beautiful uniform, and I'm real happy. In this area, I'm almost like God." He said, "I'd rather not take the money." I couldn't believe it. So we covered the hole up, and we never dug into that pyramid. But what that was, I believe, was the vault where Spaniards used to store hundreds of tons of treasure while they were waiting for the fair. You know, it's all sealed up, and it's still there. Right there at Portobelo. We got back on our boat and headed out.

We saw a reef out there with breakers on it. We headed out to that reef, off Portobelo. I didn't have any research on that area, but I said I would imagine that this was where the pirates would "hang out." I'd read about it in some of the pirate stories. Pirates would "hang out" outside the entrance to Portobelo, and when the Spaniards would come out loaded with treasure, they'd pounce on them.

We went to look at this reef right outside the entrance and anchored the boat. We wanted to get some diving in, at least. We hadn't had a chance to do any treasure hunting or diving. This was our first dive.

Everybody went in snorkeling.

Mo hadn't used a snorkel before, and fins and mask. He came up choking and coughing and sputtering. Waving his hands, he said, "Mel, I see a canyon down here." I thought, "Big deal, he saw a canyon." He said, "I see two canyons down here." Big deal, two canyons, you know?

Then it dawned on me that a "canyon" in Spanish is a cannon. He was right—there was a Spanish galleon there, scattered all over the place.

Being a novice at this, I didn't exactly know what to do. Very difficult currents. We had a gold dredge, which I'd built for vacuuming gold in the rivers in California, and floated on a big truck inner tube. We floated the dredge over the site. We also had a Briggs & Stratton engine, and we worked a hookah compressor and a water pump for operating an underwater jet venturi dredge and a sluice box. A jet venturi dredge with a built-in sluice box to catch gold. We vacuumed around there for about half an hour and didn't find anything. So we went back to the boat, gave up, and moved on.

We worked that galleon, and there was "nothing there."

I didn't realize that you had to work for years and years and years, do lots of digging, to find treasure. I thought you'd just go down and find it.

Nobody knows. That wreck might still be a big, good bonanza. One of these days I'll have to check it out again. I've never been back there. But I think it deserves about at least a year's hard work on it, and maybe a million dollars' investment.

We headed south and went to a very secluded area called San Blas Islands off [Panama]. We checked in with the Captain of the Port there. They actually have Immigration and Customs in San Blas. There's only one small building in the whole place, and that's it. That's Customs, Immigration, and Captain of the Port. They're all one guy. I anchored there, and it was nice and calm.

San Blas is a group of islands; each island has coconuts growing on it, and basically, the natives grow coconuts. That's the way they measure their wealth. Whoever has the most coconut trees is the wealthiest guy. There are a lot of native rules there. They won't let any strangers stay in their islands after dark. They come out in dugout canoes, and all the guys and gals have gold all over them—gold chest plates, gold brassieres, gold earrings, gold bracelets, gold rings, gold all over 'em. They also live from the selling of these "molas," which are brightly colored, woven mats, similar to dinner place mats, of all different designs.

You try to buy the gold; they won't sell the gold. They'll only sell the "molas." I asked them where all that gold came from, and they said, "Oh, right over there in the hills." They pointed to these mountains. I asked about those mountains, and they said, "Well, anybody who goes up there never comes back." So we didn't go up there.

We did some scuba diving there, in San Blas Bay. It's unbelievable scuba diving. The life underwater seems very gigantic. Everything is huge. There are huge kelp plants, huge black coral plants. Everything you've ever seen under the ocean anywhere else in the world, they've got there. Only it's much bigger and much more plentiful. For some reason, that entire area is just frighteningly abundant, overnourished, big. When you're down there, it's like being in the middle of a huge jungle.

I tapped Deo on the shoulder, pointed, and pinched my thumb to my finger a couple of times. That means "shark." She looked over, and there were a couple of sharks, gray ones, cruising by. They were big too. We got out of the water.

The next day I took some underwater movies.

The day after, we went on land. We went to one of the native islands, went in their huts, and looked around. They had grass shacks and dirt floors, but the floors were immaculately clean. They had lots of "molas" for sale. We saw they had a little bronze cannon. That interested me, but they wouldn't sell it. They use it every year to celebrate something. They actually fired it.

Then we headed back in the other direction. North again. We went out to a reef offshore. There we found a huge pile of what looked like silver bars, about twenty-five feet long, and about eighty feet long. "Hundreds and hundreds of silver bars!"

We broke a couple of them loose, swam them back to the boat, and hammered on them. Then we got out a cutting torch, and started burning them, to try figure out what they were made of.

We finally figured out they were made of cast iron. It was kind of exciting—for a little while.

The shape of the iron ballast pile was just like that of the *Atocha* "main pile" where, years later, we found millions of dollars in real silver bars. The cast iron was ballast from a shipwreck, and there was a whole shipwreck there.

Then we headed north and went past Colón, on up north to Fort San Lorenzo, which is a fort way up on a high cliff. The fort is on top of a perpendicular cliff about 120 feet above the water. That's where the entrance of the Gatun River dumps into the Caribbean. It comes from Gatun Lake, in the center of Panama, down to the Caribbean, and the Spaniards used to use that to transport treasure.

There were two means of transporting treasure. One was by water, and one was by mule train through the mountains and jungles. When treasure went by water, they'd go across Gatun Lake, paddling, then portage it down a ways to the Gatun River. They'd get to the Caribbean, then they'd take little sailboats—they called them "pataches"—from there down to Portobelo with the treasure.

Henry Morgan at one time had sacked this fort. I believe he was the only one who ever took this fort over from the Spaniards. He sent an army of 1,200 men by land from the back side, while he was attacking from down below. He had a secret weapon, which was a catapult machine, on his ship. It had about a hundred-pound cannon ball; it was hollow, full of fuel and explosives. He'd light that, lob it up into the fort, and try to set the fort on fire, blow up the munitions, or something. We found his sunken ship and catapult machine there. I salvaged them.

When we were up in the fort, I went diving in the cistern. There I found about a half dozen of those huge things that he had lobbed up into the fort. They had evidently picked them up with sticks and dumped them into the cistern to put them out, so they wouldn't blow everything up, catch everything on fire. I took that catapult machine back to Colón and put it underneath the shipping dock there with a lot of our other artifacts that I'd found. They're still there. Maybe we'll pick them up someday.

I did ship and crate a lot of things, sent them back to California by boat.

Then we went up the Gatun River there instead of staying out in the ocean for the night. It was weird anchoring in a river in the middle of the jungle, with all the parrots, other birds, and everything else screaming and growling all night long.

Mo told us that river was all full of alligators, sawfish, and sharks, and [said], "Don't go in the water." But we did anyway.

We got off the stern. We didn't swim too far away, though. We'd swim a little bit and come right back and get on our dive platform. Then we went out diving and scouted around. We split up, and everybody went in a different direction, with metal detectors. Just searching to see if we could find anything. Everybody came back, and everybody said they found something in all directions. They talked of cannons and other things. I'd found a stack of things underwater that looked like ingots. They gave a reading on the metal detector. We went back to the boat, and everybody said they had seen things to check out.

But we only had one day left of our vacation. The kid who'd put the fiberglass resin in the engines said he saw a bronze cannon out there in one direction. That seemed to be the nicest thing that anybody had seen. The next day we all decided to go get that bronze cannon, bring it up, and see what else we could find all around there.

We went out diving again. It was right in the middle of where the water came out from the Gatun River, so it was really muddy there, although everywhere else it was clear. We couldn't find that darned cannon.

But we found something that looked like a beer stein, a great big beer stein made of heavy bronze. That was evidence that he was telling the truth. Because it was the breach block for a bronze cannon. They'd fill it full of gunpowder, and they'd set it in the breach and wedge it in and fire the cannon.

Well, we didn't find that cannon. But we found another smaller iron one, and we brought it up. It checked out. Those ingots I'd found so quickly turned out to be batteries, a bank of batteries from a ship wrecked there.

We checked out another shipwreck that another guy found, and it was, I believe, Henry Morgan's ship. We brought up the catapult machine from it and put that on board. That was what convinced me that we had Henry Morgan's ship—the catapult. Several of us had read about that in pirate books.

Morgan lost four ships there in that battle. But he took the fort.

The Spaniards had American Indians working for them in the fort, and one of the American Indians shot an arrow through one of Henry Morgan's captains. That captain said in a report that the arrow went clear through him; it was halfway sticking out his back and his front. He told his lieutenant to pull the arrow on through him, and he did. The captain had then said, "Now put the arrow in my rifle, instead of a ball." He put a bunch of cloth doused in oil, and lit it on fire, and fired the arrow back at the fort on fire.

It blew up the powder magazine. Then Morgan's men rushed the fort.

They had trees they would lay across the moat. They all went across the trees, captured the fort, and took the treasure they had there. That actually happened. It's not a story. It really happened.

That was the last day of our vacation that we could spend treasure hunting. We packed up and went back to Colón. There we shipped off all of our finds that we could. What we couldn't ship, we started shoving underneath the Customs officer's place, under the dock, and it's still there. Nobody knows where it is but me. It's like a safety bank there.

I don't think I have anything left of what I originally kept from that adventure. It's all gone.

I finally asked Mo, who was then in his twenties, if he wanted to stay on, go back to the States. He said he did, so he came on up to San Pedro, and I signed a paper saying that I would be his "protégé" and be responsible for him for five years. I had to send him back down to Panama by plane to fill out all the papers and bring him back in to the United States.

Later he got married and became a US citizen. He's still treasure hunting with me—but as a partner or associate now. In 1988 Mo found lots of gold again on the same shipwreck where we first found a lot of it in the spring of 1964.

Eddie Tsukimura was captain of the boat, and so he brought the *Golden Doubloon* back through the Panama Canal, up the coast of Costa Rica and Mexico, and back to San Pedro Harbor.

We flew back to California and went back to normal business, teaching people how to dive and selling equipment. I'd gone in the hole quite a bit on that trip. I was surprised when I got back and looked at my Texaco credit card bill. At the time I had run out of money, so I was using my Texaco credit card, and I chalked up $27,000 in debt. So I went and talked to them and asked them if I could get time payments.

It took me a year of working to pay off my Texaco credit bill from that treasure hunt. I remember that. Also, the credit bill was over the money that I had invested.

But it was a great adventure. Lots of romance and adventure. We didn't find any gold [but] we were a lot smarter. We learned a lot more about how powerful the oceans are, how powerful Mother Nature is, how things can go wrong out there.

Men can make mistakes, and women too, engines keep breaking down, and I don't know if it was worth the price. I guess so.

One adventure after another, without getting seriously hurt or having a comrade hurt, and Mel Fisher kept on a-going. Every day was a new day full of new opportunities, and with his family and like-minded friends beside him on his adventures, what more could an adventurous guy want? This time, again, the goal was Silver Shoals, but it was not yet to be a "reef of silver." But certainly for all it was an education on the sea, the winds and weather, on nature, and on man's engineering. They foolishly called the trip "the big one." Little did they know they would find "romance and adventure," but no gold, save in Mel's imagination—which never stopped. He learned a lot, about how powerful and ever-changing the oceans are, how powerful "Mother Nature" is, and how things can go wrong. But Mel was only a little bit hedging on his bet with nature and the universe—not sure, but guessing it was so.

The original crew in the 1960s. From left: Bob Moran, Demostines "Mo" Molinar, Dick Williams, Walter Holzworth, Mel Fisher, Deo Fisher, Fay Feild, and Rupert Gates. FISHER FAMILY COLLECTION

CHAPTER TWELVE

Pioneering Treasure Hunting for Spanish Galleons: Florida's Treasure Coast

Adventurous thinking, intuition, and physical strength, boyish curiosity and savvy business thinking all combined in Mel Fisher, the man who as much as anyone represented twentieth-century life in the United States and believed in the ideals of democracy that spelled opportunity for all who would recognize and work for their goals. Having served in the US Army in WWII, including being one day plus at Normandy landings, Mel's patriotic, all-American ideals mixed with actual life experiences in postwar times gave him the ability to dream big while calculating the odds before going into action.

My dive shop business was going real good, and I made a lot of money. I did especially well manufacturing and selling gold dredges for use in the rivers in California. They were used to find gold by diving in the creeks and vacuuming out the gold and other minerals, then sorting it out from the sand and rocks.

We had just returned from a ninety-day expedition out to Silver Shoals, and I told Deo that if we'd have stayed a couple more days, we'd have "hit it." We'd just found the stern of a ship, and then it was time to leave.

When we got back to the shop, we had a ping-pong table in there that we threw the mail on. We had a mail-order business going too, and a jobbing business as well as a retail business. This whole ping-pong table was piled high, with mail all over it, after three months. There were letters thrown all over the floor all around the table. My mother, Grace, didn't bother opening any of the mail. She just piled it all up. My mother was taking care of the dive shop while I was gone, and so it was Deo's job to open the mail.

I said, "Honey, do you want to open all that mail, pay all those bills, and cash all those checks? Or do you just want to sell that whole pile of mail unopened, and we'll take a one-year vacation and go treasure hunting?"

She didn't even stop to think. She said, "Let's go!"

I sold that pile of mail to my head instructor for $50,000 without even opening it up to see how much was bills and how much was profit. About a year later I asked him how he came out with that pile of mail. He said he made about $50,000 profit on it.

So I guess I should have let her open the mail and pay the bills. But I sold the business "as is," with unopened mail, and I sold my yacht, the *Golden Doubloon*. I sold my extra two automobiles. Sold my home and everything we had. We paid off all our time payments on everything, cashed out, and got our equity after paying off all our bills.

I got four or five other guys to do the same thing.

Their names were Rupert "Rupe" Gates, Walter "Walt" Holzworth, and Demostines "Mo" Molinar, joined soon by Fay Feild and Richard "Dick" Williams.

It was the spring of 1963 when I retired and went treasure hunting.

We came as a group to Florida in 1963. A guy at Vero Beach first showed me a Spanish shipwreck. We moved there just because it was close to that galleon—close to "our" treasure ship. Vero Beach was a nice little town. That's where the tropics begin, when you're driving south. A tropical atmosphere, which seemed pleasant, with a little jungle all around.

We drove across the country from California to Florida in a caravan. We had some trailers and hauled all our equipment across. Took a boat with us. Finally, we got to Vero Beach, Florida.

It was sure good to see the ocean after all that driving. We were all standing on the beach there, looking out at the ocean.

I saw a lifeguard, went down, and asked him, "Hey, you know where there are any Spanish galleons around here?" Just in a joking manner was how I put it.

His reply was something I couldn't believe. He said, "Yeah. There's one right down there. About a quarter of a mile." I said, "You've got to be kidding!" He said, "Yeah, there is one. I go diving there every morning—to catch lobsters underneath the anchors and the cannons."

I said, "Well, you mind showing me where it is?" He said, "If you promise not to mess with my lobsters and leave the cannons and anchors there so they can hide under them." I said, "OK. You've got a deal." He showed me the location. Sure enough, it was a Spanish galleon that had been sitting right there; there was no wooden ship, but there were cannons and anchors. There were four great big anchors. One of them was about twenty feet long, with a great big, huge ring on it.

Deo and I decided to buy a house right there, near that wreck in Vero Beach, and we did.

We found a house, made a down payment, and moved in. We lived there more than four years, but we never did go out and work on that wreck that we'd found the first day we were there. The problem was it was about fifteen miles to where you could get out to the ocean with a boat, at Fort Pierce, Florida. We parked our big salvage boat down the Florida coast at Fort Pierce, and we'd drive down there every morning. We'd get on our boat and go out through the Fort Pierce Inlet.

The first galleon we worked on was just about a quarter of a mile north of the Fort Pierce Inlet. That kept us busy for quite a while. The first wreck that we started working on was shown to me by Kip Wagner. I was fifty-fifty partners with him. I have only once ever done a handshake deal with anyone. That deal was with Kip

Wagner, when I started into the treasure-hunting business. Since then, I have done some deals first on a cocktail napkin, but most of them are just ordinary partnership deals. That first shipwreck I salvaged with Wagner was off of Humiston Park, Florida. We also swam back and forth to work there sometimes. We called that the "Wedge Wreck," because the first thing we found was a silver wedge. It looked about like a piece of chocolate cake with frosting on it. I found it with the metal detector that Fay Feild had built, which discriminated nonferrous from ferrous metals. The detector said there was something nonferrous in there, and it looked about like a ball, a ball of coral about eight inches in diameter. It looked more like a rock or ballast stone. But I hammered on it with a sledgehammer, and it broke apart. There was a silver wedge inside. Because of my silver find, we called that the "Wedge Wreck." We also found a few silver pieces of eight and some Kangxi china and olive jars and things.

But we found no vast amount of treasure, just enough to tease you a little bit and keep you going. At that time, I didn't realize how scattered out Spanish galleons could be. We just worked right around that immediate area where the ballast pile was. There were a few timbers there too. We moved all the ballast stones over to one side. We cleaned everything up there, but we never did hit any treasure.

This was part of one of a fleet of eleven ships that sank and became known as the 1715 Spanish Plate Fleet, lost in that year. We guessed that ship was called the *Urca de Lima*, or that's what Kip Wagner thought it was. The reason was that it appeared that the area where we found the wreck had at one time, about 250 years earlier, been more or less in the middle of an inlet, going in from the ocean to the Indian River. It appeared that since that time, the inlet had closed up, and man had made what is now Fort Pierce Inlet, about a quarter of a mile south of there. Also, in old documents somewhere, it mentions a wreck in the mouth of the inlet. So Kip Wagner figured that was the *Urca de Lima*, lost in 1715.

***

Taffi: A brief history of 1715 wreck sites by locations/names. No one has been able to prove for sure which wreck site is which ship of the 1715 Fleet, it is all really speculation, so landmarks were used to name the wrecks until such time as it can be determined. Until now, [September 2021] no proof exists.

The beach/park one-quarter mile north of Fort Pierce Inlet is [Claude] Pepper Park, and the wreck site is called the "Wedge Wreck." Where the silver wedge was found, some people refer to this as the "Pepper Park Wreck," and many salvors believe the State of Florida has erroneously labeled it the *Urca de Lima* (1715) in all of their literature. This park itself was a landmark, because it was the only cluster of many tall pine trees just north of the only group of tall condos just north of Fort Pierce Inlet at that time.

Humiston Beach Park is in Vero Beach, about eleven miles further north from Pepper Park. This is near the "Riomar Wreck," just offshore from the Riomar Golf Course that is visible as a landmark from sea; a couple beautiful gold crosses were found here.

"Sandy Point Wreck" is in between the "Riomar Wreck" and the "Wedge Wreck," at South Beach Park in Vero. It is called "Sandy Point Wreck" because the beach is white and sandy and juts out into a point in the ocean, another landmark visible from sea.

The "Cabin Wreck" is the northernmost wreck positively identified as a 1715 wreck to date. It is offshore of where Kip Wagner's weekend cabin was/is, and is about ten miles north of Vero Beach, about two miles south of the Sebastian Inlet. At that time, it was the *only* cabin for miles and a very good landmark.

"Corrigan's Wreck" is just south of Wabasso Beach Park, in between the "Cabin Wreck" and "Riomar Wreck." There were only two cabins on the beach here, one that belonged to the local Corrigan family—hence the landmark and site name. The other cabin, slightly north, was painted green, and the 1618 shipwreck, the *San Martin,* was found offshore of there. Before that shipwreck [*San Martin*] was identified, it was referred to as the "Green Cabin Wreck."

"Douglass Beach Wreck" is a couple miles south of the Fort Pierce Inlet. This wreck has produced the most gold.

Interspersed with the known 1715 shipwreck sites, we have found several other wrecks from other centuries, such as the *Spring of Whitby* [1824], the "1810 Wreck," the *San Martin* [1618], and more.

***

Mel resumes: Then we started working on a shipwreck about four miles south of the Fort Pierce Inlet. It was very convenient, and you didn't have to go very far. Our boat went very slow—the *Dee-Gee,* we called it. If we went up to Vero Beach, it would take us most of the day to get there. Then we wouldn't be able to do any diving and get back before dark. We were finding plenty of gold down there at Fort Pierce, anyway.

In the ocean, the first piece of gold I found was off Vero Beach, Florida, on what became known as the "Sandy Point Wreck."

We had just found our first chest full of silver "pieces of eight." They were all worn out from the wave action, just very thin coins.

I had something invented by Rupe Gates, one of my men, that was like a pistol with a three-way valve. You could push the trigger one way, and it would blow sand out of a crevice underwater. You'd flip it another way, and it would reverse and slurp up anything in the crevice into a little bag, so you could get gold dust. There was another valve—one would blow, one would slurp, and I guess the other one was neutral. I was using that thing, and I saw a glint of gold on edge.

It reminded me of the late 1940s or early 1950s, when I was in the river out in California looking for gold. There I was slurping up gold dust and mercury, and I found a coin on the edge in a crevice. It was a dime. We were way down in a canyon where there were sheer cliffs on each side of the creek. Nobody had been there for a hundred years, and I found this dime way down there, and still on its edge. I looked at the date on it—1850. It must have been in the gold rush days in California, the days of the '49ers.

A century later, I found it as it was left. The same thing—with about a 250-year time span—happened in 1964 offshore from Vero Beach, only this time it was gold.

This time what I discovered was a gold coin on edge. I picked it out of the crack. It was a two-escudo gold coin. I bought it—we had a corporation by then and a group of guys who shared in everything—and this was the first gold coin I had ever found.

Since it was the first gold I had ever found in the ocean, I paid the group $700 for that coin. They were selling for $200 or something like that, but I bought it for $700. Now they're selling for $2,000 and more. Inflation.

I had that coin mounted on a ring, and I think I've still got the ring sitting around somewhere. I haven't worn it for quite a while. I got fiberglass in my fingers when I was a kid, installing fiberglass in the attics of homes for insulation. The fiberglass is still in my skin where I had a ring on. When I put a ring on now, it irritates me. I don't wear the ring, but it's special to have it.

***

What we called a "mailbox" is one of the keys to the success of our treasure hunting. Talk about a successful invention—that was it!

Originally, I wrote a letter to Fay Feild, who was in California at the time, and told him that the water was very murky down there, that I was talking to the other guys, also on the telephone, about building something to make the clear water go down, to make the water clear. He agreed with me and told me he thought it would work.

Then I told the other guys what Fay said, but they didn't agree. So I didn't argue with them. I just went down the next night and started building one.

The first one I built looked exactly like one of these big blue mailboxes that sits on the corner all over the country.

Dick Williams came down about 12 o'clock and asked me what in the hell I was doing down there at midnight. I said, "Welding this mailbox, and it doesn't look like one." He told me I was a lousy welder. I said, "I know. I took a course at Purdue University. I know this isn't good welding. But this is difficult to do because the metal is so thin. I never had sheet metal material this thin in welding classes at Purdue University. I had angle iron and good conditions."

Dick said, "Well, let me do it. I'm a pretty good welder." So about midnight he took over, and was welding for about three hours. We got the thing about halfway built. I was holding the pieces for him, and he was welding it together.

Next morning, we showed it to Walt and Rupe. They said, "We'll help you too." So they joined in. Soon they all helped finish it. The day after that was when we tried it out.

The first "mailbox" tryout was on April 1, 1964.

It was April Fool's Day, but what we found that day was no "fool's gold." It was real treasure!

Originally we tried the "mailbox" out on what was

called the "Douglass Beach Wreck."

On that April Fool's Day, we had been working most of the day without any great finds. But in the afternoon, we decided to try out the "mailbox" there because I had found a silver piece of eight earlier.

I wasn't using an airlift then, I was using a "Braille system," with an underwater gold dredge from California that I'd made myself. It was so murky that we had to just feel around. I found an old Spanish piece of eight. I felt the cross known as the "Cross of Jerusalem" on that coin with my thumb.

That afternoon we went back to the exact same spot, put the "mailbox" on it, and pushed the clear water from the surface downward.

The depth was only about fifteen feet. So we turned the engine on very slowly, and the "mailbox" worked beautifully.

The water was pouring in, washing away all the sand and mud. Soon we started uncovering bedrock on the bottom, and there were gold doubloons all over the place!

Once you see the ocean bottom covered with gold coins, you never forget it!

At the time, Mo Molinar and I were all alone diving. Dick Williams, Rupe Gates, and Walt Holzworth were up on deck. We signaled them and went back down again.

The other guys were trying to get all their diving equipment on. Mo found a gold disc.

I think he was teasing me and asked, "Is this brass?" We laughed as though that was the first time he ever asked me if something was brass. That was because before, he always asked me if it was gold, and it was always brass. Now, Mo thinks I'm just teasing him with that recall, and maybe he's right.

A storm came up suddenly that same day. After we found gold, everybody else went into the water. We found two heavy gold discs.

Then everybody was in the water. There was nobody up on the boat. But all the engines were going. The main engine was going, the compressor engine was going. All the engines were going, and the air compressor, and the gold dredge. But nobody was up above.

I brought up a whole bunch of gold coins. I couldn't hold any more gold coins.

Then I saw this tornado coming. Real dark, ominous looking. It looked like that tornado was coming right at us.

I went down and signaled for everybody to come up. A couple of the guys came to the surface. I had to get them to go down and get the others to come up. Soon all the other guys surfaced with all the gold. Thirteen hundred gold coins!

The tornado actually hit us and was so severe that we cut the lines on the stern, because we were in real shallow and dangerous water.

We had to get the hell out of there. The rain would hit your eyeballs and blind you. I put a face mask on to protect my eyes so I could see a little bit, but it was very blurry, because the rain was hitting so hard. I could see only a little, but at least it didn't hurt my eyes.

I crawled out to the bow of the boat on my hands and knees because the wind was blowing so hard—and the big waves would have knocked me overboard—and I pulled up the anchor line.

We started heading out to sea—we thought. We weren't even sure which way was out to sea, it was raining so hard. We thought we were headed seaward, but the fathometer kept getting shallower.

Then we thought we were going the wrong way, so we stopped, started checking the compass, and checking the wind, the depth of the water, and started to head the way the compass pointed. We went that way—which was east.

I doubt that our lives were at stake that day. We

probably would have swum to shore or something. We were very close to shore. We were just afraid the ship was going to be blown backwards, and it seemed that it was, because we thought we were heading out to sea, yet the water kept getting shallower. Maybe we were being blown backward by the tornado from the direction we wanted to go—which would have made the water deeper.

The water got shallower, so the wind was so powerful it was blowing us backwards against the prop wash of the engines.

Yes, the treasure was just sitting on the deck. We weren't even worried about it. We were worried about getting out to sea, away from the dangerous reefs and the shallow water. About fifteen minutes later the tornado was gone.

The sun came out and the ocean got really flat, calm, and beautiful. It was just a typical, warm, beautiful day in Florida.

All this happened within half an hour. I had some thoughts of what conditions were like when those galleons sank in 1715. But excitement took over, because what occurred was an epic event.

What we did was to place the gold doubloons on my diving suit and take pictures of them.

I'm sure the storm that day was a full-blown tornado. It was too big for a waterspout. It was a *big* one! A waterspout is a smaller tornado compared to what we used to experience on land.

After the weather calmed, we put all thirteen hundred gold coins on my diving suit on the deck.

During the storm the coins were just laying on the deck. They didn't blow off.

With the power of the storm, some of the guys said, "Well, maybe this is the curse of the treasure, or something." I said, "No, that's a bunch of baloney. It's a beautiful, sunny Florida day, and it's just that a tornado went by, that's all."

Today's the Day!

On that second tryout day, we went to check out an "anomaly" recording on our magnetometer, or a "hit," indicating the presence of ferrous metal, such as iron ship's nails, on the sea bottom, that we had gotten straight out off the Fort Pierce Inlet, about a half mile out.

We dropped our new, metal, elbow-shaped "mailbox" down on its frame, outboard of the propeller wash off the stern, and we turned the engine on. Our successful idea was to bend or deflect the force of the prop wash downward to the search area on the bottom. The conditions were such that day that the top ten feet of the water was crystal clear. From there down it was pure mud.

The water was about fifty feet deep. We'd go down about ten feet, and it would get very, very muddy and dark, and you couldn't see anything.

Then we turned on the "mailboxes," and the propellers carried all the clear water down, in a clear column moving downward. I got in the water and hung onto the bottom of a "mailbox." I let go, and it pushed me down very rapidly in this column of clear water, going straight down.

I could see myself landing on the deck of a huge barge, a shipwreck. We could see winches, and diesel engines.

At first, I could only see about ten feet all around me. But after a column of clear water kept coming down, it gradually made a big bubble that was growing bigger and bigger and bigger. This bubble was all clear water being brought down from the surface. It spread out all over the whole shipwreck.

After I had been below about five minutes, with so many millions of gallons of clear water coming down into that bubble, I could see the entire deck there. I went around looking at everything. It was very obvious the shipwreck was all modern.

It was not a Spanish galleon. It was not the target we were looking for. So we came up, pulled anchor, and moved away. That was the second time we tried our "mailbox" invention out, but we also wanted to see what the wreck was. We thought it was a treasure ship.

The boat we were using, *Dee-Gee*, had what I call a horrible power plant. I think it was a Cummins diesel, a war-surplus engine. They didn't have any modern-day factory supplies or parts. There was nobody who knew how to repair those engines or work on them.

When something went wrong with our engine, we had to drive down to Miami and go to a war-surplus depot to scrounge around for war-surplus parts and engines. We found out that there were about fifteen models, and that gaskets from one model wouldn't work on another model. Parts from one model wouldn't work on parts for another model. It was just a horrible mess trying to repair one of those diesel engines. I think it was about 80 horsepower.

But the "mailbox" was about a million times better than using an eight-inch gold dredge or airlift, and about a million times better than fanning with your hand.

It really was excellent. Compared with dredging, we could do about a month's work in one day. So one offset the other.

About four or four-and-a-half years after we moved to Florida, we went to dive at "Douglass Beach Wreck" south of Fort Pierce. It was really muddy for diving. Water was coming out of the Fort Pierce Inlet heading south, and that just made it so that you couldn't see anything at all.

So I told the guys, "Why don't we go on up to Vero Beach and dig one hole on that wreck up there?" The guys said, "Oh, by the time we get there it'll be dark. Let's go somewhere else."

I kept saying, "Aw, c'mon, let's go." So they finally decided, "OK, let's go up there."

We set up off Vero Beach. The first hole we dug, we couldn't believe it. A gold cross came up. Weighed about half a pound.

Heavy-duty thing, with studs sticking out all over it. There were 120 little gold studs sticking out of it. Nine of the studs had pearls on them. Evidently there had been 120 pearls on that cross.

Then we dug another hole and found another crucifix. This one had a gold statue of Christ fixed to a golden cross with gold nails—three gold nails. That was a beautiful thing.

Next, we found a six-pound gold disc.

Then the air compressor quit.

My son Kim was quite young then—about ten or eleven years—and he wanted to go down and find some gold. He didn't have any air. So he kept bugging me, asking if it was all right if he would just free dive and go down. I was afraid he might go down there, come up and hit his head on the boat. But finally I said, "OK, go ahead."

He went down and he didn't come up. He stayed down, and down, and down. It seemed like four or five minutes.

I put on my fins and mask, and was just getting ready to jump in, go down and look for him, when up he came. In his hands he had seven gold doubloons that he'd found down there in one dive. Kim just held his breath for a long time because he was so excited at finding all that treasure. That turned out to be a very good wreck.

A little later we found a beautiful, teardrop-shaped emerald there. We just found the match to it in the mid-1980s. Evidently it had been a matched pair of teardrop emeralds. I think that first one I sold for $7,000 without having it appraised or weighed or anything. This last one, I think, went for $24,000.

We called that the "Riomar Wreck," because it was located off the Riomar Golf Course at Vero Beach, in the ocean right out in front of the golf course.

A kind of Mother Nature's fish trap is right there. The reef starts at the shore and goes out on an angle to the south-southeast. The reef makes a "V," and as the fish are swimming up the coast in a northerly direction, they all, more or less, get trapped in that big "V," and they just seem to circle and mill around in there.

The sharks like to come in and tear through there about dawn and dusk. It's easier for them to have dinner, because the fish haven't got but one direction to swim to get away. They've got the shore on the one side and the reef on the other side, and they're trapped in there. The only problem was that we had to swim through there every morning and night to get to work and get home.

We had set up a system where we'd leave our boat there, so we didn't have to make that long trip back to Fort Pierce inlet every day, every morning, and every night. We'd just leave our boat parked out there with one or two guys on it, babysitting, while the other guys could swim in and go home, go to a movie, or sleep in a bed and be with their families.

After a couple of weeks of that, the State of Florida notified me that they would not allow us to swim to work anymore or swim home, because it was too dangerous— the state agent might get eaten up.

With that state decision, we broke down and bought a Boston whaler.

When we were all swimming through the sharks, nobody ever got bit, but we did see them eating in there. Even in the beginning we had a state guy who would go with us when we went out and keep track of everything.

This "no swimming" order was four-and-a-half years later, or even after that—when they made us stop swimming ashore.

I'd been working in the Vero Beach area for about four years diving for the 1715 galleons, and we were doing very well. We brought in many beautiful things.

One year the weather got bad very early, right at the end of August. It was just horribly rough and muddy water up there at Vero Beach, so I decided to come on down to the Keys for the winter season.

I arrived, and I couldn't believe how the water was flat, calm, and clear.

That was about 1967, and I threw a party in Marathon for all of the guys who were treasure hunting. They were just a bunch of guys mainly doing it for a hobby.

At that party they dragged out a book we called "Potter's Treasure Divers Guide" [*The Treasure Diver's Guide*, by John S. Potter Jr.]. We were all going through the book and reading the Florida section about different shipwrecks: "Look at this wreck! It's a two-star wreck." Or a "three-star wreck."

The *Atocha* was a "four-star wreck." That was the best one. These guys were arguing about whether the *Atocha* was off Marathon, or whether it was off Alligator [Reef] Light or Coffin's Patch. Or off all those places.

I decided I'd just check it out. We searched all three of those areas, and it wasn't at any of them.

Then the next year, 1968, I decided we'd go ahead and take about a hundred days and just go all out. We'd search the entire area very thoroughly and meticulously, looking for the *Atocha*.

It wasn't there. We searched all up and down the Matecumbe Keys. Even though a map said the *Atocha* was off the Keys of the Matecumbe, it wasn't there.

We found a lot of other good wrecks in the Middle Florida Keys. We found *Tres Puentes* and the *San Pedro*, the *Animas*, and several other galleon-type shipwrecks, but not the one with the "four stars" on it.

Help in relocating my search for the *Atocha* to the ocean west of Key West and the Marquesas Keys came from a man I had met in Vero Beach named Eugene "Gene" Lyon, later Dr. Lyon. I met Gene in what was passing for church at the time, in a high school gymnasium where we were having church meetings before they started building a church.

Deo and I were in a Bible class, and Gene was running the Bible School. He would be translating the

Bible, and I would put my two cents worth in: "Well, yeah, but you could translate that another way. It could mean this, or it could mean that." We'd get a big debate going.

After Bible class one evening we were having coffee and doughnuts. I got to talking with Gene and found out he could translate old Spanish documents and books as well as the Bible.

I took him home with me right then and there and showed him several old books I had bought in Madrid, Spain. I'd gone to Madrid and gone around to all the secondhand bookstores and bought any book I could find about the Prado [museum] and old treasure.

Then I got them back to the United States, and I couldn't read them.

That night I got Gene to start reading them to me, and it kind of turned him on. He said, "My gosh, I can't believe how many tons of silver, all those emeralds, how much gold and everything were on these ships!"

So he became interested in the *Atocha* too.

I told him I would give him $10,000 and one percent of the treasure if he would research the *Atocha* for me when he was over there in Spain working on his doctoral degree. I recall he was doing his doctoral thesis on something like Spanish history in Florida.

Gene had only been over in Spain about two weeks when I got a letter from him. He had found this old document that mentioned a "Marquis," who was trying to locate and salvage the *Atocha,* and they named an island about thirty miles west of Key West that they used as an early salvage camp base after him.

Instead of answering the letter, Deo and I jumped on a plane and flew to New York. By the next morning, at 9 o'clock Spanish time, we were sitting at the Archive of the Indies in Seville, Spain, on the stairs, waiting for him to come to work.

It was chilly. They don't have any heaters in the archives, and it was wintertime. Gene arrived wearing his heavy "GI" overcoat, stocking cap, long underwear, and mittens, to work in the archives.

We went across the street and had a cup of coffee. Gene told me he had found another document before I arrived, and then we went back over to the Archive of the Indies. They wouldn't let me in, because I didn't have clearance, but he went in and got the document, brought it out, and showed it to me.

I decided that was it. We were going to move all the way down to Key West and go for it.

I knew the *Atocha* would be way out of sight of land, and so I had another bonus in there for Gene if he could pinpoint it within a quarter of a mile. He didn't do that, but at least he got us in the right general area.

Maybe gold was waiting for him on what would become the "Treasure Coast" of Florida. The family had returned from their Caribbean adventures with a new crew member—"Mo"—and new energies. They had found the stern of a ship, and it was time to leave. But Mel just shrugged it off and went home to his ping-pong table of waiting business mail. Then Mel decided something in an instant—did Deo want to just go on another "vacation" treasure hunting? "Let's go," she said. And it happened. Teaming with his likeminded, self-sufficient buddies, Mel sold his business and possessions—yacht, cars, home. And they departed (traveling together in a caravan) for Florida, and the new world of "treasure hunting." As Mel's luck would have it, he called to a lifeguard standing on the first Florida beach they came to and asked if the man knew where any "Spanish galleons" were around there. Yes, he was told, but he had to promise not to bother the guard's fishing spot. The Fishers bought a house nearby, and for other reasons looked elsewhere for their Spanish galleon treasures. The Fishers' daughter Taffi has explained more fully the information on the wrecks of the 1715 Spanish Plate Fleet and has contributed therefore to clarify Mel's information. But here is where he found his first gold, a two-escudo gold coin on its edge. And here he saw the ocean bottom carpeted with gold Spanish coins. With the help of inventions like a "mailbox" and a refined proton magnetometer, the group did find treasure in searches that continue to this day. But Mel tired of fighting "the state" and the changing weather conditions, and at the same time his inner "intuitive" feelings were lighting up over research in Spain's Archive of the Indies, where a man he met in church in Vero Beach was at work on his own kind of studies.

Conch Republic King Mel Fisher was originally voted into office in the 1980s, when Key West "seceded" from the USA in response to roadblocks set up during the Mariel Boatlift affair. The annual elections for king are held for charitable purposes, but twenty-four years after his passing, Fisher retains the honorary title in perpetuity. PAT CLYNE PHOTO

CHAPTER THIRTEEN

Quest for the *Atocha*: Dare to Dream Big

The greatest adventure lay ahead, and had already begun, but not yet in the real locations where Royal Guard ships of the 1622 fleet were lost. This was in the time before GPS and LORAN *(long range navigation)*, and unlike in Vero Beach, there was no land in site at the Atocha search area, no landmarks from which to gauge one's location. And so, the quest of years would take Mel Fisher longer than the "one hundred days" he usually anticipated. More elusive than sirens, the "Big A" called. Challenges from government lay ahead that could seem as bitingly merciless as those of the actual sea quest. But he was as hardy and enduring as the country and its "hard work" values. An amazing combination of dreamer, adventurer, and shrewd businessman, he wanted to "finish the job" and be rewarded. "Today's the day!" would be true every day for years, and also, of course, for the rest of his life.

We all packed up and headed down to Key West. We knew we were going to be doing some searching, probably west of the Marquesas. Before that I had figured that I could find the *Atocha* in the hundred days that I had taken in our Middle Keys search. But I couldn't, so I began to think that maybe it was going to take six months to do it. First, we thought maybe we could do it in the winter season, but we didn't.

I decided to just stay there until we found it and forget about mainland East Coast Florida and Vero Beach, where the state had given us a hard time with the 1715 wrecks. They had so many new rules and regulations about them owning the treasure—you just couldn't run the business.

We sold out our interest to the Real Eight Company and in 1969 started hunting for the *Atocha* full time. We searched back and forth for a year. By then we hadn't found it, but decided to go another year.

At the end of the second year, in June of 1971, we found the first sign of it—one lead ball. One lead musket ball. I personally found it, fanned a little, and found another. I came up and told the crew, "This is it." I told them, "Dig for another five minutes." They dug about five minutes and found about six more balls, pottery, and an olive jar there—which indicated that it was Spanish for sure, and the right "circa"—right around 1622. The pottery was heavier than the pottery from 1715 and 1733.

To start our search for the *Atocha*, in 1969, we went first to the site of the *Valbanera*. We never dreamed that we would be going back there to put up a treasure hunting tower. That's where Deo and I had made the movie *The Other End of the Line* for Voit Rubber Company. We were honeymooning and on a working vacation—right on top of where we'd later start our *Atocha* search. Amazing.

In 1985, after we finally found the "main pile" of the *Atocha*, Deo—I don't know how she found out—but she noticed one of the charts, with some bottom readings, and the start of our search at the *Valbanera* was the same date as her birthday! Boy!

With the discovery of musket balls, I knew intuitively it was the *Atocha*. But with my logical mind, I wasn't sure it wasn't the *Margarita*, her sister treasure galleon, because we weren't sure what a "brazza" was. We knew what depths the Spanish said the two ships had been wrecked in, but we didn't know the exact meaning of a term those early Spanish used—a "brazo." That means an "arm" of water, and some of us thought that people back then would measure an "arm" of rope from elbow to fingertip, and that would be an "arm" of rope, or "brazo."

Others would go from shoulder to fingertip to measure the rope. But I knew it had to be either the *Margarita* or the *Atocha*, one or the other, because one was sunk in three "arms" of water, and the other was in ten "arms" of water. This was in arms "arms," so it was more logical that it was the *Margarita*. But it didn't matter, because we knew that one league away from there would be the other one, the sister ship. Also, we had actual readings indicating sea bottom "anomalies" or "hits" one league away in both directions from the *Atocha*. There were two more wrecks, so we thought had found both of them, regardless of which one it was. We just blissfully kept digging to try to determine which treasure galleon wreck it was.

The next thing we found was a galleon anchor. After dusting away the sands from the anchor, we found next to it something that looked like a stack of poker chips about six inches high, but askew or cockeyed. There were nineteen coins stuck together. We carefully opened them up with some dilute muriatic acid and found a dated silver coin—the date was 1619. We were almost certain then that we had either the *Atocha* or the *Margarita*, so we celebrated on that one.

That was about the time I met Don Kincaid, and we hired him as a photographer to work with us. The first day out after Don joined us, we dug a hole in the Quicksands area, and there was something like an anthill down in the sand bottom. He went down to take a picture of me, and he saw a chain—a gold chain—there. Don thought first that we had thrown it in to trick him. He started pulling it out and it got bigger and bigger. When Don got up to the top, he finally realized that gold chain was for real—it was the real thing! He was so excited he not only forgot to take a picture underwater, but he forgot to take a picture of the chain or himself or anything! Everybody was just celebrating. We got on the radio. Chet Alexander, a salvage master and good friend, was in the neighborhood. He came out with about forty people, and several other people came to where we were working at sea. We had a big celebration right out there on the ocean with that gold chain. We found a few gold coins too. A short while later, we found a couple gold bars right near there. So we knew we were onto something good, no matter which shipwreck it was.

It had been the spring of 1969 when I decided to launch our search for the *Atocha* about thirty miles out of Key West, near the Marquesas Keys, at the site of the same shipwreck where Deo and I had been on our honeymoon. We built a theodolite tower on top of the overturned sunken hull of the *Valbanera* wreck. That wrecked ship had its own sad history. A load of women passengers were among those aboard that were refused entry to Havana, and the ship was continuing to Key West with a hurricane coming on; the ship was ultimately wrecked there, with everyone aboard killed.

The day we started to build the tower we didn't need to use metal detectors when we got to the *Valbanera* site. We could see it a block away, a big dark spot on the west end of the Quicksands area. There was a ripple of water over it from the high tide that was going by. We had brought along a couple of "burning bars," which are pieces of pipe with magnesium inside. We went down and burned four holes through the steel hull of *Valbanera*. When you light up a "burning bar," you light it with a cutting torch. That starts the magnesium burning, and you have pure oxygen going through the pipe. It makes a big ball of fire about six inches in diameter. A "burning bar" keeps burning when you go underwater, and it makes a lot of bubbles. It's pretty spectacular. When you get to a hull, you just press the end of it against the steel, and it's so hot that it burns a hole right through the steel. After we cut the holes, we went underneath the ship—which was upside down—and entered the decks. We went down some stairs that were going up, and down a hall, through a doorway. We went down a stairway to the next deck—going upwards. There were all kinds of shadows moving in there, probably grouper and jewfish. We were using underwater lights and got into the engine room.

Finally, we saw some shafts of light coming down into the total darkness. I hammered on the bottom. I think it was a fellow named Gino who was on the outside, responded with a bang. I had the bolts with me, and I put washers on them and then pushed the bolts up through the holes—one at a time. He would put the nut on from the outside with the washer. Now we had somewhere to start to build our "Eiffel Tower." We built that tower out of angle irons, until it stuck up above the water, about ten feet high. Then we tried it out with a theodolite, which is a survey instrument for measuring angles, and a communication radio to navigate by. But we found the tower at first was a little shaky, so it wasn't very accurate. We had to run four cables in different directions to it to hold it steady.

That first search day after we'd built the tower, I told the crew, "Today's the day, men! I know there's big squalls all around. And it's really rough. But with Gene Lyon's pinpointing the area where he thinks the *Atocha* went down, we very well could find it today. It's a big, powerful ocean out there. It takes men and ships. But we're gonna reverse things, find this ship, recover its treasures, and let everybody in the world look at it!"

Then we set up a search pattern, and the *Virgalona* headed out from the *Valbanera* site for "Tail End Buoy," which we were going to use as the other end of our baseline. This was to be a baseline from the *Valbanera* shipwreck, on which we had constructed our theodolite tower, and the Tail End Buoy, which is a distance of about seven miles. The boat headed out, and after about three miles, began disappearing and reappearing from sight on the theodolite, because it was going over the horizon.

So I told the guys to take a break, and put up a long cane fishing pole. I took one of the black plastic bags and stuffed it full of newspapers, and tied it on top of the fishing pole, then I tied the fishing pole to the antenna so that after the boat went over the horizon, I could still see that big black ball floating in the sky. And that way I could keep them on course heading out toward Tail End Buoy.

Sometimes they'd get ten or twenty feet off to the west, or ten or twenty feet off toward the east, so I'd just talk them back. I'd say, "ten west, nine, eight, seven, west, five west, three, two, on course." And they'd keep heading for Tail End Buoy, dragging Fay Feild's underwater proton magnetometer to detect iron.

Once the fathometer on the *Virgalona* showed they had passed the edge of the reef and dropped off into the Gulf Stream deep water, they made a U-turn and came back at me. I'd move the theodolite over a couple of seconds on the compass and guide them back toward the *Valbanera*, where I had my tower. This way, they were searching the whole area like the spokes of a giant wheel out from the tower. Back and forth.

We did get quite a few readings on the New Ground–Quicksands area, near our first tower location, but we didn't check those out, because our information from the archives said the *Atocha* should be in fifty or sixty feet of water. Maybe one of these days I'll go back out and check those anomalies that we originally located, since they could mean one or more of the sister ships that went down the same night.

At the time, I guided my crew back and forth for about three or four hours. The squalls kept getting more ominous, and the winds kept getting higher. Sometimes a big squall would go between me and the *Virgalona*, and I couldn't see them. So they had to stop and wait for the squall to move by. The *Virgalona* was engulfed in the middle of one of them. They told me on the radio it was like a miniature tornado, blowing things off the boat.

But after it passed, we continued on the search. I looked around, and while the boat was turning around, I could see about sixty or seventy squalls in all directions. I'd never seen that many squalls all at once before. It was kind of frightening.

A waterspout headed for me, and I was wondering if the tower would hold up if it hit us, hit me. Fortunately, it went on by, off to the side. But a big squall did engulf me, with winds about fifty miles an hour. So I had to shut down the radio and hang on for dear life to keep from getting blown overboard. I got thoroughly soaked and was unprepared to keep my logbooks dry.

I learned on the radio a couple of days later that this was the beginning of a hurricane named "Celia," which formed south of Cuba and hit the Gulf of Mexico, turning into a Category 3 by the time it hit the coast of Texas with more than hundred-mile-an-hour winds and a bad flood. It really didn't matter about the logbook, though, because they hadn't yet found any anomalies in the proper depth of water to check out to see if it was the "Big A," the *Atocha*, we were looking for. That logbook got wet and ruined, so I threw it away. That was just the first day of our hunt out at sea. So I told the guys, "Well, I figured we could find it and recover it in about six weeks, but considering the storms and the big powerful ocean, it might take us a little longer. Maybe tomorrow will be the day!"

We continued searching down the "spokes" of that giant "wheel," gradually working toward the east for a couple of months—until we could no longer see the boat. Then we decided we would have to move our tower—which was the hub of the "wheel"—to Cosgrove Shoal Light. That lighthouse is about twenty miles east of the *Valbanera*, and about seven miles south of the Marquesas Keys. It stands on the edge of the Gulf Stream, where the bottom comes up rapidly, and there is a ten-foot shallow reef that could have been the reef that the *Atocha* struck. There we found several anomalies along that outer reef near the drop-off. One was a Civil War ship, which I may go back and dig on someday. Another was an extinct lighthouse that had been blown over and destroyed by the ocean, by the powerful ocean! Also, we found several more modern shipwrecks.

But I'm thinking of that day when we started our search, and I was on this tower, way out of sight of land there, all by myself, and I could see squalls in all directions. As it happened, this was the first time I'd ever been in the eye of a hurricane as it was forming. The thing started right there on the *Valbanera* spot where that ship had had its disaster back in 1929.

Our converted treasure-hunting boat, *Virgalona*, was making runs back and forth under my guidance. I was talking to them on the radio, and I was telling them, "ten feet left," and, "eight left," "seven left," "five left," until they got on zero, and I'd tell them, "straight ahead." If they got off to the left, I'd tell them to "go right five feet," or "ten feet," until they got on zero.

They disappeared into one of those squalls of rain that was coming down very hard. So we took a break for a while.

But the wind kept getting stronger and stronger and stronger. Soon it was blowing beyond gale force, up to about fifty miles an hour, in a hurry. The squalls were getting thicker. There were lots more of them all around me. Quickly it became one big storm.

The crew was out of sight. I couldn't see the *Virgalona*, and they couldn't see me. And I was hanging on for dear life with all that wind and rain out there. I was hanging on to the angle iron railing we had around it. Finally, they found me. I jumped off, and we headed for the Marquesas—where the palm tree was. They picked me up, but we had a rough trip going back to the Marquesas.

I could imagine if you were on deck of the *Atocha* trying to hang on. It would have seemed almost impossible. I guess that's why most of them were down below. Or those that were up, two or three that were up topside, they were tied down. I remember I was thinking about that, thinking how it must have been back then.

That storm went on down to Texas and hit there with hurricane force, giving them flooding and a lot of damage. But in Florida, I was just out there hanging on. The waves didn't get high enough at that point to be coming up over the platform, because we had about a ten-foot height over the water. But it was close. If the waves would have gotten much bigger, then I would have probably gotten swept overboard, or the tower would have been knocked over. Fortunately, the boat got to me. They saw me between the rainstorms and picked me up.

It was ominous in the first place when we started. It was spooky-looking weather. It just kept getting worse and worse. We didn't know that a hurricane was coming. I think this hurricane was spawned right where we were—right on the side of the *Valbanera*. That would be kind of unusual, I know. Most usually, hurricanes start way over by Africa and come across the ocean.

But I have seen a couple of others start out here since then during the last twenty years. Several other hurricanes have started right here and then went over and hit in Louisiana or Texas.

A few days later I decided to search in the opposite direction from where Gene Lyon told me to look, because we didn't find the *Atocha* where he said he thought it was. I saw a marking on a local chart that said "Rock Pile," and I thought, "There are no rocks out here, so if there is a rock pile, it must be ballast stones," which meant an old shipwreck.

We searched the area where it said "Rock Pile" and still didn't get any magnetometer anomalies. I thought the pile might be that of the *Margarita*, which sank in three "arms" or, we believed, eighteen feet of water.

Much later, in 1980, we found about half of the *Margarita*, which had been scattered for about five miles. We still have to find the other half of the *Margarita*, which was described in the archives as being to the east quite a ways.

We have found a scattered underwater "trail" going to the northwest. This scattered trail goes into a gigantic sandbar, which has deep water on each side of it. About twenty feet on one side and thirty-five feet on the other side. In this deep sandbar, we've got several anomalies showing as "hits" with a magnetometer, but we have never had a boat capable of getting through all that sand. We need a big vessel to "dust out" these anomalies.

Perhaps that sand pile will be the missing half of the *Margarita*. The documentation said she broke in two. Duncan Mathewson, the marine archaeologist, believes that the *Margarita* section that we located in 1980 was part of the side near the stern, a section of the side of the ship, the side of the hull, near the stern.

We still have not found the keel of the *Margarita* or the *Atocha*. With all the amazing finds, in 1986, we were still missing more than forty-eight thousand manifested coins from the *Atocha*, 264 manifested silver bars, 111 gold bars, eight bronze cannons, as well as the items not manifested, such as gold chains, gold coins, emeralds, and personal belongings of the wealthy passengers. We were also missing about half of the manifested objects on the *Margarita*, so there is a lot more treasure to find!

Even with what the Spanish salvaged off the *Margarita*, she's still got some spectacular secrets. There's still even some bronze cannons missing from the *Margarita*. We're still missing more than eighty thousand manifested silver pieces of eight, and 169 silver ingots, four bronze cannons, and twenty-two copper ingots, as well as an unknown quantity of silver biscuits, gold bars, gold chains, gold coins, emeralds, and jewelry and other personal effects of the wealthy passengers.

For me, the greatest moment of the *Atocha* hunt was finding the two round lead musket balls, because we had already been searching for two and a half years. In an article for *National Geographic* magazine, Gene Lyon recalled that, on June 1, 1971, I had "dived and found the first signs of a sunken Spanish ship—some ceramic shards and a single lead musket ball." He says that two weeks later, a diver located the ring and buried shank of a huge anchor. Later, a blackened silver coin came up, and then Don Kincaid discovered the gold chain. That's pretty accurate.

Normally we didn't dig on the shallower waters, because we weren't going after the *Margarita*. We thought that we might have located the *Margarita*, and that is where we finally worked on it. We knew we thought we had found it, but we didn't want to work on it then.

We wanted to go for the *Atocha* and try not to get sidetracked with all these other shipwrecks we found. That day I found the musket balls, we had completed all of the search and survey that we could in deep water, in fifty to sixty feet of water, and we had gone full circuit and completed searching the entire area of deeper water from Rebecca Shoals to Key West.

We had failed to find the *Atocha*.

That day I decided to start checking anomalies in the shallower water, where it is about twenty-two feet deep, to see if we could find the *Margarita*—which was said to be in twenty-two to eighteen feet. The first anomaly I dug on, I found the musket balls. I just had them dig lightly with the "mailboxes," just gently dusting the sand away. They dusted away about six inches of sand, and I found two lead musket balls!

I got all excited, because after searching for two years, hundreds of thousands of miles, and finding thousands of modern objects, we had finally found something that appeared to be made a long time ago and was obviously a musket ball made of lead.

Two musket balls made of lead.

I came up on the dive ladder, showed the balls, and told the crew that, "This is it! Today's the day!"

Somebody answered, "This is what?"

For some reason instead of saying it was the *Margarita*, which it would seem because of the depth of the water, I said, "This is the *Atocha!*"

The guy said, "It looks like two lead balls to me!"

I had them dust another five or ten minutes, and I stayed right in the hole, right underneath the down current of the "mailboxes," to make sure I didn't miss anything.

This is extremely difficult to do, because the water current is blowing you away. I saw six more lead musket balls, and then I watched an olive jar neck uncover. It had a cork still in the neck.

I came up with the six balls and the olive jar neck, and I could tell from the shape of the olive jar neck that it was Spanish, circa 1622. Then we all got real excited.

We dug down deeper in the sand. It didn't seem to have any bottom. It was just underwater sand dunes, which they call the "Quicksands," and it seemed as though it really was quicksand. During that year I don't think we ever did get down to the bedrock through the sand.

But we found the anomaly that had originally indicated that we should dig there—and it was three intact iron barrel hoops. Evidently the barrel had been long since devoured by teredo worms. The "mag hit" was on the metal of the three iron hoops.

So another boat we were using, *Holly's Folly*, surveyed more intensely in that area and got a good reading on the galleon anchor of the *Atocha*.

I believe that was the stern anchor, because it was a smaller size than the bow anchors. I don't think they ever threw that anchor. I believe it stayed with the ship—was lashed to the ship. Then we dug out the anchor. We decided to keep digging a huge hole where the anchor was. There I found a stack of coins that were stuck together like a stack of poker chips that had been bumped slightly to one side, so that it was a curved stack of coins.

I think it was about a dozen coins. We cleaned them right then and there to try to confirm the nationality and age of the ship.

We broke out our bottle of champagne to celebrate

because—sure enough—one of the coins had a date of 1619 on it and bore the crest of Philip II of Spain. It was minted in Potosí, Peru, which I guess is now Bolivia, and we knew we either had the *Atocha* or the *Margarita*. We weren't sure which.

During our first two years of searching before we found those two musket balls, we worked and searched all the way back into the Key West channel here. We had gone back out to Boca Grande Key and set up our theodolite tower on the west side.

From the time I applied for a permit to search an area of the ocean, and before the State of Florida agency approved it, I had it all searched and completed. Then I applied for a new one and by the time they issued that, I would have it done. I applied for about three or four more in advance, so that by the time they got around to giving me a permit, I'd have checked it all out.

We found an old Navy Avenger aircraft, which was used during World War II, underwater south-southwest of Boca Grande Key. I was really fascinated by it and wanted to salvage it, because it would probably be a clue to the "Bermuda Triangle" mystery of the six missing Avengers.

But I decided in those early search years of the 1970s that I didn't want to slow down on the hunt for the *Atocha* and get distracted by other things.

We just marked our charts, left it there, and kept on searching. We had a nice anomaly halfway between Boca Grande and the Marquesas Keys, and we dug there for three or four days—a huge hole—but never did find the anomaly. We finally got Fay Feild out there and made some magnetometer surveys with a search "head" on the bottom and a "head" on the top. Fay finally computed that it was a meteorite.

Even stuff from the sky was screwing up our search. Whatever it was, was way down deep. We later found that there are hundreds of meteors out there that have buried themselves pretty deep down under the sea floor. In fact, probably both Boca Grande and Marquesas were formed by gigantic meteorites striking the Earth and splashing the dirt out to make a circle like an atoll. That was probably what formed the Marquesas Keys.

I've been asked whether there was another shipwreck called the *Candelaria* that was part of the same fleet that went aground by Ballast Key somewhere. That's possible. I believe the *Candelaria* was a guard ship sent out from Havana to guard the ships against pirates. It wouldn't have been part of the Spain-bound fleet; it was a guard ship based in Havana, like a Coast Guard ship.

They normally did have a guard ship or ships go out ahead of the fleet from Havana. One would head to the left and one would head to the right scouting for pirates, so the fleet ships wouldn't get pounced on as they came out of Havana Harbor. These guard ships would accompany the fleet until it got into the Gulf Stream and headed north, and then they would turn back to Havana. So it may have done an escort guard duty and also been caught in the same storm. We found a ballast pile there, but we haven't really investigated it.

Records of actual ships lost from the fleet indicated that nine were sunk or stranded of twenty-eight that sailed together from Havana. I believe my son Kane found another one of them during 1987, which is also in addition to the guard ship. We are not sure what vessel Kane found; it is not identified, but it appears to be circa 1622, Spanish, so it is probably one of the fleet. I don't want to say what I believe is the name of the ship we've found, because people criticize when you can't verify it.

Of the fleet that sailed, other than the *Atocha* and *Margarita*, I believe several more of the wrecked ships have been spotted in the federal park out in the Dry Tortugas. The *Rosario* was stranded, I believe, near Garden Key in the federal park area, and the Spaniards themselves, within a week after the hurricane, boarded and salvaged the *Rosario*.

They also saved 128 people that were on a small

key; I guess it was Garden Key, I'm not sure. They left the people there, but they let them help unload the ship. They had to put most of the treasure and objects from the ship under the island, because their ship couldn't hold all those people and all that treasure. The *Rosario* had more than seventy tons of silver bars on it. The rescue ship could not hold all of that, couldn't hold the people or the treasure, so they parked it all on an island there. It was really just a sand bar that stuck above the water, but it had mangroves on it.

I remember the description from the archives that on the equinox of the moon, precisely thirty days after the morning that the *Atocha* and the *Margarita* sank, another hurricane more violent than the one that sank the ships struck the area.

The people and treasure on Garden Key were inundated with huge waves, high tides, and high winds, and the island went underwater. The people had to hang on to the tops of the mangroves to keep the waves from sweeping them away. Many of them were swept away, or they had to hang on for a day and night until the storm blew over.

Much of the treasure and other things that they had salvaged was scattered, covered with sand and mud, floated away, or blew away. Probably today if somebody wants to go detecting on that sandbar, they'll probably find some fabulous treasures. That ought to get a bunch of people out there. I think they can go out there, because I know Florida now allows beachcombers to beachcomb and keep what they recover.

They once tried to claim it all.

Back in 1965, I believe, Florida had been claiming any beachcombing finds belonged to the state. But there was a blind man detecting inshore from where we were working at "Douglass Beach Wreck." He had a seeing eye dog, and instead of a cane, he used a metal detector. Every time he got a reading, the dog would dig it out for him.

He found a magnificent golden bumblebee with an

emerald body, and the state tried to take it away from him. He wrote to the Blind People's Association and to the American Legion, and they put on enough pressure to change the law so that beachcombers can keep what they find in Florida.

So maybe now people would be able to keep it.

I had hoped to find one of the large galleon anchors of the *Atocha* along the outside edge of that reef, because in the research it mentioned that as they were approaching the reef from the south, headed north in the hurricane, the navigator was sounding with a lead weight and got a reading in about two hundred feet of water, and got another one in about one hundred feet of water.

Then they prepared an anchor with three of their longest lines on it.

As the water got shallower, they threw the anchor in.

Because of the huge waves in the hurricane, the shortest line snapped first, then the second line snapped, and soon the third one parted.

They went over the reef, and the *Atocha* opened up from below in about "three arms" of water. That's "two arms" and a little more of water—which would probably be about twelve or fifteen feet.

Then the *Atocha* passed on over the reef and went on a little farther. She sank suddenly, with only a broken tip of the mizzenmast showing above the surface. The ship opened up from below. All people on board perished except for five souls, one of which was a young cabin boy.

They all hung onto a spar for five days and nights. They existed because the boy was agile enough to catch sea gulls and other birds when they landed on top of the other survivors' heads. They devoured the birds, feathers and all, to exist.

As I stood on the Cosgrove Light platform, I could see the shallow reef below, and a short distance away was a reef called Marquesas Rock. I figured that, since the owner [commander of the Guard Fleet] of the *Atocha* was the Marquess de Cadreita, perhaps that reef was where the *Atocha* first struck, and that they named the rock after the Marquess, the Marquesas Rock. I'm still not sure, perhaps it could have hit any one of fifty other shallow coral heads that lie between there and the forty-seven tons of silver bars that we found in a big pile.

We have yet to complete a meticulous survey of that large area. It will probably take us from now through the turn of the century to discover all the anomalies along the trail of the *Atocha*, which already has developed to be more than ten miles long.

I had always thought that the *Atocha* was sitting there all in one pile and very easy to salvage. So I had my six weeks' outline for finding and salvaging the wreck.

However, I have changed my mind and decided it's going to be thirty-five years instead of six weeks. That doesn't discourage me. I'm sending boats out regularly.

Each time I tell the captain and crew, "Today's the day." Of course, they have heard that several hundred times. But they always have agreed with me.

Even though the weather may be very cold "today," they are always heading out "gung ho."

We know there must be somewhere between $200 million and three and a half billion still out there. We know that there are thousands more emeralds, the deep dark green kind that little girls like. Thank God for little girls, or the emeralds wouldn't be worth nearly so much.

I have never seen anything about emeralds on the old Spanish ships' manifests. However, through the years Dr. Gene Lyon has continued his research in such documents. One day, for example, I got a note from Dr. Lyon saying that he came upon a document in our research materials, and that he had written to Seville, Spain, and the Archive of the Indies, to seek a copy of what he saw noted, about a lawsuit in 1623 over a chest of emeralds. The emeralds weren't on the manifest, but there was a lawsuit over that chest of emeralds after the *Atocha* sunk.

This material at the Spanish archives is adjoining in sequence the material about the 1622 shipwrecks and may pertain to a seventy-pound box of emeralds, which the admiral supposedly smuggled on board the *Atocha*. I believe the thousands of emeralds we have already recovered from the *Atocha* site were from many small stashes of emeralds. Probably everybody on board, if they could possibly afford it, were taking emeralds back to Spain with them, because it would put them on "Easy Street."

I would have no way of accurately documenting how many shipwrecks, and deaths from them, have occurred worldwide. There are so many shipwrecks. So many people went down at sea, it's mind-boggling. Hundreds and hundreds and hundreds of huge treasures are out there, shiploads full of gold bars and all kinds of things. There are lots of lists of shipwrecks. The federal government compiled one. I think the State of Florida had one. The State of California had one out there. But there are so many ships going in all the time. Lloyds of London, which has insured ships through the centuries, probably has got a couple of million wrecks in their records.

Out of all those shipwrecks, people ask me, "Why did you fasten on the *Atocha*?"

First, I thought it would be relatively simple to do, because the wreck was in about sixty feet of water, where scuba diving is very plausible. The water would be clear and warm. It should be all in one pile, I thought, and not scattered out in the breakers like the other wrecks we'd been working, such as from the 1715 fleet. There probably wouldn't be any waves and breakers there.

The *Atocha* was a large target, with an estimated $400 million on it. That's why I picked it.

Also, it was in an area where my children could go to good schools and people spoke the same language. I'd thought about going to Colombia, and Panama, and other places where there are a lot of huge treasures. I was invited by Jamaica to work on Port Royal, and by Panama, to work down there.

I just decided that Florida would be better for the family.

I first read about the *Atocha* in John Potter's book *The Treasure Diver's Guide*. But unfortunately, it didn't mention in that book which sentences were quotes from the archives, and which sentences were written by the author. Some of the sentences were accurate, and some were very much inaccurate. So that's when we were all at the beginning.

Key West is home base now. My children and I all own our own homes on that island; we call Key West "home." We now own the big building that houses the Mel Fisher Maritime Heritage Society and its museum, and that is a good anchor.

During the 1970s, in our search for the *Atocha*, we once used a lighthouse platform. It was way up high, maybe fifty or sixty feet above the water, and it was quite a hassle to carry all the equipment and batteries up and down the steel rung ladder on that lighthouse. So we left them up there overnight.

We came back one morning, and everything was gone. We thought somebody had stolen it. We called to report the "theft" to the Coast Guard, and they said, "Oh, we've got it here." They explained, "You're not allowed to trespass on government property." We'd been working out there at Cosgrove Light for a long time too.

We decided we'd better set up at the Marquesas Keys and work from there.

When we found the lead musket balls, what I said was, "This is it, the *Atocha*! It's so close I can taste it." I did say that. I think I also said, "Today is the day. We've found it."

Instead of "Today's the day," which I usually say, I said, "This *is* the day!" when I found the ball.

That's what I said. "So close I can taste it!"

However, it didn't quite work out that way. I didn't think it was going to take so long.

I kept on going, really, because we kept finding exciting things.

Just when we were ready to get discouraged, we'd find a gold bar.

Or we'd get all disappointed, then we'd find a gold chain.

After working for I don't know how long in the Quicksands, my son Dirk found the nine bronze cannons, so adrenaline was high again.

We thought for sure the whole pile was right there. The entire treasure. It was just buried in the mud there. Then we dug up all the mud there, and there was nothing! A few little bits of jewelry and a copper ingot or two.

I can't say the process of the hunt is what sparked me. I don't know. I just wanted to complete, to finish, the job.

Now, even though we're not bringing in huge amounts of treasure, I want to complete the job of recoveries from the *Atocha* and the *Margarita*.

Often I've been asked about a negative "leave you with only a jockstrap" quote that was supposed to have been said by a state agent in the 1970s and heard by or said to Don Kincaid.

They—State of Florida officials—told us in those years that we couldn't recover anything. We could go out and detect, but we couldn't pick up anything. That seemed kind of ridiculous, because first you detect, and then you dig. If you find a piece of gold or something, you just can't leave it there, because the ocean is gigantic and always in motion, including the bottom.

The best way to describe it is: You are searching a gigantic ant hill, and you find treasure or other artifacts down in the bottom of the ant hill. If you just leave the material there, the sand will cover it all up the next day, and you'll never ever find it again!

Because of that, we started taking the objects, artifacts, over to the galleon anchor still on the bottom, and setting them all around the anchor. We always measured how far away from the anchor we found something, and in what direction on the compass from the anchor. We used the anchor as a baseline, or point of reference, to locate all the other things.

When, after that three months the state finally sent down an archaeologist, we thought maybe he was going to study the archaeology. But instead, he had pulled alongside but didn't get on our boat. He had gone down and brought up all the gold and goodies, put them in his boat, and he was preparing to leave.

That was when I told him, "Wait a minute," that he had to come aboard and count everything and inventory it by serial number and description and sign a receipt for the items. He just gave me a big smile and "the finger," and took off for Key West with all the loot. So I never did get an account of all the stuff he took or a receipt.

Whether this was the same time as the incident when Don Kincaid said he heard a guy saying that if we didn't do what he wanted us to, he'd leave us with nothing but a jockstrap, I don't know. It sounds familiar, but I don't remember when that was, or hearing it myself.

The greatest dangers that we have faced over the long haul can't be pinpointed, and they don't happen one thing at a time.

***

Wendy: *As a journalist and photojournalist, I wrote the story, and I took the pictures, describing a time of tragedy for the Fisher family and the whole treasure "family."*

This is part of the story I wrote for The Key West Citizen *and the wire services:*

"It's a powerful ocean,' said Mel Fisher as he stared blankly across the sun-shimmered waters of the Gulf of Mexico. 'It *takes people and ships.'*

"In the 17*th* century, the ocean took to its bottom a Spanish treasure ship, the Nuestra Señora de Atocha. *Last week Fisher, head of Treasure Salvors Inc., triumphantly announced his team had discovered the* Atocha *and its valuable cargo.*

"Sunday, triumph turned to tragedy. The sea struck back and claimed Fisher's son, a daughter-in-law, and one of his divers.

"They died when the firm's converted sixty-foot tugboat, the Northwind, *capsized and sank in predawn darkness while its crew of 11 slept.*

"Dirk Fisher, 21, the skipper of the boat, his wife, Angel, 25, and Rick Gage, 21, a diver for Treasure Salvors, were trapped below deck and drowned.

"'It's an unfortunate accident—a helluva tragedy,' Fisher, 52, said in a barely audible voice. 'I'm just very sad.'

"The accident came one week after the discovery of bronze cannon and other artifacts from the Atocha. . . .

"The search for the treasure was suspended temporarily, but Fisher said it will resume.

"'Dirk would have wanted us to bring in the rest of the treasure,' he said."

***

Mel resumes: It's a whole lot of dangers out there that add up. Usually, it's not just one thing to cope with. It's a multiple of things that add up to disaster and danger.

Number one, it's probably just weather, and waves, and currents. The currents on the *Margarita* are so strong that it's impossible to swim against them—with fins and arms. That's a definite danger. It exhausts divers trying to fight the power of the tides, the moon's pull on the ocean.

In the 1980s, one of my salvage boats was caught in gigantic waves off the coast of Africa. We had a very large salvage boat, but even this big vessel was rocking and rolling dangerously, and a submarine we had aboard broke loose on deck. One of the "R.O.V." [Remote Operating

Vehicle] operators tried to stop it from sliding across the deck, and it broke both of his legs. So the crew had to put in near one of the islands off the coast of Africa, the Azores. They didn't have to actually go in, because we had a big helicopter pad on board. They took him to shore by helicopter and flew him to London to get put back together again.

We had to fly another expert from London down to meet our vessel.

We're working now on various nationalities of shipwrecks.

In the past I've always tried to stay clear of deep diving.

I have gotten in trouble with deep diving, and I didn't want any of my guys or gals try to buck the deep water. I felt it was too dangerous.

However, starting in the latter 1980s, I have been doing some deep-water salvage, much to my own surprise. But the way I'm doing it now, I don't feel that I'm responsible for the welfare of the divers. That is because they are all professionally trained experts, and they're under the supervision of highly qualified divemasters and hyperbaric physicians. They have a 100 percent excellent safety record.

There are always dangers, because any boat owner knows that all ships malfunction, and they are constantly rebuilding and renewing everything on the ship. One fact is that seawater is an electrolyte and causes extreme electrolysis and corrosion. Sometimes, for example, bronze foot valves, nonreturn valves, and through-the-hull fittings rapidly deteriorate and fall out of a boat or malfunction, allowing water to come in quickly and sink a boat.

I can think of about three occasions through the years when lightning has struck our boat or struck near it. That is very dangerous, because you're way out in the ocean, and you're the tallest thing around—to attract the lightning.

On one occasion, a lightning bolt burned out all the wiring on the entire ship, burnt all the insulation off all the wires, blew up all our electronics equipment, and sank the boat! That was at Fort Pierce, when we were working on the "Fredrick Douglass Beach Wreck." We had to make a decision the next day what to do—whether to leave the boat sunk, or whether to salvage it and refurbish it.

We decided to salvage it, make it float again, rewire it, and buy all new equipment. That's what we did. The boat was called the *Buccaneer*. It was a thirty-three-foot Chris-Craft, with two big Chrysler engines in it. We had to take the engines apart, clean it all up, and put it all back together again.

Then there are the creatures of the sea, which I think everybody knows about. One of the worst ones for this business is the Portuguese man-o'-war. Sometimes they drift in on us by the thousands, huge schools of them. Even after they are sucked into our propellers, and chopped into thousands of little pieces, all those little pieces still sting you, very badly!

We had to wear wet suits that cover every part of our body, so that the only thing left exposed is your lips around the mouthpiece. We'd coat our lips with Vaseline. This happens up off the Vero Beach-Fort Pierce area as well as off Key West. It could happen anywhere. When it does, you have to have a special hood that fits right around your mask and really covers you, doesn't allow anything to go down your neck.

Then there are, of course, sharks and barracuda. The barracuda are always there, everywhere you go, every time you jump in, it seems like. There's nowhere in the ocean you can jump in without a barracuda being there. We just ignore them.

But sometimes they get too rambunctious and come in grabbing crabs and worms and things right next to the divers' hands. Then we have to spear them in self-defense.

We had one called "Ralph" out there on the *Atocha* search, and we just ignored him for almost five months. He was almost like a pet. But he got so threatening that, finally, we had to have him for dinner.

I saw a video a couple of months ago with a guy feeding barracuda with mackerel, by hand, and right in the video you can see a barracuda come up and bite his finger clear off. The man didn't realize there were two barracuda. He had his eyes on the one, and when one would come in, he'd let it have the fish. But there was another one behind the first one that came in and grabbed for the fish, and he didn't have it sticking out. He had the fish sticking in his hand, and it grabbed his finger too. Cut it right off.

For our treasure hunting, most of our crew members are in their twenties and single. That's because a lot of times wives don't want to be away from their husbands, who are out at sea for a long time.

Then, during the lean times, we weren't making big enough wages to support a family. One of the ways we used to cope with lean times was with our "hard times parties." That's when it was just good to have fun, perk up your spirits, and get full, chip in whatever we each had on a big dinner for all.

Another reason I picked *Atocha*, decided to go out there, was because the state and the federal governments harassed me so much when I was working inside territorial limits that they made it virtually impossible to succeed.

Also, another reason I went outside the territorial waters of the United States and Florida was so that I could work long hours and weekends. The state wouldn't let us work more than eight hours a day, and they'd only let us use one boat.

On the *Atocha*, I finally complained so heavily that the state said, "OK"—they'd hire two more employees for the State of Florida—if I would pay for their salaries. I agreed, and then they came back and said I'd also have to pay for their diving equipment, scuba gear, and suits, and pay for their diving lessons and their food, and miscellaneous expenses. This was while we were searching for the *Atocha*, and I believe also after we found it.

After we found it, I wanted to have two or three boats diving for treasure, and another boat searching. My goal was to let the *Holly's Folly* keep searching for the rest of the shipwreck. They wouldn't let us do it unless I paid for it. I think at that time, the first time, they hired two more people. I had to give the state a lump sum of cash in advance for their employees' payrolls, equipment, and food. They wanted me to pay for their housing too, but I told them that was a little far-fetched. I squawked about food too, but I think I ended up buying their food.

There were different state agents from time to time, but they really gave us a hard time. They wouldn't show up in the morning to go to work, so we'd have to go wake them up and try to get them down to the boat to go out. For a while there, they said we could only work eight hours a day, because that's all we were paying them for. They didn't want to stay out there all night long without getting paid—which makes sense, I guess. Then they decided we couldn't stay out overnight. So by the time we'd get out there and bring the state man back, we'd only have two or three hours to work a day because of the travel time. These were long supply lines. The state agents could only work five days a week, and we couldn't work on weekends. I told them I wanted another state man to work on weekends, if that's the way it had to be. Finally, we did that.

Even so, the state hassled us in other ways. Once, the automatic bilge pump in the *Virgalona* went on, at night, and some oil from the bilges leaked off the engines, went out into the water. The state man reported it to the federal government, and they sent down some inspectors and gave us a big fine.

Over the years, people got to know me as the guy who took on the state and federal governments and kept winning. Hard as it may be to believe, at one time I agreed to give the federal government 50 percent—to settle the *Atocha* case. I offered them 25 percent first. I told them I wanted to make a settlement with them, so they said, "OK, come on up to Washington, and we'll negotiate."

I figured this was a pretty important thing to be negotiating, so instead of my one attorney, David Paul "Dave" Horan, I took four attorneys.

When we got into the meeting, there was a huge conference table, and the government had thirty-four attorneys, plus the Attorney General of the United States. And they talked all day long about general principles, about the boundaries of the state and federal governments, about shipwrecks in general. They didn't even talk about the matter at hand—which was who's going to own the shipwrecks, and who's going to own the treasure. It was very expensive for me to pay those four attorneys 125 bucks an hour, and all their expenses and plane tickets, the Hay-Adams Hotel, the $200 meals, the cocktails, and everything in the evening.

So that night I told my lawyers I couldn't afford it, and I couldn't pay them, and so tomorrow, they had to strike a deal with the federal government.

I said, "Go ahead, and let them take 25 percent of our gross." At that point we'd brought in about six million dollars' worth of treasure, and we'd spent approximately six million dollars to bring it in. So I thought, "Well, we'll go ahead and take a million-and-a-half-dollar loss, and hope that we can recuperate next year, or in the next few years, and gain that loss back by finding a lot of treasure."

That was the only way we could make it, by finding a huge amount, because normally for the last fifteen years, we had not been finding a huge amount. We'd just find a small amount of treasure each year. Each year, in every case, even without the government being in the picture, we were then operating at a financial loss.

And we did operate at a loss—every year.

So with the government taking 25 percent of the

gross, or 50 percent of the gross, all those years were really a loss, a huge loss. And there's no business in the United States that can have the government take 50 percent of their gross income, or 25 percent, and still exist, and make a living. Especially when they keep it for five years in a row without giving you anything!

I brought up, too, the fact that they wouldn't let us exhibit the treasure to anybody. They wouldn't let us preserve it. They wouldn't let us borrow money against it. They wouldn't even let me look at it.

When we'd just found it, that same day they wouldn't even let me look at it; they'd whisk it off to Tallahassee. Then four or five years later, I'd ask them for it, and they'd say, "Well, we're still working on the archaeology."

For example, there were the emeralds that the state agents were "cleaning" right out of their fastenings. There were hundreds and hundreds and hundreds of items that were listed by the state as "lost in cleaning."

Years passed, and more years passed, and still only elusive but tantalizing signs were found of the rich prize Nuestra Señora de Atocha, *and her sister Royal Guard galleon, the* Santa Margarita, *of the 1622 Spanish Fleet, lost together in one hurricane in September 1622. That was followed a month later by a second storm that did more damage than Mel and his crews could even imagine. He kept changing the time to find her—from weeks, to months, to years—and his family was growing up, the seasons changed, but still no luck. But Mel clung to his original clues, lead musket balls, signs of the times in which they were lost. First one musket ball, then a second. He told his crew, "This is it," and to dig for another five minutes. More little signs, more musket balls, pottery, and an olive jar neck of the right "circa." Then they found the anchor and some silver coins, one dated 1619. A wondrous golden chain came, and celebrations, but they were still premature. The storm that blew up around him on his first search day, where he started with a theodolite tower above the sunken* Valbanera, *was nothing but a signal there would be problems, but nothing insurmountable. Mel told his crew, "We're . . . gonna find this ship, recover its treasures, and let everybody in the world look at it." More weeks, months, years went by. Mel said, "That doesn't discourage me. I'm sending boats out regularly." Always, as was his nature, Mel just wanted to "finish the job."*

A happy Mel displays some of his finds. PAT CLYNE PHOTO

CHAPTER FOURTEEN

Today's the Day!
Mother Lode and "Heeeeere's Mel"

TODAY'S THE DAY! *Almost everyone in Key West that day—July 20, 1985—remembers where they were when they heard the news that Mel Fisher's team had finally discovered the submerged "mother lode" of the* Nuestra Señora de Atocha. *Intuitive as ever, Mel felt the find was at hand. Where once he found musket balls, he learned the day before from sea that the "trail" had now led to the ship's ballast stones. His Treasure Salvors "family" was at last to be world-renowned for finding the historic "primary cultural deposit" of the richest-ever Spanish Royal Guard treasure galleon shipwreck.*

July 20, 1985

It was raining, I was just walking down the street from the dive shop back to the office—a couple of blocks walk—and I must have had thirty or forty people stop me on the street and say, "Hey, Mel, you hit the Pile!"

Evidently Bleth McHaley couldn't find me, and didn't know where I was, so she told the local radio stations to announce on the air, "Anybody who sees Mel Fisher, tell him they found the Big Pile!"

They sure did.

I got back to the office, and it was just mobbed with two hundred to three hundred people, and cameras, and videos. Really wild!

Over the marine radio, I remember, Kane told me I could put away the charts. I had been looking at these charts and plotting everything that he found, that everybody else found, and trying to figure out which way the trail was going to go next. So my son Kane told me, "You can put away the charts, we found the Big Pile!"

I had planned to go out that day. In fact, I knew he was going to find the Big Pile before he found it. I just knew he had it. Because he started getting into the ballast stones. A big pile of ballast stones the day before and some copper ingots.

And I knew that had to be it.

That was why I went out the first thing in the morning and bought some new fins, mask, regulator—got all the equipment together that I needed to dive on it.

But there was such pandemonium that I couldn't even get out of the office. All the news crews showed up, the television stations, the newspaper writers, and magazine people, so I was snowed under.

July 21, 1985

I finally got out there the next day, and it was the same way out there. There were dozens of boats rafted all around Kane's boat. I had to climb over several boats to get there.

When I got out to the site, I got kind of scared, because the boat was real low on the water line. They had a couple hundred silver bars on it and about three hundred people.

I told them to start shifting silver bars to other boats, to take twenty over to that boat, ten over to this boat, and twenty over to that boat.

We spread out the weight, and I told the people they would have to get off the boat and only have about a hundred people on there.

It's a good thing we did that, because about an hour later, lo and behold, here came a big old squall blowing about fifty mile an hour, and it just scattered everybody.

Good thing we transferred the weight and the people.

Mel at sea, July 21, 1985, headed back to Key West:

Today was a fantabulous day!

We headed out on the *Hatteras* about 10 o'clock this morning. The *Magruder* followed us, and Ted Miguel went out with a bunch of photographers.

We went out to the site, and there was all kinds of mayhem there. There were, it seems, about fifty photographers from newspapers and magazines taking pictures of me, asking me hundreds of questions. It was very exciting.

There were silver bars all over the decks, and copper ingots. They opened the bilge hatch, and gosh, the bottom of the bilges was all piled with silver bars!

I went to the stern, and they have a beautiful silver box, very ornate, carved just like the gold poison cup we found, only this one's made out of silver. It wasn't closed, though. I imagine it was a jewel box, but the lid was missing, and there were shells on the inside. I'm going to ask our attorney, Dave Horan, where he found that box, because there might be some jewels right near there—within a foot or two. It looks quite similar to the box where we found the emerald cross and the emerald ring, so that's exciting.

I didn't get down right away, because there was a lot of work to do.

There were so many people on the *Dauntless*, and more boats kept coming out—a lot of friends and well-wishers. Before we knew it, we had about a hundred people on the *Dauntless*, and all that silver and copper. I was beginning to worry about whether the *Dauntless* might sink.

We all got on the stern and had a big champagne celebration, clicking our glasses together and yelling, "Today's the day!"

Very enthusiastic group!

Then I started worrying about getting all this weight off the boat. We sent ten silver bars over to Mike Alexander's boat, the *Salvor One*. Then we sent fifteen silver bars over to the *Hatteras*, and we sent twenty copper ingots over to the *Saba Rock*. We sent ten silver bars over to the *Saba Rock*, and then we sent 'em ten more silver bars.

That all sounds real easy, but these silver bars weigh seventy-five pounds each. When everybody's bringing 'em out of the bilge of the *Dauntless*, carrying 'em across the deck, and putting them into a bouncing Whaler, then lifting 'em out of the bouncing Whaler up into the big boat—man, that's one heck of a lot of exercise!

What you never think about with finding treasure is, it's like weight-lifting all day long.

And this was after the guys had already brought the silver bars up from the bottom of the ocean and wrestled around with 'em down on the *Atocha* main pile. So everybody's gonna sleep real good tonight!

The *Magruder* came alongside, and I said, "Well, let's put ten silver bars on the *Magruder*." I said, "Well, let's give 'em ten more! Well, let's give 'em twenty more!" We put forty bars on the *Magruder*!

I was beginning to feel a little more that the *Dauntless* was going to stay afloat after all.

Finally, I put on a tank and went down to look around, to see what it was like down there.

It was just mind-boggling.

I got to the bottom.

It was about fifty feet deep, and I used a descending line to equalize my ears.

The first thing I came on was a copper ingot. I hung onto it and looked around. I could see about a dozen more of them all around me.

There were a couple other divers down there in the distance. One of them motioned to me to follow him. So I did. I went over there, and he had fanned out something with his hands.

He had fanned out a silver coin chest!

It was a complete, intact chest of "pieces of eight." Two of the sides were still on the chest, and the coins were all shaped like a rectangle. I'm pretty sure there are two thousand of 'em in that box. It's still there. We didn't bring it up or anything.

We just fanned on it a little bit, looked at it. I started wandering around some more down there and found a silver bar.

I thought, *"Wow, a silver bar!"*

Then I went to roll it over. But I found out it was stuck to about thirty more of them, so I didn't roll it over.

Then I swam a little farther on. There was a stack of about fifteen of them right in front of me—seventy-five-pound silver bars! I went on a little farther, and there was a whole stack of 'em, laying there.

I went on a little farther and there are some *huge timbers down there!* I don't know if they're the ribs, or the hull, or what, but there are some big timbers, probably part of the main hull section of the *Atocha*.

When we uncover all this, I think we may have to build us a gigantic swimming pool in Key West to reconstruct the *Atocha* hull, only we won't be able to use city water, with chlorine in it.

We'll have to have it all full of rainwater or distilled water. And then change it to alcohol, and how long can you tread water in a swimming pool full of vodka? Or tequila? I met a guy who owns a tequila factory. Maybe I could talk him into filling the swimming pool full of tequila to preserve these timbers of the *Atocha*.

I think we're going to put this on display at the Smithsonian in 1989 instead of the *Margarita*. This looks much more impressive! Then after we displace the water with alcohol, we have to displace the alcohol with polyester glycol. It'll take us a couple of years, but we've got plenty of time. It'll be worth it. That's for Smithsonian's Bicentennial Celebration—1989!

I looked around some more. Decided to come up and relax. After I got up on deck, and after I got off my tank and weight belt, mask, fins, I couldn't believe it. On the horizon there's a boat coming in. I thought, "Boy, I hope it's not pirates."

Damned if it wasn't Jimmy Buffett! Our good old Key West country folksinger! He came on aboard and went into delirium. He couldn't believe all the treasure he was looking at. Everybody admires Jimmy and his singing. Everybody wanted to get their picture with him. It was pretty exciting.

Then I told the crew to stack up those forty bars they had in the middle of the *Magruder* and make me and Jimmy each a throne to sit on! Made of silver bars!

Sure enough they did it, and I yelled out, "Anybody got a gee-tar?" Jimmy said, "Yeah, I've got one. I just happen to have a guitar!"

And so he sang us a good ol' pirate song. He kind of had a little hangover from celebrating about our treasure find the night before, but he apologized.

My son Kane wanted to have his picture with me and Jimmy Buffett. Then my son Kim wanted to get in the picture too, and I got an idea.

I said, "Hey! Let's let everybody get in the picture! Everybody get in the stern of *Magruder*! They did, and so I let Wendy Tucker's and about thirty other cameras take a picture of all the crew out there.

And Jimmy Buffett sang us another song, "Margaritaville." It was excellent! A good time was had by all. We drank up two cases of champagne, celebrating.

Well, yesterday was *the day*!

Today was a good one too!

I think we're going to have a lot of good days from now on.

I figure it's gonna take another two-and-a-half years to pull all this treasure in from the *Atocha*. Then we've got the *Margarita* to do too.

One hand for the boat! I didn't have one hand on the boat—and we just hit a big wave!

Anyway, it was a fabulous day! Everybody had a lot of fun, romance, and adventure!

We got everybody on the *Hatteras* for the last boat to the City of Key West, and I placed out three more buoys! One white one, one green one, and one red one. The white one's on a real good hit for the *Swordfish*. The green one's on probably another pile of treasure—for the *Magruder*. And then I put a special red buoy over there for the *Saba Rock*. That's just all gold and silver.

We'll find out tomorrow whether my predictions were right from my gold head detectors, magnetometers, and side scan sonar that we've been using out here.

Tomorrow could be a better day yet. Could you believe that?

We don't have to match any serial numbers. This is it!

This is the "Big A"!

The *Atocha*—with all its tons and tons and tons and tons and tons and tons and tons!

I lost track. There were twenty-seven tons, and then they put on another mess o' tons, and then they put on twenty tons of copper, and then some more tons of silver. I'll tell you, it's a mess! I saw a bunch of it down there today, that it's all there!

Actually, I figured out about five years before the discovery that "Kane's trail" would lead us to the "Big A."

I figured out which direction the *Atocha* came from. That was possible because of one of our innovations—we rented this huge pump, it was four feet in diameter, and we built up what I called a "hydro-gyro" that hung down under the *Arbutus*. This was a gigantic new type of underwater "mailbox" that worked hydraulically. We tested it, hanging it down under the *Arbutus*. I was down in the "hole" under the "mailbox" and came up and out. There was a ballast stone, a big one, half in the mud and half out. I brought up the ballast stone. Then I looked at our buoys. We were way out from being on line with our buoys, our spar buoys.

We were cutting into the Quicksands, and the "Bank of Spain" area—and so, I just was thinking about it logically.

That stone couldn't roll that far. It was so heavy nobody could throw it that far. So the *Atocha* had to be there, and that was on this line, Kane's "trail."

At that time, I had the *Arbutus* start digging out that way. I was very disappointed when I found out that they'd moved off that trail and went out looking around the seventeen-foot reef with the *Arbutus*, because I knew we only had rented that big machine for one month for $7,000 a month, and we were wasting valuable digging time cruising around. It was too late to tell them to move back. I told them to dig wherever they wanted to dig, because we only had a few days left.

And then what? Well, of course, if you're a big dreamer like Mel Fisher, you share the dream. And so there are people who are grand in the history of sharing dreams "live" on modern television, like Johnny Carson. He helped Mel share the dream—and the "pot of gold at the end of the rainbow" was really there.

A couple of weeks after we found the "Big Pile," we got a call from a man with *The Tonight Show*. Johnny Carson wanted to have us on his television show

We flew out there, and it was exciting. There's a room where you stand by. They put your name on the door like a star. They actually have a star on the door. I recall it says "guest star," and they put your name up there too. This was for NBC-TV, and the studio was around Los Angeles, at Burbank, California.

They had me come and wait behind the curtains, where Johnny always walks out. They started the show. It came my time, and so I walked out through the curtains.

Just before I walked out, I took my six-foot gold chain off my neck. I just held one end of it in my hand, and I started swinging it around. I was swinging this gold chain around when I walked out, and the band was good!

The musician and bandleader in me realized they've got a very good band. They were playing, "He's in the money, dah, dah, de dah dah!"

On camera, I sat down, and Johnny started interviewing me. We got into it; I'd been somewhat primed by my son Kim. He said I ought to ask Johnny something about his alimony. On the show, Johnny kept telling everybody I'd ". . . found four hundred million dollars down in the ocean." So I said, "Well, Johnny, I think I might have found enough to take care of a couple of your alimony payments."

He just sat back and laughed, and it really cracked him up.

The audience really applauded. Johnny was having so much fun with the show, holding the gold bars, the treasure, silver "pieces of eight," and everything, that he just kept on going with me.

Three other people were supposed to appear on that show. None of them got to come on, because he was having so much fun with the treasure. Johnny just had me stay on, and while we were having fun, I did get a plug in. I told all the people in the audience what was happening in Washington.

Johnny mentioned something about how the government was trying to take all the treasure away from me—and I told him, "Yeah, that's right. They claim it's all theirs, and that's a bunch of baloney, because you know we'd been working for seventeen years, and spent $12 million, and it was ours!"

I told the audience too—I pointed the truth out to the audience and urged them to write a letter to their congressmen and senators and tell them the government doesn't own treasure ships, and should not in the future.

At the end of the show, when it was winding up, I had this thing—it looks like a grease gun—with a plunger on it. I showed that to him. He took it in his hands and said, "What is this thing, anyway?" I said, "Turn around, bend over, Johnny, and I'll show you." He said, "Oh, no, no! No goosey!" It was an enema machine. I told him they mixed up gun powder, sulfur, and saltpeter and really kept your bowels in good shape.

Johnny asked me if he could come on down to Key West. I told him, "Sure," he was welcome to come on down and dive on the wreck.

Sure enough, he did. The next Saturday he came down to Key West. We took him out in a fast speedboat. He enjoyed that. He got to drive the speedboat a little. There was a Panamanian fellow with what they call a "Force 10" speedboat, and he was staying at the Ocean Key House. That's where the boat was. Johnny Carson and I, the boat owner, and his wife went out.

At the *Atocha* site, there were several television crews making documentaries. One of them was from Lima, Peru. They were doing everything in Spanish. They got a shot of us getting our equipment on—tanks, weights, fins and all. Also, my associate Pat Clyne was taking video footage as usual.

I didn't know if Johnny could dive very well, so I was explaining things to him. He said he had a little trouble equalizing his ears.

I told him I was putting down a really good descending line, that it had a knot every 12 inches. I explained to him how to slide down just one knot at a time, and, maybe, two or three knots—if it didn't hurt his ears. I told him to go down about three feet, and stop, build up a little pressure inside of his mouth, then to swallow or gulp, and listen for "eich, eich, eichhhh," a squeaky noise where the Eustachian tube opens inside your mouth to your inner ear. That makes you get the same pressure inside your ears and sinuses as there is outside in the water, and then your ears and sinuses don't hurt. He seemed to understand everything.

I told him we weren't in any big hurry. "Let's just take our time." I said we'd get down there sooner or later, and the treasure wasn't going anywhere. It was about fifty-five feet at that point.

We jumped in and cleared our masks; we started to go down, and I stopped at about twelve feet because my sinuses were hurting very bad. I had a cold. Johnny came down and went right on by me. He went "chung, chung, chung" all the way to the bottom real fast. I was still hanging up there trying to equalize my sinuses. He started to swim away from the line, but I think he realized that he didn't know where he was, which direction he was going, and he couldn't see anything. Finally, he stopped and waited for me to get down.

Johnny couldn't find any treasure. He was looking all around and couldn't find anything. He held his hands up to signal, "Where is all the treasure?" He was pointing this way and that way. "Which way to go?" He's a comedian underwater too, as much as he is up on deck. I got him started fanning with his hands down in this little gully, hoping he would find something. But he wasn't finding anything. He just didn't know what it looked like.

So I picked up a "piece of eight," and put it about a foot in front of him where he was fanning. I knew he'd get to it. Sure enough, he got to it and he reached down. I thought he was going to pick it up. Instead, he picked up a seashell right next to it. He held it up shortly. I waved my hand, "No," and shook my head. "No, no, that isn't a 'piece of eight'."

Then I pointed down at the "piece of eight." He reached out and grabbed to the right of it. Picked up another seashell. He held it up to my face, and I said, "No, no. That isn't treasure. That's a seashell."

Finally, I pointed my one finger really close, right at the "piece of eight," and he picked it up. Oh, man! He was so excited! He was jumping up and down and giggling and screaming underwater.

I tapped him on the shoulder and told him to "follow me," then went over and showed him a whole chest full of money! There were about two thousand coins all stuck together, like a box of money that's all stuck together. It was black. You could hardly even tell it was coins, because the box was all gone. There was no more wood left. There were just the coins sitting there.

Then I took him over a little farther, and I showed him about ten chests full of coins, all stuck together. Each one of those boxes was worth about $2,640,000. I took him over and showed him some silver bars.

Much to my surprise, I saw a wheelbarrow sitting there, upside down. I didn't even know it was down there. They were using it to haul the treasure around, to get it to the baskets, instead of just carrying it all. The wheelbarrow had a pneumatic tire on it, and wooden handles, so it floated.

There it was, sitting upside down with a great big ballast stone on it to hold it down. I took off the ballast stone and put the wheelbarrow right side up. Pat Clyne was down there, shooting underwater videotape. He got a video of me and Johnny down there, exploring around.

I signaled for Johnny to throw a silver bar into the wheelbarrow, just so we'd have some action for the TV footage. Johnny reached down to grab this ninety-two-pound silver bar, but he's kind of a little guy. He went to lift the bar, but instead of the bar coming up, he went down. His face was pulled right down next to the bar.

Then he waved around, and signaled, "OK, now, I've got it all figured out how I'm going to do it."

He held his hands up, and he put one foot on each side of the bar—that's hard to do when you've got your fins on.

He squatted down, he took hold of the bar, and he gave a big pull. Johnny threw that bar so fast at that wheelbarrow that it caught me off guard and flipped the wheelbarrow upside down. Then I let go of it, and the wheelbarrow started to float up.

I had to go catch the wheelbarrow and pull it back down. By then, I guess, he was breathing pretty heavy. He was excited, and he ran out of air.

Just about then I found a big silver pyramid, which weighed about forty or fifty pounds, a real heavy thing! But Johnny signaled me he was out of air. He was excitedly signaling he was out of air and didn't know which way to go.

I signaled to him just to stand there a second, and I handed him this fifty-pound silver pyramid. He had this big, big-eyed look, like, "Gee whiz, here I'm out of air and you're handing me this big heavy thing to hold?"

He tried to hold onto it. Then he was still trying to bend over and signal he was out of air while he was holding it. In the meantime, I'd taken off my weight belt. I had about a forty-pound weight belt on. So I held the weight belt out with my left hand, and I reached out with my right hand, and I got the silver pyramid. I dropped the weight belt, and then I signaled, "Let's go up." I knew which way to go; he didn't.

We got up fine. Sure enough, when we got to the top, the TV crews were shooting footage of us coming out of the water, bringing up the silver pyramid. Actually, he wasn't totally out of air. You've always got a little more, it seems.

We sat down on deck, and the television crew from Peru was interviewing me and Johnny in Spanish, although neither one of us know very much Spanish. It's kind of fun listening to the interview. That's because even if you don't know Spanish, you can figure out what they're talking about. It was a very good show.

Johnny did a good job of autographing a lot of things for people and shaking hands with people. I know how it is. I've had quite a lot of that myself, and it can get old. But he just kept pleasing everybody, smiling, and cracking jokes.

Same old Johnny you see on TV—all day long! He just keeps on a-going, laughing and cracking jokes, being friendly and happy with everybody.

I had mentioned that I was planning on having an exhibit of the treasure down in Lima, Peru. They asked Johnny what he thought about that, and he said he thought that was a nice gesture, that it would be exciting for the people to see the treasure. A lot of this silver came from the mountain of Potosí, Peru.

That's the Johnny Carson story, I guess. Except that he went back home and took this video footage and showed it on the air the next week.

Johnny told his audience, "Now folks, this is what I did on my vacation." He did a "show and tell," just like we all did in school.

I knew Johnny had a good time on his first dive here, because the next day, he went out to the site again. I didn't go the second time. I had some work I had to do in the office.

While I stayed in, Johnny went out by himself, did some more diving, found some more treasure! I think he was fairly experienced. He seemed to handle himself very well underwater.

One day I got a call from one of his right-hand men who wanted to know if it was all right to use that footage from those two shows for a small company that's trying to help sell coins for some of my investors.

I told him, "Yeah, that's fine," I'd let them use the footage, and help them all sell some coins and make some money. I think Johnny's waiting until we find another big pile of treasure, so a return visit would be really exciting.

We'll probably do that today. I'll call him up—after we hit it.

Television is where it is, along with books, on how you find treasure, where and how to look! The ideas for gold and silver and jewels, though, actually can mean any kind of "treasure," and so the idea of "treasure" goes on and on, just like the real "finds," and that's why Mel Fisher's story is real but also an inspiration for us all.

I just gave the captain of one of our boats out there the location "numbers" of where I saw a chest of money out there about fourteen years ago. It's still there. We never did get it. So he's going to do some digging around that area. He's got a good shot at it!

I enjoy doing television shows. I just did one for another guy who wanted to sell some coins. I think he invested about $100,000 with me, and he got about $2 million worth of treasure. A lot of it was coins, so I did a twenty-four-minute television show and just talked about nothing but "pieces of eight" for twenty-four minutes. I enjoyed it, and it's good documentary evidence to get all that information about coins permanently recorded.

I think there's enough, out of that one conversation, to do a half-hour television show all about "pieces of eight." I may do that, and then we might even play it here in our gift shop. If somebody wants to know about coins, we'll turn it on. This would be good for the nonprofit Mel Fisher Maritime Heritage Society to have as part of their resources for educating the public about the Spanish New World and other maritime history, and about our twentieth-century quest and discoveries.

When I think of the gold treasure that we find now, I remember that it just keeps on a-going through the centuries. It doesn't rust, it doesn't turn green. It just keeps on going from hand to hand, man to woman, on through centuries and centuries, and lots of lifetimes.

The gold just keeps on a-going, and I'm a custodian for a while.

Mel "kind of knew" his son Kane was going to find the "Big Pile," the "Mother Lode" of the Atocha *because he always was*

Today's the Day!

looking for clues, and this was a big clue. His son started getting into ballast stones, which signifies a very old wreck, along with some copper ingots. And so, THE DAY *the world was discovering the* Atocha *had yielded up her main treasure pile. "That had to be it," which was why he went out to buy new dive gear. The world, in Key West, told him on his way back to the office that he had "hit it." He couldn't get out of the office for all the excitement until the next day, when he headed out to sea to see the piles of treasure he had been hunting for so many years. So for Mel and all his "Golden Crew" members, family, and friends—from Key West and from around the world— the day was "a fantabulous day." For him, it was the 20th and the 21st, because it took him a day to get to sea to see it all. And, of course, he was more worried about the weight of the treasure brought up, and the load of well-wishing people, and not wanting any tragedy to occur with any sinking boats. Moving the treasure, he said later, is like weight-lifting all day long. But finally, Mel got his chance to go below, to the ocean bottom, and "it was just mind-boggling." He didn't bring anything up. He just looked at it. When he came up, there was a boat on the horizon. Mel hoped "it wasn't pirates'; it turned out to be singer Jimmy Buffett, who had brought a guitar with him. Picture time, and lots of cameras were used, including mine, with a photo that went on page one of the* Key West Citizen *and out to the wire services. So of course, Mel concluded, the two days were "...fabulous. Everybody had a lot of fun, romance, and adventure!" He figured there would be a "lot of good days from now on."*

    Johnny Carson invited Mel to come to his studios for a live Tonight Show *appearance, and Mel in turn invited Johnny to come see what he and his "Golden Crew" had found off Key West.*

Mel's friend Jimmy Buffett sings "A Pirate Looks at Forty (Mother Ocean)" to him while sitting atop a pile of newly salvaged, eighty-pound silver ingots on the boat deck over the Atocha *site.* PAT CLYNE PHOTO • USED BY PERMISSION

CHAPTER FIFTEEN

Treasure Is Where You Find It

And what are the real treasures? Life itself, dreams and the doing, family, friends, nature, challenges, action, achievement, gold masquerading as many things, as varied as the dreams and realities of people themselves!

My mother, Grace, was as proud as any of us when we finally found the "Big A" in that summer of 1985, and I'm grateful she was there to see it.

After she moved in with us when her health was failing, she always kept a framed, hand-colored picture of me in my high school band uniform on the long counter between our kitchen and dining room. She had kept pictures and scrapbooks of my adventures all through the years. There really was even a picture of me as a baby on a bear rug. The bear had been shot by one of my relatives.

About a year and a half after the big find, I was still explaining to people that the search for treasures from the *Atocha* and the *Margarita* is going to continue probably past the turn of the century.

People would ask, "Do you have any new ventures planned for your treasure-hunting career?" Others who know me would tease, "Are you going to retire again for the third time?"

By then, I had slowed down on Treasure Salvors Inc. It had been growing so fast, by leaps and bounds, that it was getting into real big business. I just didn't want to have a public corporation and business, so the board and the stockholders agreed that we would sell out the company and liquidate the assets to the stockholders. That is what we did. We made a deal to sell the rights to the *Atocha* and the *Margarita,* and we sold off the assets. What was left we planned to divide up for the stockholders, including the cash and the treasure that we haven't sold. Let them all have their fair share. I also agreed to act as a consultant of the group of businessmen that bought out Treasure Salvors Inc. So we are more or less going on the same for a couple of years. I expect to keep working with the same crew, captains, and divers, and we'll keep on a-bringing in lots of emeralds, gold, and silver. I think there is another big pile out there. About another 150 million dollars' worth on the *Atocha,* and also another 180 million dollars' worth on the *Margarita.* So there is plenty more out there. There's no use giving up right in the middle of it.

Everybody thinks we are finished, but we are not.

What is more important, the dream or the doing? Both, actually. And of course, you just "keep on a-goin!"

And there is probably another—you never know, because the emeralds were being smuggled and they are not on the manifest—but there could be as much as three and a half billion dollars in smuggled emeralds out there.

I guess we might as well go for it. The possibilities sure make the hunt exciting.

My son Kim found a nice box of emeralds one day. At about the same time he found an emerald cross and a brooch with a great big green stone in it. The dredge sucked these up too.

I'm looking at a gold bar, studying a little bite that's visible. The Spanish didn't have money to pay the assayer to test it, so he got to keep that little bite of gold.

There's a mark showing the carats that he tested it at—21 carat. I see how deep he dug in the back side of the bar. That's the "circumcision." I guess if they want to make change, they just cut that out. Somebody cut it off.

I just got back from a DEMA show—that's the Diving Equipment Manufacturers Association—and I saw several little robots—little machines that go down and go round by themselves.

There you go. Technology is improving each year, and each year it gets a little bit easier to find treasure.

Then there is something called "on-the-job" training. Something else that has been important over the years, which our consulting marine archaeologist R. Duncan Mathewson III has spearheaded, is continuing—on-the-job training of the divers in artifact recognition and handling.

One of Duncan's goals, he stressed in more active times with us, is that he wanted to see people in our company ". . . as expert at handling the objects as they are at finding them."

"That's my goal," he said in my office one day. "I want to see the divers, at least half a dozen, who really have a feel and, as I say, can talk to the objects after they are found. Divers have been finding them. But I want them to understand how to handle these objects. That comes from on-the-job training. It comes from learning a lot about objects that they don't already know. I think that possibly would mean that they would have to become familiar with our uniform procedures. They would have to go to school within the company."

Duncan, in fact, suggested that about every six weeks or so, we should have little discussions about whatever we want to talk about—gold bars, ceramics, little things that we want to learn, so that we could become better at handling artifacts of any kind.

Some months after that suggestion, the decision was made to liquidate Treasure Salvors Inc., which occurred in December 1987. As a result, Duncan's ideas weren't all implemented right away.

But Jim Sinclair, archaeologist and conservator who has continued much that Duncan began, is educating all of us, all of the time, consulting both with my Cobb Coin Company and the nonprofit Society.

"Today's the Day, Every Day!"

Outside the huge stone former Key West Naval Station building that was bought with Mel Fisher's personal treasure division in 1985, a sign by the large outdoor emerald cross reproduction says, "Today's the Day!"—encouraging people to visit the famous Mel Fisher Museum and be "amazed by the jewels and beauty of the past." Other signs say, "Come and See Mel Fisher's Treasure Exhibit, 200 Greene Street." A transition is occurring, as the nonprofit Mel Fisher Maritime Heritage Society renovates the former Treasure Salvors museum it now owns and operates. Much material has been being removed from the front of the building, but one sign still says, "Headquarters, Treasure Salvors" and "Melvin A. Fisher, President," and over the main gate, near the main front door, another sign says: "Mel Fisher and Treasure Salvors Inc. presents the Treasure of Nuestra Señora de Atocha.*"*

Inside, a television crew is busy interviewing Mel. The anchorman is urging Mel to "say that" again. "Today's the Day!"

***

Today's the day! Life after finding the "Big A" is still exciting!

For any project I do, I start with dreams, but that's not all I do.

The television people usually ask me something like, "It was such a determined effort for you for so long, over fifteen years, what happens after? There's the excitement of it happening in 1985, and now the ultimate dream seems like it has happened. What does it mean now?" I tell them, "It's still happening. Every day it's still exciting. We keep bringing up more and more. It's mind-boggling. Very exciting."

On a day-to-day basis, everything is more or less the same as it always was. I just manage things. Have an office. We have our treasure exhibits for the public. They can come to Key West and see all the gold things, all the things the navigator had in his chest, what kind of tools they used. We've also got a nonprofit Mel Fisher Maritime Heritage Society. There is a preservation laboratory. We're starting a video library too. Also, we have books about underwater archaeology and shipwrecks.

Then there are always people coming in with stories about treasures here and around the world. It is amazing how many treasures there are, everywhere. I'll usually be wandering around, chasing down some of those bronze cannon stories, treasure tales here and there. Just for a little variety and excitement.

I am happy, but motivation is the key!

One television interviewer asked me: "How is the Mel Fisher of ten years ago—in the middle of going after treasure and having been doing it for years—well, how are you different today, now that the *Atocha* has been found? You said you've got all the gold and emeralds you could ever want. How are you different from before?" I told him, "Really not much different. I seem to be traveling around on jets quite a bit more, but I have the same home, and other things are about the same. I am happy."

He kept on asking: "Did you have anything that you—did you have anything in your mind, like, 'Well, if we find it and it all comes up, I'm going to do this.' Or any personal things that you wanted to change? No new car or things of that kind?" Not really. I never did have any goals like that.

I just wanted to just keep working along toward completing the project on the *Atocha*. I told him, "Most people seem to think it is all over, like you are kind of saying. But in reality, it is going to take us about fifteen years, just on that one shipwreck, to get the job done. People think you just go in, and in one or two days you work a shipwreck. But the ones in Fort Pierce and Vero Beach I have been working on for approaching thirty years. Can you imagine that? I still have a fleet of ships working up there every year.

It just keeps going on and on and on. It's a lot of hard work and costs a lot of money. You have to be real patient, and you have to preserve everything you find. It's quite different from what most people think.

The same interviewer asked: "Tell me a little bit about the lean times. I heard somewhere that it was costing like a million bucks a year to keep the operation going. After the Plate Fleet up there—Vero Beach and that area, and then when you first started finding stuff off the *Margarita*—that was millions and millions of dollars. I've heard that you traded bits of treasure for food and fuel before?"

"Oh, yeah," I told him.

He asked what they all do—if they have really watched our story over the years: "I mean if there was that much of a find, how come it was still so hard and so lean?"

It is hard to explain, I suppose.

We took in a lot of partners over the years. There were limited partnerships and contracts and stockholders. Then when we find something, we have to reward them for their help financially, so we give them treasure.

That's the way I've done it. Instead of selling the treasure and giving people money—I let them have it in kind.

So maybe three-fourths of everything I would find would go right out to my partners and investors. We did sell coins and things from time to time. But we just keep spending that for fuel, food, and repairing boats. You have heard about the boats you shovel money into. I've got a whole fleet of them and really shovel money.

"Holes in the water," he laughed, and, since those people are always looking for the ultimate answers, he asked, "What was the toughest part? If there was one thing that was the hardest over the years?"

The toughest was losing my son Dirk. But I'd rather not talk about that.

Today's the Day!

His greatest loss: Mel with Wendy Tucker

Pressed about his greatest loss, Mel's eyes clouded as he looked back in time, thinking of his sons Kim, Kane, and then Dirk as ". . . the brother who had passed away out there." Mel, in the late 1980s, recalled:

"I recently visited the gravesite, a couple of weeks ago, and it was just beautiful. I couldn't believe it.

When we lived in Vero Beach, Dirk and I were out hunting one day in the jungles, just complete jungle, and we had his dog, Admiral, with us. We didn't find any wildcats or panthers or ducks or anything, but we had a lot of fun tromping around in the woods. And we came across this real small graveyard. There were just six or eight graves there, and Dirk was kind of impressed with it, and he said, "You know, Dad, when I die, that's where I'd like to be buried."

I never thought about it at all, because it wouldn't make any difference to me where he wanted to be buried—because I was going to die first. But as it so happened, he went first, and so we granted his wish and took him up to Vero and had a hard time finding that graveyard again. It was way back in the jungles. Just a real back dirt road and a lot of wilderness.

And now I went back a couple of weeks ago, and it's all millionaire mansions around there! They cost half a million dollars for one lot to build to buy a house on. They've beautified and restored the graveyard, and it is really nice.

***

Yeah, Kane knew that his brother Dirk had gone out in that direction [searching for the *Atocha*], so he started up from there and searched all directions from where Dirk found nine bronze cannons and found some spikes, signs, barrel hoops, and things to the south. A little bit to the west and east and north and a little bit more to the southeast. But when he started going more in the easterly direction, it was the only way that he could find things farther and farther away from the bronze cannons. So it really took about six months or a year of digging just to find out which way the trail would go from the cannons, and which way it went to the farthest from the cannons.

That's the way he [Kane] kept going then, even though there was no treasure—just a rock now and then, or maybe a nail. Kept doing that for four and a half years without any treasure. When he would get bored or say, "I don't want to go in without any gold or silver," he would either jump on the *Margarita*, or jump on the Quicksands at the Bank of Spain, and bring in a few coins and things to make the payroll and buy some fuel.

One questioner reflected, "The big picture is the treasure, it's the archaeology, it's the history—it's so many different things!" He was right. So when he asked, "All things considered, what do you think's the most significant thing about the *Atocha* and the *Margarita*?" I say, "I think, probably, motivation. I've been able to motivate thousands of kids, and older 'kids' too, to hang in there, to stick with it, persevere and complete their education. To study harder, to pick out their goals in life, and go for it, to hang in there 'til they get it done."

For example, we're always using trigonometry, or "trig," out here treasure hunting. I would like to point out that every course that I took at Purdue University, I am using out here treasure hunting. At the time I was taking the courses, often it just seemed mundane or even ridiculous for me to be taking these courses, because I really didn't think that I needed that know-how. I took a course in welding, for example. I knew I was never going to be a welder. But one recent week when I was out inspecting the *Swordfish*, I looked underneath a section where the guy had been doing overhead welding—which is tougher than ordinary welding because you are doing it upside down. The guy had done an excellent job, because I remembered how the professor had explained how to "lay a good bead." So I looked at it and told him that that was a good job, that he had "laid a good bead." He was very happy, appreciative that I knew what a good bead was.

All the courses I took in college have helped me all the way through life.

Young people ought to appreciate and realize that college training is good for them, no matter what the courses are. Even economics, which I did not enjoy, or history, Shakespeare, or whatever it is—they are all good for you, and you will use them the rest of your life. That was true in high school too. But college training is much more specialized, much more intensive, and more practical to use than the high school courses.

I keep using my education skills all the time with detection systems, and treasure is very hard to find, so you have to figure out and keep trying different systems. All the different shipwrecks have different problems and different depths of water and different currents and different waves and different temperatures and different firmness of the bottom—some of it's like concrete, and some of it's mud, and some, sand, and some, coral—there's all different conditions that you have to put up with. Sometimes all these different things will come up right on one wreck site. You have to be flexible.

Having the opportunity to hear Professor Albert Einstein when he was at Purdue University, formally and informally, I learned a lot, although I never did understand all of his advanced theories. I wasn't that smart. He was smart! A lot of things he would be saying would kind of go in one ear and out the other, because I didn't understand it. But at least he got the ideas out. I still use things from him as they come to my mind. I guess you could say he was an idol of mine. For example, I am still piddling around with some of his ideas on the "mailboxes," and on gold head detectors—there are some other guys out in California whom I met who are working on some of those concepts. I am always experimenting with some equipment to see if it won't find treasure better.

More than he knows, a fellow from PM Magazine, John, was right on target when he commented, "It sounds to me that for you, the search was more fun than the actual find." That's true. It still is true. There are eight more bronze cannons on the *Atocha* that are still out there under the ocean that we have not found. You know that I am going to keep going until we find all eight of them. They are hard to find.

Treasure "division" was another Mel Fisher "five-minute job."

It was almost an impossible task for our team to prepare for division of the 1985 treasure finds in September of 1986, but we did it. Can you imagine—in our museum in Key West, we had forty-seven tons—huge stacks—of silver bars all over the floors? You can't even imagine how many times we moved them. People don't think of that.

They think you just bring it in and hand it out to people.

We bring silver bars up from the bottom, and you can't leave them on the top of the boat, because it makes the boat top-heavy. So you have to hand them all down. You pick them up from the deck and hand them down to a guy in the engine room. He has to carry it down to the other end.

One day we had so many bars in the *Dauntless*, and so many video cameras and people on board, that it was getting dangerous. The boat was on a list, and I could see a storm coming. I said, "Hey, you guys, get twenty of those bars out of the bilge and take them over to that boat." So they had to hand them back up on deck and stack them, then hand them into a Whaler, and they had to stack them. They would take them over to this other boat, hand them up, and stack them on deck. Then they had to stack them down in that engine room.

So we fed twenty bars each to about six boats. Then you take them into the dock, and it is quite a height to hand these bars up. You get the silver bars out of the engine room and put them up on deck. Every time you pick one up, it's a superhuman effort. It's just about all you can do. You go to pick one up, and it seems like it's nailed to the deck. Then you lift it up. Another guy grabs it and puts it in a truck. You fill a whole truck load with a ton and a half, and then you drive over to the museum.

"What are we going to do with them now?" You stack them in the front of the museum and carry them up the steps. Stack them just inside the door. The next day you have to pick them up again and move them into the museum and stack them in there. There you have to turn them all upside down and stamp a number on them. You have to lift them again, and then you have to lift them again to weigh them. You put them all on scales, and you weigh each one with the serial number. Then you've got huge stacks of silver bars in there and you think, well, we'd better stack them all up in little stacks all around the wall because we have to be able to find one when somebody wants one. When you want *that* bar, we have to know where it is. We can't get one out of the middle of that big pile. So you restack them again and get them all organized.

Then you think, "Well, now we're going to preserve them." So you pick all these bars up again and put them in the elevator. Put them on a pushcart and take them up to the third floor, where we have this big laboratory. You put them in some tanks there, where we preserve them for about three or four days. It stops them from corroding; it cleans them up and takes off the silver sulfides. Then you unhook them, lift them out of the electrolyte, put them back on the carts, take them back downstairs, and stack them up again.

By the time you go through all this, and then

deliver them to one of the investors, you are glad to see them go. You put one on their shoulder. Then they are leaning over with inhuman effort to get it out to their truck or their car. Then the back of their car sinks, you know, and they take off up the highway.

We have moved about forty-five tons of silver bars that way, and still they are getting moved all over the country and all over the world. They get on airplanes, and people carry them on pushcarts down the aisles of the planes. They sometimes ship silver bars by air freight, and they mark them as being stones, mud samples, or something, disguise them. It's amazing.

Gold is the same way. It just keeps going through the centuries. It just keeps going and going and going, from man to man, man to woman, woman to man. They buy this, they buy that, and they buy something else. Maybe the boat sinks. Then somebody finds it and brings it up. It buys something else, and it goes to some other country. The gold is made into jewelry. Later it is melted down and made back into gold bars. It just keeps going forever, shining forever. Everybody keeps wanting more of it.

People ask how we convert treasure into "liquid assets"—into money—so that people can do whatever they want to with it. First, a lot of people donate treasure. The wealthier people donate it as tax write-offs. Some people sell treasure just to collectors. It's not an easy thing to market treasure either. That's another whole ballgame. So if we say the *Margarita* finds, in 1980, yielded $20 million, you'd think, "$20 million! My gosh." But that $20 million amount is what I call "optimum fair market value." That means the highest price that you could expect to sell treasure for under retail conditions, with a willing buyer and a willing seller. In real life, many other business and other factors are involved. There's also a wholesale value, for example. About half that. There's also a distributor's value or manufacturer's price, which is maybe one-quarter of the optimum fair market value.

So we consider ourselves something like manufacturers. We're like a factory. We don't just find this treasure, and it's not instant money. It has to be sold through distributors, jobbers, dealers, and stores, or in auctions. Everybody along the way gets their fair profit out of it.

As Deo points out, though, a lot of people don't even want to sell their treasure. They want to just keep it. People ask how many millionaires are being made through the *Atocha* and *Margarita* finds, other treasure discoveries. I have no idea. I really don't care either. Quite a few, I believe. I finally realized I was a cash money millionaire when I sold $1.7 million worth of coins to one guy. Then I had $1.7 million.

Very soon, I bought the museum building we are in for $1.4 million, and I more or less spent the rest of it. Money doesn't really matter. It is really kind of silly to even talk about it pertaining to the treasure, because as I say so often, treasure goes from hand to hand, from one museum to another. It's just not money. These are antiques, valuable metals, valuable jewels. Money is paper. Money is just paper. These things are for real. They've got history and archaeology connected with them. A lot of the people just don't even want to sell it. For a long time, I didn't really try to sell any of my treasure, to tell you the truth. I just let people look at it, pick it up, try it on their necks. It educates people about the past, and the way they did things in the old days. Money is really not important at all. Only when you run out of it. When you don't have any of it, and you've got a bill to pay. Then you can go hustle, sell a coin or two, and pay the bill.

Probably the biggest misconception I know is that people think you just go out there, find treasure, and become an instant millionaire.

Would-be treasure hunters get disillusioned real quick when they get out in that big ocean and start looking. They look in all directions and just see water, water, water everywhere. Then they get a little seasick. They go back and forth for three or four days. It gets boring to them, and they give up. They have no concept of how long it takes, how much it's going to cost, the hardships they are going to have to go through.

One guy who really knew about it was the Spanish soldier and salvager, Francisco Núñez Melián. He evidently had had quite a bit of experience, because when he came here to look for the *Atocha* and *Margarita*, he came with four tons of bat guano for fertilizer, a ton of pitch, a lot of seeds, and all kinds of things that you never think of having for a treasure hunt. He knew it was going to take several years, and he knew that it took a lot of perseverance, time, money, and hard work. He imported the bat guano from the caves in the Cayman Islands. They came to the Marquesas Keys, where it's relatively sandy. The ground is tough to grow things in, so they had plenty of fertilizer. They started their own vegetable gardens and grew their own wheat and other crops. They dug a well and had a caisson they brought for that. They knew they were going to need water. They were really well prepared. They also had specially made diving bells, believe it or not, and they successfully used them. That's how they found the *Margarita*. They would drift with the tide. The tide would go for six hours in a northerly direction, and then it would stop. When it stopped, they would move over a little bit. Then the tide would go in a southerly direction for six hours, and they would drift along with the diving bell hanging underneath the ship and four divers—with the diving bell being close to the bottom and no waves and sun reflection, so they could see the bottom and look for wreckage.

In that manner they drifted for several weeks back and forth searching with this diving bell, and they came upon the *Margarita*. They didn't come upon it. They searched for it and found it! They found half of it. Then they stayed there and worked for four years. We've got a day-by-day inventory of the auditing records of four certified accountants they had there writing down in longhand everything that happened: how many coins came up this day, and how many bars came up that day. It was even embarrassing, though, because I think of the first two hundred silver bars that they recovered, none of them were on the manifest. The other half of that shipwreck is still out there, and we found a portion of that. We found, well—optimum or most favorable value—about twenty million bucks worth of things down there, but really there's still roughly another $180 million still out there. So we are searching for that today. We've got all of our fleet and ships working on the hunt for the other half of the *Margarita.*

The questions keep being asked: "A lot of people think that when we are talking about many millions of dollars' worth of stuff, hundreds of millions of dollars sometimes, it seems that by now, since treasures from the *Atocha* and *Margarita* have been found or are still being found, that there have been dozens of millionaires made because of all of this. Is that true? Has that really happened?" My answer is, "I believe so. A lot of people have been very well rewarded. One couple invested $90,000. I recall they got about ten million bucks worth of stuff. There have been some millionaires made. That's all right. That's fine. There's plenty there for everybody."

But most people who are investing also know it takes time to get a cash return, just like in other businesses. When people get greedy, they sometimes forget that. For example, when we found the *Margarita* treasures in 1980, it was several years away from being twenty million dollars' worth of assets that were distributed, a couple of years away from being anything because of the cataloging process, and because of the requirement for an admiralty award of title to the finds from the federal judge in the US District Court system.

Same Trouble, Different Wreck

The same kinds of problems we had on our 1960 Silver Shoals trip happened in the late 1980s on an expedition, down in the Curaçao area. The water was bad—big, thirty-foot waves; the wind was blowing, engines breaking down. Everything was going wrong you could think of. But I thought we were succeeding. There were quite a few people in that expedition of the 1980s, and there were in 1960 too, that just think negative. They're pessimists, and at the same time they just think the whole thing's a lark, or a wild dream, and it "really isn't there." That discourages some of the other people. So I'm getting to go back again on this one, and I'm just not going to let the negative people go with us. I want some positive thinkers, people who are optimistic, and are enthusiastic; they want to "go for it." I always believe we're going to succeed because of that. Some of the negative thinkers on the late 1980s venture wrote me a letter and said, "It ain't there." They wrote: "As you know, our recent search efforts off the coast of Curaçao were unsuccessful. We are not only disappointed but frustrated as well. We are not accustomed to failing. And including some of our own equipment problems, this project did not go well." I had to laugh. I couldn't believe it when I got that letter—because I thought it went great! Regardless of all the problems, bad weather, engine breakdowns, equipment breakdowns, and human error, miscalculations and misjudgments, underfinancing, and all the problems that you ever have, we hit it! We succeeded! We found out what we were looking for, and now we're going for it.

Keep On Keepin' On

Wendy, you asked me about my dreaming, motivation, my own self-drive? What is there about Mel that makes you see things that other people don't? I told her, "If it wasn't for that type of attitude, we'd just have received this letter and said, 'Well, too bad. We failed.' And we never would have found it." Instead, we're forging ahead and going for it. In three or four weeks we'll just have tons of gold and all kinds of stuff! Wendy said, "Well, what will that 'tons of gold' let you do?" I replied, "I don't know—go on more adventures!"

Always the Water

Wendy asked, "Going back to your earliest days, Mel. You were doing this sort of thing long before anybody else. Why did the ocean appeal to you, since you came from Indiana? How did you come to become a 'water man'?"

I'm not sure. I always liked the water as a kid in Indiana too. From the swimming pool at our high school to the public swimming pools and the lagoon in Marquette Park near Lake Michigan. Back then, Lake Michigan itself was beautiful, clear water. The water was clear and good then, in the gravel pits and stone quarries around. Even a little pond in the cemetery. I just went to the water. I don't know why. I'd follow creeks and rivers to see where they started and where they ended. I'd go hiking for two or three days, following a creek and river until it dumped into Lake Michigan or whatever. I got to go through a lot of wilderness that way, and bump into a lot of birds, and fish, and horned things along the way. I enjoyed it.

Getting Past Your Fears

Wendy asked: "Did you feel a special affinity, once you got in the ocean, for the creatures there? You seem never to know fear. You do things that might scare other people—going out there on your own. Yet you speak in understatement about things that might terrify a lot of citizens. In the end, I've seen you bring a lot of people past their own fears."

Of course, looking back now on the things I did when I was younger, I must have been crazy. They called me "Fearless Fisher." I really shouldn't have been stabbing sharks, and hitting them on the head with sledgehammers, and spearing them, and making movies of them eating each other. I should have left them alone and got out of the water—like I do now.

One day I was talking to a guy about that that is doing research on shark-shocking machines. I did research on that several years ago too—about twenty-five years ago. Fay Feild was working on it. It seemed to work pretty well. We had this probe. If we'd touch a shark with it, or just get near him and push a button, like a cattle prod, it would give him a jolt, and he'd take off. He'd never felt that before, and it scared the hell out of him.

So one day Fay tried it on what looked like a seventeen- or eighteen-foot hammerhead. He jolted it, and it took off. The shark went just barely out of sight, about fifty or sixty feet, and he made a U-turn and came right back at Fay, with his mouth wide open, his jaws kind of wavering back and forth past him.

Then Fay shoved the shark-shocking prod right down his mouth, and the thing ate up the machine. We gave up on that. We haven't used it since. That shark just ate the shocking machine. I guess he was mad. They've got such good acid in their stomachs—he probably devoured it and consumed it.

But years later, this new guy is working on it. I told him I wanted one that we can have on the bottom of the boat, instead of us having to go down and touch the shark with it or be real close to them. Before we get in the water, we can push a button, and all the sharks within a hundred yards would take off, and they'd learn pretty soon that whenever they come near that boat, they're going to get a jolt. So that would train the sharks. Then if we're down there diving, and sharks come in on us, like they do once in a while, we can do something about it. When sharks come in, they're usually not attacking us, they're just curious, and so they're coming in looking at us—but it makes us spooky. When that happens now, we have to get out of the water and wait.

If we could develop an invention such as I have in mind, when sharks come and we get out of the water, instead of waiting around an hour to go back in and see if they've had lunch, I'd rather get out of the water and give those sharks a jolt, make them all take off, and then go right back in the water again. The fellow said he'd work on that model and see if he could make a shark-shocker that'll work as I suggested. I hope he does.

The question comes up, "What about sound, as opposed to electricity?" I didn't talk to the guy about that, but I know it does work. I've done some research on that too. There's one sound that, unfortunately, you can't make with electricity. The sound is a kind of *poomph*. It's such a low frequency that a speaker won't make it. I think it more or less imitates a sound similar to that of the thumping of the tail of an attacking porpoise, and it must put the fear of God into a shark. Because when they had heard that thumping, a porpoise was chasing them before, so they don't like it. That sound meant a porpoise was about ready to hit them in the side with their snout, so when sharks hear that low, thumping sound, they take off. I haven't followed through on that yet.

"How do you have time to go in all these directions at once?" I am asked.

I don't. I work seven days a week, but I still don't find time to do it all. So I try to get other talented people working around me, and with me, who can do it. I just help them, and give them the ideas, and help get the money for it, or do research on it to try to accomplish it.

So we'll be working on that too—shark-shocking machines and shark sound machines. We'll probably have to do it mechanically. But we haven't been able to recreate it yet.

Then There's the Government

Knock around Washington, DC, go through several of the congressional sessions, and you begin to realize that those guys are powerful. Even though each one, individually, is just an ordinary guy, collectively they can do anything. Much of it is done unknowledgeably. They just don't have time to do it all. Just like me. I don't have time to do everything that I want to do. So they very often just barter and bargain with each other. They say, "Well, I haven't read your bill about preserving shipwrecks, but I've got one here on a dam. So you vote for mine and I'll vote for yours." They choose words—"preserving shipwrecks" or "preserving history"—to make legislation sound like it's something real neat. Instead, they are saying that the government's going to take title to all the treasure and not let any private enterprise work on it. Disappointing as it is, that's the actuality of it. When the senator or congressman gets up there and says he's "working to preserve historic sites," it just sounds good.

In my claim to the *Atocha*, I thought that once I won in the Supreme Court of the United States, that was it, it was over and done with. But these guys can just come in and with a stroke of the pen create a new Act of Congress. They can completely set aside anything that the Supreme Court's done.

They can pass a new law and say: "From now on all shipwrecks and all treasures belong to the federal government." They wrote a law like that first in the early 1980s. I went up to see US Senator Paula Hawkins from Florida. I explained to her how that wasn't the way it is, that admiralty law was created to take care of salvaging. I explained how the Constitution also stated that.

At that time, she had it shelved. She helped me that year. But each year's different. That's something else I don't understand about Congress. Once they bring up a bad idea like that, and it gets voted down, I should think they would throw it in the wastebasket, forget it. But they don't do that. Each year they keep reintroducing it. Then it gets voted down again, and the next year they reintroduce it again.

That went on for five years. Each year it was turned down. But, finally, in 1988, it looked like bad legislation was going to get passed, because they had just worn me down, and other people too. It costs an awful lot of money to go lobbying all the time and to hire lobbyists. There's a lot of travel expense, there are so many expenses, just to be heard.

I testified in the congressional hearings and the Senate hearings for four straight years.

But in 1988, I was just busy. I was on an expedition, treasure hunting down in Venezuela, and I just couldn't be at the Senate hearing. That time I didn't get go to Washington to defend private industry.

So up there, they just said, "OK that sounds good. The government can 'preserve shipwrecks' now." They didn't explain—nobody explained to them—that really they're just taking possession, stealing all the treasure, for the government, when it doesn't belong to the government.

Under admiralty salvage law, it belongs to the finder. They're just taking the entire concept that we've had for two hundred years and turning it around and trying to let the government take it all. They're just not capable.

Can you imagine the government spending several million dollars a year treasure hunting? They would have to build a huge building bigger than the White House to handle the offices.

The night I returned to Key West by air from a congressional appearance in 1988, I was really tired and almost discouraged when I opened the door of my house, set my briefcase down, and headed for the kitchen. As I got ice from the refrigerator, opened the cupboard for some rum, and poured Coke on top of it, Deo asked me:

"How did it go up there?"

I told her, "I think they really had it stacked against us up there. I had to listen to about fifteen or twenty testimonies before I got to talk, and they were all state agents and government agents talking about why they should own all the treasure."

Deo asked whether any of them were as truthful as the woman who had once said at a hearing that they needed "title" before they could get their funding.

That's what it boils down to. I pointed that truth out to the congressmen and their aides when I talked, that all these people wanted were government grants, big government grants! And that's why they're doing it; it was just a matter of greed. Instead, they just were talking about archaeology, and using all the nice words that sound like "preserving Plymouth Rock." I read something that we had prepared, and I just read it verbatim. I didn't do that the year before. I couldn't find the papers I had there, so I had just talked. This time I read it verbatim.

But as I was listening to the people before me, I made a few notes as to the questions the congressmen and their aides were asking. It seemed like they were going backwards about five years and getting even more greedy, wanting to have ownership of all ships that were outside the United States and outside the state and federal boundaries.

I realized that they didn't even know what the boundaries were—nobody there did. They also didn't know that the state boundary was the same as the federal boundary. They were trying to say, "Well, anything out of the state boundary but still in the government boundary, we can own." So when I got up, I informed them that they were one and the same, that the state's boundaries were the same as the federal boundaries, and that it was three miles in the Atlantic Ocean and three leagues in the Gulf of Mexico. I tried to point out that if they went beyond those boundaries, then they were really in big trouble, because

134 nations had agreed in a Geneva treaty conference, and they all signed this treaty, which stated that no states or governments own any shipwrecks or bullion lying on or under the subsea floor, and that's it—they all signed it.

So, I explained, if they wanted to try to claim that they owned everything outside the state's boundaries and the government's boundaries, then they really had an international problem.

Also, I pointed out, even on the stuff that was inside the boundaries, they had a problem with the US Constitution. I beseeched them to refer this question before the Judicial Committee rather than Fisheries, because it was a Constitutional violation, and the same guys that wrote the Constitution wrote the admiralty laws concerning shipwrecks, and so it should go before that committee.

Also, I pointed out that they were getting into time troubles. They were saying they wanted to own all shipwrecks after they've been down for a year and a day. I told them that I'd been through this thing for many, many years, and if they were going to pick a time to call something a "historical wreck site," it should be a hundred years, and that that's no problem, we could easily identify the date—"circa"—of any shipwreck.

I pointed out that if they didn't, then they were going to have a horrendous liability—the federal government and the states. That would be because there are thousands of shipwrecks out in the ocean that are sunk but are just beneath the water surface, and any interests in any ship that hits it, also relatives if people die, will all sue the states and the federal government—if they own them. So they really shouldn't do that.

Then there's the Jones Act, which is very, very powerful, and there would be no question whatsoever but what the states and the federal government would be completely liable for the loss of any seamen or ships that hit these sunken wrecks.

What was frightening was that they seemed much uninformed.

They just seemed to have faith in whoever came in there to discuss this thing. The only one who seemed to know what he was talking about was Mr. [US Representative Norman D.] Shumway from California. I knew he'd probably done quite a bit of research, because he had introduced one of the bills. The other fellow, from Florida, had been trying to get his bill passed for five years, and it had been turned down every year, because the bill was just ill-conceived and had no provisions for free enterprise, the American system, and it gave complete title and ownership to the federal government, and said then they could give it to the states.

That's directly against the Constitution, and it's directly against admiralty law.

I told them all that up there, after I read the regular talk I had. I took notes on all the things I told them about.

Deo asked me if I had told them about a basic contract that I've worked out with some foreign governments that seems pretty fair to all. I didn't go into that. But I told them I'd been working very well with the compromise agreement we made with Florida.

The main thing was that about ten of the people who testified said that there were no provisions in admiralty law to protect historic shipwrecks.

I told them that wasn't true, that the judge has stated—and it was a matter of law now—that the archaeology guidelines had to be complied with, and that in the event that the state felt that we had found something that would be usable as a museum piece, in a public museum, that they could present a claim for it and probably get it.

I told them that we had been working for the last five years under a system like that, and it had been very smooth; everything was going fine.

And that not one case had ever had to come up before the federal court, because in all instances, ourselves and the state agreed as to what items should be donated by us to the state of Florida for their museums. And that without that, it wouldn't work at all, because without the judge's gavel above our heads, we would not be able to come to an agreement.

I also got on the record an idea I have to restructure the tax law.

It came out that South Carolina is taking 50 percent of the gross of anything recovered from any shipwreck, and they've been doing this successfully now for five years. But there's only been one salvager that was naive enough and—must be an awful bad businessman—agreed to give them 50 percent of his gross.

I told the congressmen that the main correction needed to any new legislation was that the shipwrecks and the treasure do not belong to the federal government. For the rest of it, I agreed that there should be archaeological guidelines. That was included in Shumway's bill—which was the one we should use if either was going to be passed. I had talked to Shumway in the past, but I never did claim that any of his bills were my effort. I didn't have anything to do with it. He just wrote it out on his own. I didn't even know he was going to have anything to do with it. He had asked me questions the year before, because I read the testimony from the year before, and he asked me what I thought. I told him, and I guess he took that answer and tried to fill out a compromise. I ended up concluding that we were probably going to have to have some kind of law go through just to keep everybody happy. So as long as it didn't give the government title to the shipwrecks, I thought it could be a clarification of what's already going on, having that spelled out a little more definitely, so that everybody would know that history and archaeology is being preserved.

All they did, in the end, was say that they wanted everything.

In 1988, I considered making a videotape to send to all the senators and congressmen and putting a little treasure in there. I hoped that some of them would take it home and show it to their families, get to talking about it, and realize that the government doesn't own shipwrecks and treasure. I wanted to try to convince them to vote against it. But I couldn't afford to do it at that time. I decided instead to try to get the general public to write letters, send telegrams, call up their senators and congressmen, and tell them they were against the government taking over the salvage industry.

The message I sent out urged people to urge their congressmen to: "*VOTE 'NO' ON H.R. 74!*" I sent a similar message straight to the lawmakers themselves.

I told them I took so much flak from the state and federal governments during these past twenty-seven years that I just don't want to see my grandchildren have to go through what I did. What I tried to do was get together a knowledgeable group of people who know the most about admiralty law and the US Constitution, the ways they affect treasure hunting, and the ways they affect archaeology and history.

We wanted to write up a "Bible" for treasure hunters, archaeologists, historians, and legislators, and have a "Mini-Bible" to summarize things for the legislators, their aides, and also the state governments. We planned to also publish a thick "Bible" to distribute free to legislators, aides, and governments all over the world. We thought perhaps we could sell some at a low price or a very narrow profit margin, and that way get the story out to the world about the way it should be with salvage.

Our best efforts couldn't win against a tricky timetable in Congress that year. Nothing we would have done, it turned out, would probably have made a great difference, given the misunderstanding or worse about what the real truth is about our underwater world.

We should keep admiralty law intact, and the US Constitution intact, and the international treaties intact, the way our forefathers designed them and wrote them, and not try to change them now to avoid admiralty law.

It would be tragic to have a new law saying that the government owns all shipwrecks and treasure!

Wendy, you asked me at one point, "In the long haul, which has been tougher—fighting situations offshore or people onshore?" I said that the toughest part has been fighting the governments and others who try to pirate the treasure.

I've gone through 114 federal lawsuits, some of them were eight or nine or ten days long [in court]. I've gone through the US Appellate Court three times and the US Supreme Court once. I won all of them!

Still, even after the Supreme Court decision—which I thought was the law of the land and would forever end injustice—much to my dismay and chagrin, I learned that any congressman or senator can just, with the stroke of a pen, write a new Act of Congress and get it through—one way or another, by hook or crook. That becomes a new law! Such unfair tactics can void all the things in the Constitution, the things in admiralty law, and all the court decisions in the past—even Supreme Court decisions. They can just make a brand-new law to circumvent what is just. This seems wrong to me!

They kept trying to do that for five years in a row, and each year I managed to get it stopped. However, by 1988, it looked just "touch and go." They got it through committee in the House. I was so worried about it that I thought perhaps a new book or two would help, plus I wanted to make some television videos about it and try to get the general public to help me, also educate the congressional aides and staff personnel to inform the lawmakers themselves.

It seems a lot of the senators and congressmen

don't have time to read this stuff, and they just—well, they're trading legislation. For example, they'll say, "You know, Joe, if you vote for my new Act of Congress, I'll vote for yours. I want a dam over here in Tennessee, and you want to protect shipwrecks in Florida, so we'll just vote for each other." They don't even bother really reading it, and don't have the time to delve into the serious Constitutional and judicial aspects of such new legislation.

On the surface, it sounded good—"protecting shipwrecks" sounds really great.

But really they're destroying shipwrecks, because as these things sit out there, each year they get more and more deteriorated. The wood is being eaten up by teredo worms. The beautiful silver things are corroding away—because saltwater is an electrolyte. Out there, a shipwreck is just like a huge battery. It keeps eating away all of the metal objects except gold. Gold is inert. If we don't get these things out of the ocean and preserve them, they're just going to crumble into bits through the centuries.

Not many interviewers think to ask, "What have been the roles of private enterprise vs. the government's role in actual salvage?"

The fact is—the government's never done any salvaging.

If the government was to set up a $5 billion salvage program and set up a billion-dollar laboratory to preserve things, and hire qualified archaeologists, historians, and salvage masters to do the work, then I should think they should be able to file an admiralty claim on a shipwreck and own it.

If they were to go out there with the latest in remote sensing equipment and locate a shipwreck and identify it, and "arrest" it in admiralty court, they would have a perfect right to own it and work it, just like any other salvor. But they shouldn't be able to own it just by making a stroke of a pen, and saying, "We own it. In fact, we own any shipwreck which any salvage company may find."

They're taking it away from the people, and the salvors, and the free enterprise system. They're leaning toward Marxism rather than democracy, and that's just not the American way.

Americans Have Dreams

They want to follow their dreams and be a free person to do this. They want to pay their own expenses, and do their own detection, and do their own preservation, and their own archaeology. They'd probably hire professionals to help them, but they should have a right to be in business, just like any other business in the United States, and not have their factory owned by the government, and all the assets owned by the government.

I believe that if the government went into the salvage business, it would probably never get done, unless they threw an awful lot of money at it.

Based on my generations of salvaging under contract with the State of Florida, I would imagine they have in mind doing just as the State of Florida did—using the claim of title as a club over free enterprise, salvagers, then approaching them and saying, "Hey, look, if you want to work on one of these wrecks that we own, then you've got to go by our rules, do it the way we say. You've got to give us a large amount of the gross of the treasure that you find—before you can deduct any expenses.

"If you break any rule, you get a fifty-thousand-dollar fine for each infraction or for each object salvaged. Then we'll still charge you for income tax when you finally do make a profit, if you do make a profit." But if it's a mediocre wreck or a poor wreck, they won't let you take out your expenses. They take their share of the objects recovered from the gross. So in 90 percent of the cases where free enterprise is salvaging, they would lose money because of that.

There's no business in the country that can

operate—any business—where the government takes 25 or 50 percent of their gross income before they allow them to deduct expenses.

The State of Florida held the *Atocha* treasures for five years with no distribution to the salvors. If the government wants to take a large percentage of the gross from a free enterprise business in the United States, then it should take a large percentage of the gross of all businesses in the United States, not just the salvage business.

An example of how misguided law proposals can be is one I received a copy of in 1988. In big, bold print was a notice that said: "$50,000 fines proposed in House Bill 74." That's the one they developed in 1987 and, as proposed, for using underwater metal detectors or commercial shipwreck salvage or recreational wreck diving, they could create any rules and regulations they so desire, and if any of these rules and regulations are broken, they would have a right to place a $50,000 fine for each infraction. That is very unjust. Free enterprise should be free and not cost a whole bunch of money to be handed over to the government. They're just blatantly attempting to put all salvage companies out of business and prevent the use of metal detectors and recreational diving.

That's just against the American spirit.

I've experienced firsthand some real injustices dealt out by agents of the state and federal governments. In fact, one of the federal judges wrote a fifty-four-page report eloquently describing all of the ways in which the State of Florida has harassed me, and my captains, and my divers. They've put them in jail, arrested them. The same goes for me. They've put stickers on our boats, so that they'd be impounded. They've confiscated the items that we've salvaged. They've held materials for several years so that we couldn't sell anything and make a living. The State of Florida created so many rules and regulations! They kept adding more and more. Each year they'd have another hundred rules—to the point where it was absolutely impossible to go out and do a day's work. There's just no way you could abide by all those rules. If you're going to have a $50,000 fine for an infraction of each rule, that would really throw it out, over the fence. It would mean just nothing was ever done. Everybody would have to be criminals if they wanted to go in the water.

In the old days of the 1960s, when we first started in, there were no laws, rules, or regulations. We got along fine. I took all the things I found up to the university. The professors were working with us on determining what type of materials we'd recovered, studying them, and photographing them, measuring them, trying to find out the nationality, the year, and everything.

After some years, in the late 1960s, they passed a law similar to what they were trying to do in 1987. It was an illegal law. They put it in the state constitution, saying that the state owned everything—all shipwrecks and treasure, that the state could make up as many rules and regulations as it wished, and they would automatically become law without going through the Legislature and getting it approved there.

That also is unconstitutional. But they did it. They're still trying to uphold that, although it has fallen several times in the federal admiralty court. They've determined over and over again in the federal admiralty court that the states do not own shipwrecks or treasure. Nor can they enforce these rules and regulations that they have made as law. I don't want to deal with the United States government either. They also intervened in court and said they owned it all. The lower court disagreed; the lower court said the federal government does not own shipwrecks and treasure. The federal government appealed it to the appellate court, with three judges presiding.

These three admiralty judges agreed that shipwrecks do not belong to the government—to the US government. The federal government failed to appeal that case, that appellate case, to the Supreme Court, because they knew the odds were against them, that they couldn't possibly win. So they dropped it.

And I don't want the government, the federal government, to have title to these wrecks, and I don't want the states to have title either—because neither one of them would do a good job.

I'm sure it would be just the way it was back in 1965 and later, when they just strangled the free enterprise salvagers and put them out of business. I finally left the area, moved to Key West, and started working outside the state of Florida. Then they even came out there and claimed that their boundary went out to the edge of the Continental Shelf, which is ridiculous! It wasn't until the oil companies challenged them on their territorial boundary claims that those claims were halted—when the US Supreme Court decided that the boundaries would be three miles in the Atlantic, and three leagues in the Gulf.

That ended that question.

About that time, I decided to file in admiralty court as owner of the *Atocha* shipwreck. The admiralty court, and the federal judge presiding over it who acts as a moderator, has been very reasonable. The federal admiralty judge did award a portion of the items to the state of Florida. Admiralty court does assure that proper archaeology is done on the wreck sites, that the historic research is done, and that pirates are not allowed to take any of the treasure.

The admiralty court has done an excellent job through the years, for more than two hundred years, and no shipwreck has ever been harmed or destroyed under admiralty jurisdiction.

However, in various state jurisdictions, several wrecks have been destroyed. There was such destruction on shipwrecks I was working on. Once I found a ship called the *San José*, at Coffins Patch, about three and a half miles east of Duck Key, Florida. The State of Florida came in and claimed they owned it. I had subcontracted it out to another salvage company, which was led by Tom Gurr.

The state bullied him and took him to court. He didn't have enough money to pay for good attorneys. As a result, they forced him to make a deal with them under which the state would get half of the gross income, and they would get half. They ended up arresting him, putting him in jail, and putting him out of business. He had to move to Panama to go treasure hunting.

Yes, that's what they do. If they have title and ownership, then it's theirs, and they can do anything they want, and you don't have any choice about negotiating an agreement with them. They make an agreement the way they want it, and you either sign it, or you cannot work on a shipwreck. That's bad news.

Personally, and I think a lot of Americans agree with me, I don't like the government meddling in the free enterprise business. I think that they should stay out of it and let the people do it.

We're doing a good job. We're educating people. We have things in many museums all over the world that otherwise would still be down under the ocean, corroding away and rotting away.

We have made a lot of people happy, inspired a lot of people, and educated a lot of people. We've given a lot of—thousands of—kids an interest in history, an interest in archaeology, and an interest in achieving a goal in life.

To take all that away and say, "Nobody can treasure hunt anymore." Then we might not have any more Tom Sawyers, Huckleberry Finns, you know?

Luck and Hard Work for Mo and Mel and . . .

In 1987 I sold the boat *Virgalona* to "Mo" Molinar for a dollar when I made him a partner on a wreck we've been salvaging together all through the years. Soon after, he called one morning at 8 o'clock. He said he had the boat all ready to go and he was boogyin'! He was heading out to sea. I wondered what he'd find.

At the end of the 1988 diving season, during the last week, Mo Molinar found 220 gold coins on the same 1715 Spanish Plate Fleet wreck where we first found gold in 1964.

When we had a division on that material in 1989, Mo and his three new partners came to Key West. Also, my old friend and associate Harold Holden, who has his own company, was here. With myself, my daughter Taffi, and my son Kim, we got the division done for my Cobb Coin Company and its associates, and everybody was happy.

Holden got 15 percent of the things that Mo found. That is because I had given a small search area on that wreck to Holden, on an exclusive basis, because he had been working in that area for four and a half years, even though it was not very productive.

He talked Mo into coming up there and helping him, because the *Virgalona* has better "mailboxes," and Holden couldn't work in the deeper water.

Finally, the thing paid off this year.

Mo found—it's approaching—one thousand gold coins. Then on one day in 1989, he found 120 beautiful gold doubloons, eight escudos, and all of them were dated but one. They were all from the historic Spanish Lima mint, and they're rather rare.

On the 1715 wrecks in 1988, they were leapfrogging, or hopscotching, each other, with three boats—my operations manager for the 1715 fleet, John Brandon with the *Endeavor*, Harold Holden with his boat, and Mo Molinar with the *Virgalona*.

Mo seemed to keep hitting it consistently better than the other boats! I don't know if its luck or that gold tooth he has, his radar, or the *Virgalona* being a lucky boat.

But we learned that that shipwreck, my first one, is like all of the others I've ever worked. It's scattered out for miles, instead of just being in one spot.

Today's the Day!

Grandfathered Admiralty Claim Holds

By 1989, I came up with a new theory about this particular ship of the 1715 Fleet. Dr. Lyon—Gene—said he had identified this ship as the *Nuestra Señora de las [Nieves y] Las Animas*, which means, "Our Lady of Snow of Your Soul." The new theory was that the troubled ship came in from the northeast instead of the southeast, like I'd been thinking for the previous twenty-five years. These ships were scattered, so far flung, up north and south along the beach, that some ships had a different direction of wind than the others. I now think this one came in from the northeast. It became obvious that gold was heading out in that direction. So it became a trail similar to that of the *Atocha*—very long and strung out for miles.

With that conclusion, I extended my admiralty salvage rights in that direction. I did that in federal admiralty court.

By then there was a new Act of Congress in effect that was yet to be challenged. According to that new act, this federal admiralty claim cannot be made on newly discovered shipwrecks.

But I was sure it could be done on this one, as the old salvage claims, I was sure, were grandfathered in. I made sure, though, to write a letter to the state and inform them about what I'd done, so they didn't issue a lease to somebody else for that area, because it would conflict with my admiralty claim.

Time and Treasure Finds Do Loop Occasionally

Late on Tuesday night, Aug. 22, 1988, just a day after my birthday, I got a call from my longtime associate on the 1715 Fleet quest, Roy Volker. Roy said, "Today was the day!" And he told me he'd worked all the way from the "Cabin—that's Kip Wagner's cabin—Wreck" toward Sebastian Inlet for about six miles, dug hundreds and hundreds of holes, and didn't find anything.

Then he'd decided to come back where he started and go the opposite direction. He went about a hundred feet and came into a hole about the size of a kitchen. There he found about eight hundred silver pieces of eight. He also found a few smaller coins, denominations of four reales, and two reales, and one reale, and a gold ring. I congratulated him and told him I felt very happy for him, because he had been really working long, hard hours all summer long, and he hadn't found anything. All of a sudden, he came into it! That was really great! I was very glad for him.

This is one wreck we've worked a long time. We started working on this one in 1963—that's more than twenty-five years ago. The first people who were working on it was the Real Eight Company and Kip Wagner, and then I—we—went in there with our magnetometer and helped them locate a huge pile of treasure.

At that time, I remember, we found more than a ton of these silver coins in one day! Way back then! We called it the "Cabin Wreck" from the beginning. By the late 1980s, Volker had started using a jet-powered boat, with a Navy surplus superjet engine, for his quest. Asked if it was really 888 pieces Volker had found in 8/88, I said, "Well, it was a little over eight hundred 'pieces of eight'—the big ones—and then the rest were probably the 88 smaller coins."

"Green Fire"

By January 1988, I was really focused on "green fire," the large amounts of dark green and valuable emeralds that were being found on the *Atocha* site, although they had been nowhere listed on the archival cargo lists or "manifests." Manuel Marcial [de Gomar], President of Emeralds International, Inc., told me he worked in the emerald mines in Colombia as a boy, and the only mine that he worked in and had ever found emeralds of the quality and color that we have found was in the Coscuez mine in the Muzo area of Colombia. However, they really can't find many of this high-quality stone anymore. They are also having major problems in Colombia, with battles between the cocaine smugglers, the guerrillas trying to control the emerald market, the emerald mining business, and the government of Colombia. So there is very little emerald recovery going on right now. I think all the stones in that area came into existence at the same time. But only the ones from that mine are this quality. I don't know why the emeralds weren't listed on the manifests. I don't think the king normally had a tax on emeralds. He did on gold and silver. But he did not have one on jewelry or emeralds.

Almost everybody, it seems, did their best to smuggle or carry as many emeralds as they could back to Spain. One big box, though, that we learned from other records, was smuggled aboard, obviously still has not been located, because it alone would be about one hundred times as much as what we have found.

More Finds on 1715 Fleet

Among the 1989 finds by our Cobb Coin Company and associates on the 1715 shipwrecks was a gold box that resembled either a snuff box or a cocaine box. It was gold, I'd say 24-carat pure, with an ornate top and bottom. It resembled a gold watch that would open on a hinge, but it was not a watch, just a box to hold something that someone valued, a small box you could put in your pocket.

Also there was found a very ornate gold fish. This gold fish is like a pocket knife; it opens up with two gold blades. I believe one of the blades is probably a knife for cutting cocaine, and the other's probably a sniffer for snorting "coke."

They did use cocaine in those days, we learned. It's in the documents. They paid the American Indians with cocaine instead of money, and they used it every day. In fact, they had to use it up in the mountains, or they just couldn't exist. Up at fifteen thousand feet altitude, they couldn't exist without it.

Found at about the same time was an ornate decoration, like a Maltese cross, that is made of very rich gold, with green enameling in the arms of the cross, and set with five emeralds and eleven diamonds around the outside. Another rare find of 1989 was a little Lima Mint coin, dated 1698. I told my associates that it would really be wild if that was also a Cuzco Mint coin. We learned it was.

I decided to send my son Kim up there with our *Hatteras*, have him do some subbottom profiling, sidescan sonaring, and "mag" runs, and attempt to find another "big pile" there.

Such a new treasure "pile" would be similar to the *Atocha* "mother lode," and this one, I believed by then, would be more valuable and richer, because it would be mostly gold instead of silver, and so that was very exciting.

I thought we might find the next "big pile" yet that year!

According to Gene, we didn't have any research on the cargo. So at that point it was all in my head. I was hoping that there was going to be another rich one. It couldn't help being rich, with all the millions that we'd brought up from it already.

Yes, twenty-five years earlier, my first big find of four and a half million dollars in gold coins and other treasure was found on that same wreck. One big "problem," however, was that it also looked as though we were going to find the remaining "big pile" of the *Margarita* in the summer of 1989.

Today's the Day!

Ink First Could Show Where Treasure Is

At my Greene Street headquarters space for Cobb Coin Company, in the spring of 1989, I headed into the chartroom to look over our "top secret" map records of find locations to date.

Associate Tony Kopp and I started discussing three years ago when I started experimenting with something I call a "Squark." My "Squark" uses "gold heads" to try to find gold and discriminate it. Right from the very first time I used it, it seemed to work very well. To explain what I did: I had four double-head sets for components, one double-head set located on an outrigger off to the port of the boat, and then another double-head set on the port corner of the boat. I had a magnetometer in the middle of the boat, and then a double-head set on the starboard corner, and another one on the starboard outrigger.

I would run tests using a target, like the ship *Arbutus* that was anchored at the general site. On a chart I noticed a test run on the *Arbutus* dated Sept. 23, 1983. I find one pass recorded here on the chart, another here. So it was clear that we went back, and we got the biggest reading with the set I marked to identify by a black pen. If the *Arbutus* was off to the starboard side, then the double-head set that was closest got the biggest reading. I saw the black pen mark was on the outrigger. The next biggest reading would be the brown or gold. That gold ink must have been on the starboard corner of the boat. Then the red ink was on the port corner, and the blue ink was on the outrigger, because it was a smaller reading. The ones that are farther away from the target get a smaller reading.

So one can also tell what direction the target is from the boat.

Instead of not only finding the anomaly and discriminating from nonferrous and ferrous metal, we can also tell what direction the find or anomaly is.

I looked at another test of the same thing. The black one gave a big reading, the gold one gave a rather big one, the red, a little smaller, and the blue just barely got it. We were probably away from the ship at the time, because of the small blue reading.

Elsewhere, the chart shows another test, on a small target. I believed that was bronze cannon. That "bronze cannon hit" was marked October 23, 1983. As I recall, that test was done on a bronze cannon in about twelve feet of water.

On a nonferrous small target like that, we get a double hit, one from each head, and as I look, it appears that one head set went right near the cannon. The cannon were apparently over to port side. Looking over the charts, I had marked the "Squark hits" with a square with a circle around it. I seem to remember that this "No. 36" was one of the best hits, and "No. 90."

Yeah, the *Margarita* site.

Here's a line pencil-drawn from the three anchors way out here that passes through the timbers, going right up here. I tap the chart with a pencil. This is not very far off; it's only about fifty meters off of that line.

So it very well could be the location of the remaining "big pile" of the *Margarita* that we've been hunting for quite a few years. According to Gene Lyon, there's supposed to be 189 silver bars out there, and I'm hoping that's it. Talking to Tony Kopp, I recall that " . . . back in, I think, 1981, we were towing a giant pulse detector here."

I tap the chart again. "We got one, two, three readings with that giant pulse detector there also, which would verify the 'Squark,' and that also finds nonferrous items."

I told Tony, "To me that is very exciting. We've got to dig that. The boat that's working on it is a subcontractor who tells me it looks very good." Moving over the chart, I noted, "There's a big sandbar there."

As I looked over my chart, I noted another place where I also tested with my "atomic absorption spectrometer." With that equipment, we're radio-activating the Earth, and we can discriminate gold that way too. I've been using that for about seven or eight years. But I haven't double-checked its findings yet. I've got to dig these records out and see what readings I've got on them. I haven't worked on this for about a year.

Sometimes I've had to let things like this sit until I can come back to them.

With the "mailboxes" on the subcontractor's boat, we'd just dug a couple of "holes" in the sand. In one, nothing was found. In another one, a hundred meters north, we found a bomb. On one about fifty meters to the east, we found nothing. Yet another hole that was dug to the south yielded nothing. I point out to Tony, "That's the first big sandbar, when you're coming from the south-north, and that would be a likely place for the ship to hit first. In a hurricane. There could be a real healthy pile of loot, right there." Then while I'm thinking of a digging strategy, I realize the subcontracting boat is running out of supplies. They've been out a while. I tell them that if they have to leave the spot we have other options, other vessels to pick up the hunt. They've only got a four-cylinder engine on their "mailboxes," and they may not be able to hack that deep sand. I think it's probably ten, fifteen, or twenty feet deep. I decide that if they have to leave, we'll move the *Magruder* in there with her big engines, and big "mailboxes," and let them "dust it off." We'll still give these guys, the subcontractors, their 5 percent of the treasure, regardless whether they find it or we find it. At least they're in there working on it.

They've brought new blood, excitement, and pizzazz. I think it is very exciting!

Wendy: *"You're going to be written about obviously in history books because of all of this," said one of the television interviewers.*

What do you think, what's the most accurate thing that they could say about Mel Fisher in the books?

Today's the day! Every day. And the first thing you know, today *is* the day! That's probably the best concept.

> *Mel's voice is clearly his own, as are his views, molded over a lifetime. With what he says here, one can hear the voice of twentieth-century America and beyond, into the twenty-first century, with its positive attitudes, including the view that the little guys can still win, still pursue their dreams and achieve them. His is the voice of two big oceans, the Pacific and the Atlantic, and the awesome country in between. At the center of the nation, of course, is the hardy Midwest, from where Mel began his quests of a lifetime, in company with his own family and his extended "family." The* Nuestra Señora de Atocha *and the* Santa Margarita, *of the 1622 Fleet, and the 1715 Plate Fleet wrecks, symbolize more than his treasure finds, though they show the world so much. They symbolize each man's treasure, and his right to go for it, in harmony with the nation's comforting presence of like-minded, peace-loving people.*

Mel and Deo Fisher—a lifetime together, well-lived.
FISHER FAMILY COLLECTION

EPILOGUE

Follow Your Dreams!

Mel Fisher was born August 21, 1922, and died December 19, 1998. His birth came sixteen days and three hundred years after the sinking of the *Nuestra Señora de Atocha*, the *Santa Margarita*, and the other ships of the 1622 Spanish treasure fleet west of Key West, Florida. His arrival on the planet came sixteen days and three hundred years after their loss, and it only took him a lifetime, moving from mid-America and the Great Lakes, and from one coast to the other, with time out for the Great War—in which he was a second-day participant at Normandy's beaches—to decide to chase the *most* elusive, greatest Spanish treasure ship ever found, the *Atocha*, and her sister Royal Guard galleon, the *Santa Margarita*, both lost in hurricane winds south and westerly of Key West in the Florida Keys.

He was of the same ilk as Francisco Melián, another rugged salvor, who was among the first to salvage and partially recover from the *Margarita* in the ship's own time. But Mel was more—an explorer, a carpenter-builder, and engineer, also self-taught in the world of underwater archeology, and always working with his staff to learn from the past for the sake of the future. As a salvor, he was the common denominator in the twentieth century, following in the footsteps of Melián, the most outstanding of the early salvors.

In this book, published on the four-hundredth anniversary of the sinking of the 1622 Spanish Royal Fleet, Mel spans centuries, with experiences in historical and treasure recoveries and his magical life that led up to them and watched them happen. Then he moved on through his continuing adventurous spirit and the assured love and support of his family—his wife Deo and their children Taffi, Kim, Kane, and Dirk, Mel's first son Terry, and his greater "treasure family."

Some people look forward, and some look backward in time, as they quest for their own life's adventures.

In Mel's case, and for the glory of the physical world, history, and archaeology, he chose to look backward, but in the process, he was an underwater pioneer himself, using modern technology and his innovative engineering skills, often rough-hewn to begin with, in an unforgiving undersea world.

The more he looked backward, the more forward in time he was with his achievements. Yet Mel decided to always keep the physical touch in his work, choosing not to put his divers at the advantage only of technology. He was also about the human sense of action, adventure, and mixing in a little fun and romance—always.

In the twenty-first century, Mel's daughter and sons carry on the tradition of seeking and finding treasure and other historical artifacts and knowledge, both from Key West and Sebastian, Florida. They maintain a family-directed museum in Sebastian that is still operating, and there is a separate nonprofit museum that Mel Fisher and his wife and business partner, Dolores "Deo" Fisher, founded in Key West years before he ever found the grand *Atocha*.

That will rank as only one of Mel Fisher's real contributions as an undersea pioneer and shipwreck salvager, and as a through-and-through twentieth-century American from small-town roots who made it big by following his dreams.

Mel also concluded that there are artificial separations among people that do not necessarily apply under the sea, because it takes considerable investment of money to launch uncertain quests. He also was a strong believer in the free enterprise system that undergirds the spirit of America, her government and her people, and he successfully carried out his missions and then defended them both in the halls of Congress and the court system, all the way to the US Supreme Court. And he was no stranger to the rules of admiralty law.

As a man who was born and bred in the Midwest and lived on both coasts and in the oceans surrounding this nation, Mel was an unusual, broad-based businessman, adventurer, and engineer-inventor who was also uniquely equipped to experience and feel the power, freedom, and diversity of America.

When I was in the final editing stages of this book, Mel's daughter told me that Mel and one of his dear friends were both diagnosed with bladder cancer in 1982, and they were the guinea pigs for the two newly developed options of treatment, either radiation or chemotherapy. Mel opted for chemo and his friend opted for radiation, and they had a $100 bet to see who would live the longest. With the unknowns of cancer at that time, the doctor had estimated Mel had six months to live. He lived another sixteen years.

Mel was cremated and his ashes were dispersed over the ocean, flowing above the *Atocha* site west of Key West and also into the ocean waves near Vero Beach where the 1715 Fleet ships sank. Another pinch of ashes was set into acrylic in a small glass fishbowl, along with a commemorative coin made of *Atocha* silver, and friend Pat Clyne, while on a submarine expedition to the *Titanic*, placed the fishbowl on the remains of the helm of that ill-fated ship.

Eternally the optimist, Mel Fisher saw that there are still other worlds and treasure and artifacts to find.

Eternally the achiever also, Mel wrote this letter to his good friend astronaut John Glenn, expressing himself and his goals as only Mel Fisher could, dictating to his well-loved partner and photographer/videographer, the late Patrick "Pat" Clyne, this letter, which Mel signed on his deathbed:

> Dear John Glenn,
>
> I have had a dream about searching for and finding Atlantis for more than 40 years. I have a group of financiers who have agreed to put up 10 million dollars to start and I have personally been to the site myself several times.
>
> I need another still photograph and another aerial photograph and radar remote sensing of the area. Let's do it.
>
> Today's the Day.
>
> —Mel Fisher
>
> P.S. I would be glad to loan you one of my videographers for the project.

ABOUT THE AUTHOR

Always a journalist and writer, Wendy Tucker was already working for two Nebraska newspapers, the *McCook Daily Gazette* and the *Fremont Guide and Tribune*, while still in high school and continuing into college. After graduating from the University of Nebraska School of Journalism—where she served as the university's *Daily Nebraskan* news editor and also completed a summer internship in New Mexico at *The Albuquerque Tribune*—Tucker, raised in the Cornhusker State, worked as a *Miami Herald* intern before moving to New York City and the Columbia University Graduate School of Journalism. She received a master's degree with High Honors from that institution. Tucker then worked as a reporter and photographer, again for the *Herald*, and eventually became that newspaper's Boca Raton (Florida) bureau chief. She later served as a reporter in Charleston, South Carolina, at the *News and Courier*, then moved in the early 1970s with her Navy husband to Key West, Florida, joining the staff of the *Key West Citizen* as a reporter and photographer. She rose to assistant managing editor of the *Citizen*. Tucker was also a correspondent for United Press International (UPI), the Associated Press (AP), and Reuters, and broke the wire service news internationally of the *Nuestra Senora de Atocha* discovery in 1985. She then worked for the City of Key West, ultimately in an assistant city planner role, before her retirement in the early 1990s. Meeting Mel Fisher in summer 1964 during her *Herald* internship, and again later in Key West, Wendy became a close friend of the family; she conducted and transcribed more than one hundred hours of interviews with Mel Fisher, now collected in this book and using the late adventurer's own words. Tucker worked closely with the Fisher family to provide in-depth color to his life and their collective experience.

Wendy Tucker and Mel Fisher. PAT CLYNE PHOTO

INDEX

Abt (Fisher), Taffi *6, 8, 73-74, 108-9, 207-8, 220, 303, 314*
Alexander, Chet (salvage master) *225*
Alexander, Mike *256*
Acapulco, Mexico *119, 160, 171, 182-3*
Alexandria, Louisiana *69, 70*
American Legion Drum and Bugle Corps. *52*
Aqua-Lung *7, 101-3, 105, 115, 133-34*
Arthur Murray Studios *28*
Arbalete (vintage French-made speargun) *115*
Arbutus, motor vessel (MV), (salvage vessel) *259-60, 308*
Arch of Triumph *76-77, 87*
ASTP (Army Specialized Training Program) *57, 65, 68*
Atlantic (Ocean) *4, 86, 105, 172, 291, 301, 311*
Atocha, Señora Nuestra de 1-2, 8, 10-11, 15-16, 18-20, 58, 69, 83, 127-30, 133, 164, 196, 218-20, 223-42, 244, 246-50, 253, 256-60, 262, 268-271, 273-74, 276-77, 279, 282-84, 289, 299, 301, 304-5, 307, 311, 313-15
Bank of Spain *260, 277*
Barman, Lillian (Sprencel) *26, 33*
Barman, Tony *33*
Baths, Virgin Gorda, Virgin Islands *165*
Battle of the Bulge *78*
Bel-Aqua Company *136, 158*

Billings, Montana *173*
Biltmore Hotel, Los Angeles *136*
Bishop Rock, Cortes Bank, Channel Islands, California *171*
Black, Lew (electronics expert) *173, 182*
Blackbeard the Pirate 40
Blue Ball Highway *76*
"Bolero" (Ravel) *57*
Brandon, John *303*
Bremerhaven, Germany *84-85*
Bridgeford, Kenny *107*
Brown's lily iron (arrowhead, i.e., tip of a harpoon) *107*
Buccaneer, MV (salvage vessel) *246*
Buffett, Jimmy *258, 268-69*
Bunyan, Paul *130*
Bussoz, Rene *101, 103, 133, 137*
Cab Calloway Orchestra *55*
"Cabin Wreck" (shipwreck) *207-8, 305*
Camp Claiborne, Louisiana *70*
Candelaria (shipwreck) *236*
Capone, Al *151-53*
Captain Tuna ("Chicken of the Sea") *173*
Carson, Johnny *260, 262, 266, 268*
Caribbean *1, 7, 111-12, 116, 125, 130, 148, 154, 160, 164, 182, 185-87, 189, 191, 197, 220*
Catalina (Island), California *107, 112, 146, 149, 152, 182*
Chaplin, Charlie *24*
Chicago, Illinois *28, 40, 45-46,*

54, 59, 80, 89, 94, 122
Chicago Canal 46
Chicago River 40, 45-46
Chris-Craft (boats) 246
Ciesinski, Ed "Eddie" 127, 130
Claude Pepper Park 207
Clyne, Patrick "Pat" 262, 264, 315-16
Cobb Coin Company 272, 303, 306, 308
Coffman, F.L., author of *Atlas of Treasure Maps* 172
Colón, Panama 186
Comeford, Mary (Sprencel) 26
Conch Republic 222
Concepción (shipwreck, off coast of Hispaniola/Dominican Republic) 183
Corbett, Al and Carol 172
Cornelius (portable air compressors) 114
"Corrigan's Wreck" (shipwreck) 208
Corrigan family 208
Cortes Bank(s), Channel Islands, California 169, 171, 182
Coscuez Mine, Muzo emerald district, Colombia, SA) 306
Costa Rica 182-83; 200
Cousteau, Jacques 7, 102-3, 131
Cozumel, Mexico 112, 119
Cummins diesel 215
Cuzco Mines (Cuzco Mint), Colombia, SA 307
Dauntless, MV (salvage vessel) 255-56, 279
Dee-Gee, MV (salvage vessel) 208, 215
Delta Chi fraternity 56, 62, 65

Desco (underwater equipment manufacturer) 114
Dive Air Company 134
Dougherty, John (attorney) 160
Douglas Aircraft 147
"Douglass Beach Wreck" 9, 208, 211, 215, 237, 246
Driftwood (Inn), Vero Beach 5
Einstein, Albert 62-3, 65, 278
El Camino College, Torrance, California 144
Emeralds International, Inc. 305
Endeavor, MV (salvage boat) 303
Fels-Naptha 38
Feild, Fay (electronics expert) 7-8, 17, 135, 182, 202, 204, 206, 210, 228, 235, 287
Finn, Huckleberry 40, 46, 302
Fisher, Angel 244
Fisher, Dirk 6, 8, 114, 121, 126, 242, 244, 275-76, 314
Fisher, Dolores "Deo" 2-3, 6-7, 11-12, 14-16, 27-28, 60, 104-5, 110-11, 115-28, 130-31, 140-41, 144, 146-48, 151, 154, 180, 186, 196, 202-5, 218-20, 224-26, 282, 290-91, 293, 312, 314
Fisher, Earl (Melvin) 24, 27, 39, 109, 144
Fisher, Grace Marie (Sprencel) 24-26, 39, 51, 109, 144, 204, 270
Fisher, Kane 6, 27, 126, 236, 253-54, 258-60, 268, 276-77, 314
Fisher, Kim 6, 10, 126, 130,

216, 258, 261, 271, 276, 303, 307, 314
Fisher, Terry *89, 314*
(Fisher) Abt, Taffi *(See* Abt entry*)*
Fort Pierce, Florida *8, 11, 205-8, 214-217, 246, 274*
Frankfurt am Main, Germany *82*
Frankfurt Oder, Germany *82*
Gagnan, Emile *102-3*
Gary, Indiana *22, 25, 31, 35, 45, 52, 54-57, 59, 61, 65*
Gary Hotel, Gary, Indiana *56*
Gantner (swimsuits) *131*
Garmisch Park, Garmisch, Germany *84*
Gates, Rupert "Rupe" *7, 157, 202, 204, 208, 211*
Gatun Lake, Panama *185, 197*
Gatun River, Panama *197-98*
Gibbs, Romano *35, 37, 42-45, 49*
Gimbel, Peter *167*
Gimbels Department Store *167*
Glen Park, Indiana *28, 30, 55*
Glenn Miller (Orchestra) *51, 54-57, 61*
Glenn, John *315-16*
Gold Digger, MV (salvage barge) *9*
"Golden Crew" *268*
Golden Doubloon (reproduction galleon museum) *145*
Gold Doubloon, MV (dive charter and salvage vessel) *115-16, 127, 145, 180-82, 184, 187, 189, 200*
Great Inagua *174-75*
Green Beach, Normandy *75*
"Green Cabin Wreck" (shipwreck) *208*

Groening, Homer *117*
Gulf of Mexico *45, 190, 229, 243, 291, 301*
Gulf Stream *17, 20, 174, 228-29, 236*
Gurr, Tom *301*
Haiti *116-17, 119-20, 172-76*
Hass, Hans *131*
Hatteras, MV (salvage vessel) *255-56, 259, 307*
Hawkins, Paula (US senator, Florida) *289*
High Road to Danger (TV series) *160, 169*
Hispaniola (island: Haiti/Dominican Republic) *9*
Hlodnicki, Joe *53-56, 86*
Hobart, Indiana *22, 25, 27*
Holden, Harold *303*
Holly's Folly, MV (search and salvage vessel) *234, 248*
Hollywood-Riviera, California *135, 138, 142*
Holzworth, Walter "Walt" *7, 202, 204, 211*
Hope and Page (company) *114-15*
Horan, David (attorney) *249, 255*
Horner syndrome *78*
Humiston Park, Vero Beach, Florida *206*
Indian River County, Florida *5*
isinglass *43*
Ivory (soap) *38*
James, Harry (bandleader) *55*
Jantzen Swimsuit Company *116-17, 131*
Key West, Florida *4-5, 12, 14-16, 23, 116, 127, 130, 145, 218-20, 223, 226, 233, 235, 241, 243, 246, 253,*

255, 257-59, 262, 268,
273, 279, 290, 301, 303,
313-15, 318
Key West Citizen 268, 318
Key West Naval Station 273
Kopp, Tony 308-9
La Posada (Inn), Vero Beach,
  Florida 4-7
Lake Michigan 23, 25, 35-6,
  40-41, 44-46, 57, 286
Louisiana 14, 69-71, 231
Lucite 170
Lyon, Dr. Eugene "Gene"
  (historian) 15, 218, 227,
  231-32, 239, 304, 309
Magruder, MV (salvage vessel)
  255-56, 258-59, 310
"Mailbox" (excavation tool)
  8-9, 210-11, 214-15, 220,
  233-34, 259, 278, 303, 310
Marcial, Manuel de Gomar
  (gemologist, emerald
  expert) 305
Mariel Boatlift 222
Marquesas Keys 15, 19-20,
  218, 223, 226, 229-30,
  235-36, 238, 241, 283
Mathewson III, R. Duncan
  (archaeologist) 232, 272
Mathison, Nelson "Doc" 107,
  130, 165, 166, 168
McHaley, Bleth 253
Mediterranean Sea 83-84
Mel's Aqua Shop 104, 111,
  114, 121, 126, 133, 135,
  138, 142, 161-62
Miguel, Ted 255
Miller Beach, Indiana 27, 35,
  44
Mississippi River 45, 49, 70
Moeme, MV (salvage vessel)
  167
Molinar, Demostines "Mo" 7,
  9, 45, 180, 187, 202, 204,
211, 302-3
Momsen lung (early
  rebreather) 159
Montana 11, 123, 144, 173
Moran, Bob 202
Morgan, Captain Henry 197,
  199
National Geographic (magazine)
  10, 13, 232
National Geographic Society
  13
NAUI (National Association
  of Underwater
  Instructors) 160
Noel, Edward 26
Normandy 67, 75, 203, 313
North Sea 85-86
Northwind, MV (salvage
  vessel) 244
Nuestra Señora de Atocha
  (shipwreck 1622) *See*
  Atocha *entry*
*Nuestra Señora de las Nieves y las
  Animas* (shipwreck 1715)
  218, 304
Ocean Key House, Key West,
  Florida 262
PADI (Professional
  Association of Dive
  Instructors) 160
Pacific (Ocean) 105, 113, 171,
  311
Palos Verdes, California 138,
  148-49
Pan American Airways 116,
  168
Panama 7, 116, 125, 182, 184-
  87, 190, 192, 197, 200,
  240, 302
Panama Canal 184-85, 200
Paris, France 76-80, 87
Peru 235, 262-66
Peterson, Chuck 108
Petrillo, Joe 56-57

Phips, Sir William *9*
Pirelli (Rubber) Company *136, 159*
plexiglass *170*
PM Magazine 279
Point Arguello, California *113*
Popular Mechanics 36
Port Hueneme, California *154*
Portobelo, Panama *193-94, 197*
Potosí, Peru, SA (mine and mint in present-day Bolivia) *235, 266*
Potter, John S. Jr. *10, 218, 241*
"Potter's Treasure Divers Guide" *218*
proton magnetometer *17, 220, 228*
Puerto Vallarta, Mexico *182*
Purdue University, West Lafayette, Indiana *55-57, 60-65, 67-69, 144-45, 210, 277-78*
Real Eight Company *8-9, 15, 224, 305*
Red Ball Highway *76*
Redondo Beach, California *111, 114, 125, 133, 135, 138, 148-49*
Rene's Sporting Goods *101*
Rhone (shipwreck, Virgin Islands) *165-66*
Riomar Golf Course *207, 216*
"Riomar Wreck" (shipwreck) *9, 207-8, 216*
Rosario (shipwreck) *236-37*
Rubatex Corporation *157, 159*
Rhythm Rockers *54*
Saba Rock, MV (salvage vessel) *256, 259*
Salvor One, MV (pleasure boat) *256*

San Blas Islands, Panama *195-96*
San Clemente Island, California *182*
San José (shipwreck) *301*
San José, Costa Rica *182*
San Pedro, California *140, 145-46, 148, 182, 189, 200*
San Pedro (shipwreck) *218*
"Sandy Point Wreck" (shipwreck) *207-8*
Santa Barbara, California *113, 182*
Santa Cruz Island, California *140, 149, 182*
Santa Margarita (shipwreck 1622) *1, 10, 224-25, 231-33, 235-37, 242, 244, 250, 257-58, 270-71, 275, 277, 281-84, 307, 309, 311, 313*
Sawyer, Tom *46, 302*
Scott Hydropack *115*
Sebastian, Florida *1, 11-12, 314*
Sebastian Inlet *207, 305*
"See the Sea" Dive Shop *142*
Seranilla Bank *190-92*
Shumway, Norman (US representative, California) *293-94*
Silent World (Cousteau film) *131*
Silver Shoals, Hispaniola *116, 125, 154, 172-73, 186-87, 190-91, 201, 203, 285*
Sinatra, Frank *61*
Sinclair, James (Jim) *272*
Spanish Plate Fleet, 1715 *1, 8-9, 206, 220, 275, 303, 311*
Sprencel, Agnes *24-27*
Sprencel, Gail *27*
Sprencel, Julia *26*
Sprencel, "Grandpa" Louis *23, 27*

Sprencel, Mama "Ma" *23, 27*
Sterns (First backer on films on Cortez Banks) *172*
Stillwell S. Bishop (shipwreck) *171*
Swordfish (salvage vessel) *259, 277*
Tail End Buoy *17, 227-28*
Tampa, Florida *27, 45, 49, 92, 94, 96-97, 99, 101, 103, 106, 109, 118, 121-22*
Tarracino, Anthony "Captain Tony" *12*
Tehuantepec *183*
The Blue Continent (movie Mel made for U.S. Divers) *143, 160*
The Other End of the Line (underwater film) *15, 129-30, 224*
The Tonight Show (NBC TV program) *260, 268*
Theroux, Louise (Sprencel) *26*
Titanic (shipwreck) *315*
Tommy Dorsey (Band) *51, 54*
Tongue of the Ocean *174*
Torrance, California *123, 133, 138, 142, 144, 172*
Tortuga Island *120, 175*
Treasure Island 11, 40, *181*
Tres Puentes (shipwreck) *218*
Tsukimura, Eddie *2, 127, 145-46, 180, 187, 189, 200*
Tucker, Wendy *12, 111, 115-24, 146-48, 189, 243-44, 258, 276, 285-86, 296, 310, 317, 318*
Tuscaloosa, Alabama *57, 68-69*
Under the Red Sea (Hass film) *131*
Unger, "Auntie" Marion *113, 155*

University of Alabama, Tuscaloosa *68*
Urca de Lima (shipwreck) *206-7*
US Army Corps of Engineers *47*
US Army Reserves *64*
U.S. Divers Company *102, 143, 160*
US Supreme Court *289, 296, 300-301, 315*
U.S. Steel (United States Steel Corporation) *57*
Valbanera (shipwreck) *14-17, 20, 128-29, 133, 224, 226-31, 250*
Valiant (shipwreck) *150-51*
Valparaiso, Indiana *22-24, 43*
venturi dredge *121, 194*
Vero Beach, Florida *4-6, 8, 11-12, 15, 121, 204-5, 207-9, 215-18, 221, 223, 246, 274-76, 315*
Virgalona (salvage vessel) *17-19, 45, 227-28, 230, 248, 302-3*
Voit Rubber Company *15, 129-31, 224*
Volker, Roy *304-5*
Wagner, Kip *8-9, 205-7, 304-5*
Wagner, Marietta *54*
Wauhob Lake, Indiana *25, 43-44*
"Wedge Wreck" (shipwreck) *206-7*
Welk, Lawrence *70*
Wham, Harry *155*
Williams, Richard "Dick" *7, 202, 204, 210-11*

324

www.ingramcontent.com/pod-product-compliance
Lightning Source LLC
Chambersburg PA
CBHW060500170426
43199CB00011B/1276